VOID

Library of
Davidson College

# The Economics of Export Restrictions

# Westview Special Studies

The concept of Westview Special Studies is a response to the continuing crisis in academic and informational publishing. Library budgets are being diverted from the purchase of books and used for data banks, computers, micromedia, and other methods of information retrieval. Interlibrary loan structures further reduce the edition sizes required to satisfy the needs of the scholarly community. Economic pressures on university presses and the few private scholarly publishing companies have greatly limited the capacity of the industry to properly serve the academic and research communities. As a result, many manuscripts dealing with important subjects, often representing the highest level of scholarship, are no longer economically viable publishing projects--or, if accepted for publication, are typically subject to lead times ranging from one to three years.

Westview Special Studies are our practical solution to the problem. As always, the selection criteria include the importance of the subject, the work's contribution to scholarship, and its insight, originality of thought, and excellence of exposition. We accept manuscripts in camera-ready form, typed, set, or word processed according to specifications laid out in our comprehensive manual, which contains straightforward instructions and sample pages. The responsibility for editing and proofreading lies with the author or sponsoring institution, but our editorial staff is always available to answer questions and provide guidance.

The result is a book printed on acid-free paper and bound in sturdy, library-quality soft covers. We manufacture these books ourselves using equipment that does not require a lengthy make-ready process and that allows us to publish first editions of 300 to 1000 copies and to reprint even smaller quantities as needed. Thus, we can produce Special Studies quickly and can keep even very specialized books in print as long as there is a demand for them.

## About the Book and Editor

Focusing on free access to primary commodity markets as an element of the New International Economic Order, the contributors to this book assess both the possibilities and the potential profitability of export restrictions by LDCs (less developed countries) and the impact of such restrictions on developed countries. Using a general equilibrium model, the contributors identify the necessary conditions under which restrictions will lead to increased real national income while promoting domestic processing industries. The effect of export restrictions on levels of employment, money supply, inflation rates, and economic activity and growth in both exporting and importing countries is also considered. Although, in theory, export restrictions over a range of commodities can lead to stagflation in developed countries, this effect is unlikely in practice. The contributors present empirical studies to argue that the combination of conditions (low price elasticities, lack of potential substitutes, and close cooperation among producing countries) necessary for restrictions to significantly affect redistribution of world income is a remote possibility. As a result, it is improbable that LDCs will rely on the imposition of restrictions on primary commodities as an economic tool. The contributors conclude that export restrictions are an inefficient method of solving the problems of LDCs and that trade of manufactured goods is the safer, albeit slower, means of promoting the economic development of LDCs.

Jimmy Weinblatt is senior lecturer at Ben Gurion University of the Negev, Israel.

# The Economics of Export Restrictions
Free Access to Commodity Markets and the NIEO

edited by
Jimmy Weinblatt

Westview Press / Boulder and London

382.6
E19

*Westview Special Studies in International Economics*

All rights reserved. No part of this publication may be reproduced or transmitted in any form or by any means, electronic or mechanical, including photocopy, recording, or any information storage and retrieval system without permission in writing from the publisher.

Copyright © 1985 by Westview Press, Inc.

Published in 1985 in the United States of America by Westview Press, Inc.; Frederick A. Praeger, Publisher; 5500 Central Avenue, Boulder, Colorado 80301

Library of Congress Cataloging in Publication Data
Main entry under title:
The Economics of export restrictions.
  (Westview special studies in international economics)
  Bibliography: p.
  Includes index.
  1. Export controls--Addresses, essays, lectures.
  I. Weinblatt, J.
  HF1414.5.E25   1984     382'.64      84-25629
  ISBN 0-8133-7024-8

Composition for this book was provided by the editor.
This book was produced without formal editing by the publisher.

Printed and bound in the United States

∞  The paper used in this publication meets the minimum requirements of the American National Standard for Permanence of Paper for Printed Library Materials Z39.48-1984.

6   5   4   3   2   1

# Contents

Foreword, *Helmut Hesse* . . . . . . . . . . . . . . . . . . . . ix
Preface, *Z. Y. Hershlag* . . . . . . . . . . . . . . . . . . . xi

1   Introduction, Summary, and Conclusions
    *J. Weinblatt*. . . . . . . . . . . . . . . . . . . . . . . . 1

2   The General Effect of Export Restrictions
    on Commodity Markets
    *R. Nathanson and J. Weinblatt* . . . . . . . . . . . . . . 10

3   Commodity Export Taxes as a Means of
    Promoting Internal Processing Industries
    -- A General Equilibrium Model
    *Horst Keppler* . . . . . . . . . . . . . . . . . . . . . . 51

4   Free Access to Supplies Versus Restrictive
    Supply Policies: The Ability of LDCs
    to Control Commodity Markets
    *Horst Keppler* . . . . . . . . . . . . . . . . . . . . . . 71

5   Export Restrictions as a Means
    of Redistributing World Income:
    An Appraisal
    *J. Weinblatt and R. Nathanson* . . . . . . . . . . . . . 116

6   Restrictions of Exports from LDCs
    and Their Impact on World Economy
    *J. Weinblatt and R. Nathanson* . . . . . . . . . . . . . 128

7   Monetary Effects of Export Restrictions
    on World Commodity Markets
    *J. Weinblatt and Miriam Rodrik-Farhi*. . . . . . . . . . 143

8   Exports from LDCs: Impacts on Economic Growth
    *J. Weinblatt and Nora Schrager*. . . . . . . . . . . . . 161

9  The Effects of Export Restrictions
   on Economic Growth in LDCs
   *J. Weinblatt and R. Nathanson* . . . . . . . . . . . . . . . 181

10 Export Controls:
   An Institutional and Historical Perspective
   *Michael Rom* . . . . . . . . . . . . . . . . . . . . . . . . 197

11 The Analysis of the GATT Provisions
   *Michael Rom* . . . . . . . . . . . . . . . . . . . . . . . . 220

12 Summary of Findings and Main Conclusions
   *Helmut Hesse* . . . . . . . . . . . . . . . . . . . . . . . . 258

*Contributors* . . . . . . . . . . . . . . . . . . . . . . . . . . 262
*Index* . . . . . . . . . . . . . . . . . . . . . . . . . . . . . 263

# Foreword

The David Horowitz Institute for the Research of Developing Countries, Tel Aviv, and the Ibero-America Institute for Economic Research, University of Goettingen, have been engaged since 1978 in a joint research project financed by the Volkswagen Foundation. The project stems from the conviction that endeavours toward the lasting creation of a new international economic order require first of all a solution to the important problem of access to supplies for countries such as the Federal Republic of Germany and Israel, both of which are poor in raw material resources. A closer examination of this problem assumes additional importance in the light of developments evidencing the spread of export restrictions in the world since the commencement of the seventies decade.
    The project was planned and executed jointly, the Ibero-America Institute undertaking the study of the effects of export controls on individual product markets and seeking to establish whether such controls serve to promote raw material processing industries in the developing countries, and the David Horowitz Institute dealing with the macroeconomic effects of export restrictions and the question of how they should be drawn into the framework of international agreements.
    The research work in the David Horowitz Institute was carried out under the direction of Jimmy Weinblatt and Roberto Nathanson, and also with the participation of Michael Rom, now Economic Attache to the Israeli Embassy in Vienna. On the side of the Ibero-America Institute the investigation was undertaken predominantly by Horst Keppler. Within the framework of the same project Helmut Hesse and Hubertus Schenkel concerned themselves with a survey of the extent of dissemination of export restrictions and an analysis of their shorter term effects. The findings of these studies have been published as follows:

Helmut Hesse, Exportbeschrankungen - ein neues handelspolitisches
    Problem? (Export Restrictions - a New Trade Policy
    Problem?), in: Knut Borchardt and Franz Holsheu
    (Eds.), Theorie und Politic der Internationalen

Wirtschaftsbeziehungen, Stuttgart/New York 1980, pp. 257-282;

Helmut Hesse, Exportbeschrankungen zur Vermeidung eines "kritischen Mangels" (Export Restrictions as a Means of Avoiding "Critical Shortages"), in: G. Bombach, B. Gahlen, A.E. Ott (Eds.), zur Theorie und Politik Internationaler Wirtschaftsbeziehungen, Schriftenreihe des Wirtschafts- wissenschaftlichen Seminars Ottobeuren, Vol. 10, Tubingen 1981, pp. 103-130;

Hubertus Schenkel, Wirtschaftstheoretische und wirtschaftspolitische Probleme von Ausfuhrbeschrankungen (Theoretical and Policy Problems of Export Restrictions), Arbeitsbericht 19, Ibero-Amerika Institut fur Wirtschaftsforschung der Universitat Goettingen, Goettingen 1980.

Thanks are due to Phyllis Johnson de Barrantes and Margret von Schierstaedt for their hard work in translating and typing the manuscripts originating from the Ibero-America Institute.

Professor Helmut Hesse
Director
Ibero-America Institute
for Economic Research
Goettingen University

# Preface

This report is the result of a two-year research project on the subject of free access to commodity markets carried out jointly by the David Horowitz Institute for the Research of Developing Countries, Tel Aviv University and the Ibero-Amerika Institut, University of Goettingen. The project was financed by a grant from the Volkswagen Foundation, to which we extend our grateful appreciation.

Professor Helmut Hesse, Director of the Ibero-Amerika Institut, initiated the project. His advice and counsel throughout the research period provided useful insights and stimuli to the investigation of this complex issue, which has been the subject of discussions in various international forums of the New International Economic Order. Dr. Jimmy Weinblatt, Research Associate of the David Horowitz Institute and Senior lecturer in the Department of Economics at Ben Gurion University, Beer Sheva, headed the Israeli team of investigators and coordinated the research between Israel and Germany. Dr. Michael Rom, Senior lecturer at the Leon Recanati School of Business Administration, Tel Aviv University, and member of the Israeli delegation to the UNCTAD meetings, focused on the institutional and historical aspects of the commodities supply problem. Dr. Horst Keppler of the University of Goettingen and Dr. Roberto Nathanson of Tel Aviv University concentrated on macro and microeconomic aspects of the subject. Dr. Nathanson was also extremely helpful in the coordination effort. Assistance in econometric data analysis was given by Nora Schrager; Miriam Farhi researched some of the global monetary effects; Gabriela Williams provided secretarial assistance; and Ruth Parnass was responsible for the typing of the manuscript.

Professor Z.Y. Hershlag<br>
Former Director<br>
The David Horowitz Institute for<br>
the Research of Developing Countries<br>
Tel Aviv University

# 1
# Introduction, Summary, and Conclusions

*J. Weinblatt*

1. INTRODUCTION

   Export restrictions represent an economic phenomenon that has existed for millenia. In ancient Egypt and Greece as well as in Europe during the mercantilistic period, the purpose of such restrictions was to keep essential foods and materials at home. The problem was so well known that David Hume thought it necessary to criticize it: "It is very usual, in nations ignorant of the nature of commerce to prohibit the exportation of commodities, and to preserve among themselves whatever they think valuable and useful. . . It is well known to the learned, that the ancient laws of Athens rendered the exportation of figs criminal; that being supposed a species of fruit so excellent in Attica, that the Athenians deemed it too delicious for the palate of any foreigner."[1]
   During the first half of the twentieth century export controls were introduced (1) to allocate scarce raw materials domestically and among allies; (2) to prevent essential materials from reaching the enemy; (3) to control clearing arrangements; and (4) to maximize quota gains of the exporters. Yet even in that period export restrictions were identified as a hindrance: "Chronic as distinct from temporary restriction can scarcely be in the general interest and must be the symptom of a malady which should be cured rather than endured."[2]
   In the post-World War II period, export restrictions were imposed by both developed and developing countries for a variety of purposes including the prevention of inflation and the protection of foreign exchange.[3]
   In 1973, export restrictions were related to the problem of economic development in primary commodity exporting countries on the one hand, and to the general issue of free access to supplies, on the other. The success of OPEC in raising oil prices and significantly increasing export earnings of oil exporting countries led less developed countries to the belief that export controls of primary commodities and the cartelization of their trade could be used as an instrument to redistribute world income between the industrialized north and the less developed south. At the same time, concern grew among the developed countries over the

availability of raw materials, as well as over prospects for their own industrial production and levels of economic activity.
These concerns have heightened the interest in the issue of free access to supplies and led to several research studies in this field, including this study of export restrictions.
This volume consists of studies by several authors and covers the following aspects of the issue: (1) descriptions of export restrictions in the historical contemporary setting; (2) theoretical and empirical microeconomic analyses of the possibilities and profitability for less developed countries (LDCs) to impose export restrictions; (3) theoretical and empirical macroeconomic analyses focusing on the possible effects of export restrictions on the developed importing countries and the developing exporting countries; and (4) examination of the existing comprehensive international trade agreement. The General Agreement on Tariffs and Trade (GATT), and an analysis of its relevance to export restrictions.

## OVERVIEW AND SUMMARY OF FINDINGS

Chapter 2 is a general evaluation of the performance of export restrictions in the 1970s. The study is based on information gathered by various international organizations (IMF, OECD, GATT) on actual cases of export restrictions. The systematic analysis of this information results in the classification of different types of restrictions and of the various motives for their implementation. The findings substantiate the hypothesis that developing countries imposed export controls mainly to increase export earnings and to develop processing industries. Developed countries generally applied such controls in order to secure their domestic supply and stabilize prices.

Chapter 3 is a theoretical, microeconomic discussion of export restrictions. A general equilibrium model on which the analysis is based confirms the assumption that commodity export taxation as imposed by supply cartels can in fact lead to rises in real national income and at the same time serve to promote domestic processing industries. Contrary to the findings of partial equilibrium models, these results remain valid even if the cartel is faced with price-elastic import demand. Given the price elasticities of supply and demand for a raw material and its related processed good, the general equilibrium model is able to indicate the degree of change attainable in real national income as a consequence of export taxation. The figures obtained in this manner, however, should be treated only as a rough guide, since building the model itself involves the adoption of a series of restrictive assumptions.

Chapter 4 presents an empirical microeconomic test that examines whether unilateral export restrictions do in fact lead to increased export revenues and profits for developing countries. The empirical calculations show that - assuming favorable conditions for the developing countries - this is indeed possible for five of the ten UNCTAD core commodities, namely cocoa, tea, sisal, rubber, and tin. In the cases of coffee and jute the results are heavily dependent on the composition of the export cartel. If all developing countries exporting the products concerned were to join together to form supply cartels and cause price increases of 10 percent on the world markets, then the total revenue of the export cartels would increase by $ 500 million (five commodities) or $ 1.1 billion (seven commodities) per annum.

Chapter 5 consists of a theoretical macroeconomic discussion analysing in a comprehensive framework the effects of export restrictions in commodity markets on the real income of the exporting and importing countries and on world welfare. A comparison is made between the efficiency of export restrictions and that of foreign aid in redistributing world income. The major conclusion is that export restrictions are not necessarily harmful to world real income, but that direct transfers (foreign aid) are always superior as a redistributive mechanism.

In Chapter 6 an attempt is made to estimate empirically the stagflationary effects on world economy of export restrictions on primary commodities (excluding petroleum) as they have been implemented in the 1970s. It is assumed that changes in imported commodity prices affect the volume of the imported commodities, hence the level of economic activity and the level of employment as well as the domestic level of prices and finally generate a monetary policy reaction to stimulate the economy that offsets, at least partially, the newly caused unemployment.

The focus is on ten primary commodities (excluding oil) whose exports from LDCs -- their major producers -- have been restricted in recent years. The econometric analysis shows a clear and statistically significant shortrun stagflationary impact of these export restrictions on the economics of importing developed economies. However, this impact seems to be of a relatively small magnitude. There is no doubt that across the board restrictions on exports of all or most primary commodities could cause major damage to the economic activity of importing developed countries. However, in practice, it seems unlikely that such restrictions could be applied to a large number of additional primary commodities. Such restrictions would benefit the exporters only if the commodities in question have distinct characteristics, such as low price elasticities of demand, no close potential substitutes, export cartelisation potential, etc. A constellation of such features favorable to the implementation of export restrictions seems to be quite rare, thus the developed world should not be worried about the possibility of facing large-scale export restrictions from LDCs.

We hypothesize that export restrictions have potential negative effects on the level of economic activity in the importing countries and potential positive effects on export earnings and national income of exporting countries. Higher primary commodity prices could create an expansion of the money supply both in importing and in exporting countries. In chapter 7 the effect of accommodating monetary policies in the developed importing countries is measured.

Chapter 7 focuses on the monetary effects of export restrictions and supply price shocks in both developed and developing countries. The findings indicate that money supply and international reserves do expand in both importing and exporting countries. In order to understand the effects on inflation and growth, we observe two consecutive time periods. In the first period – after the implementation of export restrictions – the rates of inflation rise in the importing countries but drop in the developing economies. As a result, accommodative policies are adopted in the importing countries and yield a larger money supply and larger international reserves in both country groups. This result stimulates inflation in both importing and exporting countries. On the whole, the findings of Chapter 7 show that export restrictions do generate a transfer of income from developing countries at the cost of worldwide inflation and possible unemployment in the developed countries.

A general issue that is only indirectly related to export restrictions is the assessment of the role of primary commodity exports from LDCs in stimulating their economic growth. Chapter 8 is an analytical survey of exports from LDCs during the 1970s. In the descriptive part of the chapter it is shown that during the 1970s the exports of manufactures from LDCs have grown more rapidly than primary commodities in terms of both quantities and values. This indicates the growing relative importance of export earnings originating in the industrial sector. A more detailed review of the facts shows that the major component in LDCs exports in manufactures is the intra-LDC trade. This fact indicates the development of economic interdependence among LDCs, which could become a basis for division of labor enhancing economic growth.

A more refined regression analysis of the export trends indicates that the world price elasticity of demand for the aggregated food commodity group is less than 1, while the price elasticity for the raw materials group is greater than 1. The obvious implication is that, on average, raw materials are not suitable for the imposition of export restrictions. The general contribution of primary commodities exports to the economic growth in LDCs seems to be relatively small, even though there is a clear positive effect of commodity price changes (from exogenous sources). This implies the well-known relationship between terms of trade and national income. Unlike primary commodities, manufacturing sectors in LDCs face high price elasticities of demand on world markets. Nevertheless, the contribution of exports from these sectors to economic growth is larger than that of primary commodity exports. The above facts imply again that the traditional recommendations for industrialization in LDCs seem to be the most rational strategy for development. This may be a slower path but it is safer and holds better prospects than the manipulation of international commodity markets.

Chapter 9 focuses on the ten core commodities and the possible contribution of restrictions of their exports on the rate of growth and export earnings in the exporting developing countries.

The study is based on the analysis of commodity exports (excluding oil) from countries that imposed quantitative controls on their exports during the 1970s. The empirical method used consists of a simultaneous equations system relating commodity export quantities to export earnings, the rate of growth, and the rate of inflation in the LDCs.

The findings show that for most of the selected commodities the necessary condition for successful export controls (a low price elasticity of demand) is satisfied. Moreover, it was found that export controls contributed positively to the growth of export earnings and to the stimulation of economic growth, although they induced some additional inflation.

However, the magnitude of this effect is shown to be rather weak. Only very drastic restrictions of exports were found to lead to a substantial takeoff of economic growth. In less severe instances the impact of such a policy is likely to be only marginal in the short-run and probably nil in the long-run.

Chapter 10 is an historical review of export restrictions since World War I. It includes a presentation of the debates on export restrictions in the League of Nations and later at the Havana Conference, GATT talks, and UNCTAD meetings. The emphasis is on the philosophy that led to provisions concerning trade restrictions in various international agreements.

Chapter 11 presents a detailed analysis of GATT articles and examines the relevance of its provisions on export restrictions. The review indicates that many articles and paragraphs that purport to control and regulate import restrictions either make no reference to export restrictions, or are unclear as far as exports are concerned. Thus, the institutional world trade agreement, which provides some protection to free trade in the context of imports limitations, is insufficient and leaves many loopholes in the field of export restrictions. It is suggested that existing GATT provisions be used regarding imports and that they be applied to exports for the purpose of protecting international free trade from export restrictions. Some scepticism is expressed regarding the prospects for reforming and expanding the GATT agreement. The success of such an operation is conditional upon the recognition by the more powerful economic and political members of GATT that a "rule oriented" behavior is more desirable than a "power oriented" one.

Chapter 12 summarizes some of the findings and expresses important conclusions.

CONCLUSIONS

A review of the studies presented in this volume leads to a series of conclusions regarding both the existing structure of the international economy and the prospects for economic development. These results are academically relevant for improving the insight into the field of export restrictions as one of the characteristics of international trade and development. Moreover, they may be useful in helping to formulate international policies in this field.

The factual review indicates that export restrictions have almost always existed, although the motives behind their imposition have changed over time. The phenomenon appears always to have a negative impact on world welfare and the allocation of resources. Since the establishment of worldwide political and economic organization in the twentieth century, some thought has been given to the possible reduction of export restrictions. However, these attempts have been relatively weak. The GATT agreement, which deals thoroughly with import restrictions, contains large loopholes regarding implementation of export restrictions. Although in some cases, the agreement is explicit in condemning export restrictions, no enforcement or deterrent mechanism was ever applied to prevent the phenomenon or to abolish the violations. That is, the world's institutional structure seems to be less sensitive to and more tolerant of export restrictions than of other trade barriers.

In the 1970s, export restrictions were carried out largely by the international commodity agreements that sought to cartelize the trade of the involved commodities. In 1974, inspired by the success of OPEC, the developing countries called for a New International Economic Order (NIEO). This call was made in a relatively favorable political climate. OPEC had succeeded in transforming commodities exports into economic and political power. The industrialized countries were in a position in which they feared the formation of other cartels. A call for the reform of the system of commodity trade was central to the proposed NIEO.

Raw materials were the first and main problem discussed in the program of action of the NIEO. The goals of that program were to check the decline or stagnation of relative prices; to expand markets for natural materials instead of synthetic substitutes and ensure "just remuneration" for raw materials exports.[4] This philosophy led to the resolution of UNCTAD IV in 1976, the creation of the Common Fund which had the purpose of financing an over-all integrated program for commodities. The declared objectives of the program were the stabilisation of commodity prices and the amelioration of the secular trend in export earnings. International Commodity Agreements (ICAs) have had only limited success in fulfilling these objectives.[5] This conclusion is backed up by some of the findings presented in this volume. The findings in chapter 4 show that some (and probably most) of the commodities in question can hardly become cartelized. The effect of export restrictions on the direct income transfer from DCs to LDCs, as measured in chapter 4, is statistically significant, but its magnitude is of minor importance. Furthermore, the overall effect of export restrictions on the economic growth of LDCs, as measured in chapters 7 and 9, though positive and statistically significant, does not justify their implementation. All of the findings indicate that the effects of export restrictions on both developed and less developed countries are of relatively little importance. Chapters 6 and 7 show that such restrictions (except on petroleum) do create stagflationary effects in the developed countries, but that these effects are not as traumatic as expected by the policymakers of the mid-1970's.

There are signs that the fears and hopes that prevailed in developed and developing countries, respectively, concerning export restrictions on commodity markets have all but disappeared. International forums continue to seek a solution for the problem of raw materials and development, but with less enthusiasm and illusions than hitherto. The 1982 Cancun Summit exemplifies this new approach to the problem. Many observers have been skeptical of the Summit's achievements. However, the establishment of the Cancun Fund to help finance "stable commodity price agreements" may have important implications for the commodity markets.

To sum up the above arguments, export restrictions can be used successfully as a device to redistribute world income and stabilise LDCs' export earnings only if the commodities involved are characterized by low price elasticities of demand, the absence of close potential substitutes, and the possibility of collusion and cooperation by the producing countries for the purpose of cartelising exports and world sales. Only under such conditions can export restrictions be used as a lever for economic development. Since such constellations are quite rare, export restrictions are clearly an inefficient mechanism to solve the special problems of LDCs.

The findings of this volume indicate that economic growth in LDCs can be stimulated (more effectively) through trade if the efforts are channeled to increase exports of industrial goods. This is an old argument that has been expressed in the past by such prominent economists as Prebisch, Myrdal, Lewis, Kindleberger, Nurkse, and others. The claim is reinforced by the findings of chapter 8, which show that in terms of both quantity and value exports of manufactures from LDCs are growing rapidly, relative to the exports of primary commodities.[6] Moreover, world prices of manufactures are relatively more stable than commodity prices and thus constitute a more certain source of export earnings. The contribution of industrial exports to LDCs' economic growth is substantial and the process is accompanied by the development of intra-LDC industrial trade. The latter seems to be a promising phenomenon because it lays the foundations for potential future economic integration within the group of LDCs, which might enhance economic growth and development.

An important qualification regarding the relationship between trade and growth in general and trade in manufactures and growth in particular must be mentioned. As shown by Michaely (1977), a positive correlation between the two can be found only for the middle-income developing countries. In the study presented in chapter 8, the group of LDCs has been analysed as a unit and no distinction has been made with respect to their different levels of development. Therefore, it could well be that the results leading to the above conclusion are relevant only for the subgroup of higher-income LDCs. Michaely concludes that some minimum level of development must be attained before export performance begins to contribute to economic growth. This statement is compatible with the implications of our study.

When looking at the composition of exports, one rates an important distinction between the two groups of LDCs. The middle-income LDCs have somewhat more diversified export sectors, including an ever increasing share of manufactured products. The lower-income LDCs are primary commodities exporters and their export sectors consist of only a few commodities. The more diversified exports of the middle-income LDCs enable them to respond better to market signals and the relative prices of their exports have shown a greater stability.

The policy implication emerging from our study - in line with the Prebisch-Lewis-Myrdal ideas and compatible with Michaely's conclusion - is that the lower-income LDCs should be given the opportunity to break through to higher levels of export diversification, especially in manufactures. This is conditional on the development of competitive industrial sectors. The establishment of an international framework for organising, stabilising, and regulating commodity trade could contribute to the welfare of LDCs. If the international community is really concerned with these problems, it must find effective methods to stimulate industrialization by accelerating the flows of resources designated to create and develop manufactures in LDCs at all income levels. This would be, as we have indicated, a slower development path but a more secure, comprehensive, and promising one than that achieved by manipulating the markets of primary commodities through bureaucratic systems, without fully predictable effects on world economy.

NOTES

1. Hume 1898, 330.
2. Keynes 1944.
3. A detailed discussion of these motives appears in Chapter 2.
4. United Nations General Assembly Resolution #3201 (S-VI) and #3202 (S-VI), May 1, 1974.
5. See Behrman 1978, 62.
6. Similar findings were shown by Balassa 1980.

REFERENCES

Balassa, B. 1980. Structural Change in Trade in Manufactured Goods Between Industrial and Developing Countries, World Bank Staff Working Paper 396.
Behrman, J.R. 1978. Development, The International Economic Order, and Commodity Agreements, Boston: Addison-Wesley.
Hume, D. 1898. Of the Balance of Trade, Essays, Moral, Political and Literary, Vol. 1, London: Longmans Green.
Keynes, J.M. 1944. The International Control of Raw Materials, Unpublished report reprinted in the Journal of International Economics, (1974): 4, 299-315.
Michaely, M. 1977. Exports and Growth: An Empirical Investigation, Journal of Development Economics, 4, 49-53.

# 2
# The General Effect of Export Restrictions on Commodity Markets

*R. Nathanson*
*J. Weinblatt*

INTRODUCTION

In this chapter a systematic classification of export restrictions is presented and their effect on commodity markets discussed. We first discuss the types of measures adopted, and the motives behind their adoption, for each country and commodity group. Tables on commodity production, exports, and prices enable the reader to draw concrete conclusions regarding possible impacts of export controls on commodity markets. The analysis deals only with free market economies. The extraordinary increase in commodity prices during the period 1973/4 is examined and the source of the boom analyzed, mainly to check whether or not it was caused by export restrictions.

Although the analysis is limited to a number of typical cases, it can be considered valid for other commodities or countries (appendix A).

TYPES OF EXPORT RESTRICTIONS

We distinguish among five different types of controls adopted by commodity exporting countries as presented in table 2.1.
The most frequent type of export restriction is the export tax, applied mainly by LDCs on agricultural exports. Export licensing measures imposed in developed countries on exports of agricultural products are second in frequency. Embargoes are also relatively often applied by LDCs in this sector. In the mineral sector the types of measures seem to be more diversified although state trading and taxes are the most frequent cases in LDCs. In total, LDCs applied almost twice as many controls as developed countries.

Table 2.1 Number of Identified Cases of Export Restrictions by Country Classification, Commodity Group, and Type of Measure, 1973-1977.

| Measure | L C Agricultural goods | Minerals | D C Agricultural goods | Minerals | Total Agricultural and mineral goods |
|---|---|---|---|---|---|
| State trading   | 10 | 9 | 2  | 0 | 21 |
| Export quotas   | 7  | 0 | 10 | 1 | 18 |
| Export embargoes| 15 | 6 | 7  | 4 | 32 |
| Export taxes    | 28 | 7 | 2  | 2 | 39 |
| Export licensing| 5  | 6 | 19 | 5 | 35 |
| Subtotal        | 65 | 28| 40 | 12| 145 |
| Total           |    | 9 |    | 5 | 145 |

Source: See Appendix 2.A.

State trading facilitates the regulation of export flows without relying on explicit export taxes. Governments intervene directly in the production and supply of raw materials; in many cases they have nationalized private enterprises in order to control output and prices and attain economic targets. By means of state trading, the government can encourage certain types of exports and achieve a preferred geographical distribution and commodity composition of production. Many LDCs, including Bolivia, Brazil, Colombia, Haiti, Honduras, Morocco, Peru, Togo and Tunisia, adopted state trading as a means of controlling the exports of minerals, fertilizers, and various foodstuffs (see Appendix A). Developed economies such as Australia and Canada adopted this measure especially on wheat exports. Very often state trading relates to production controls that may confuse the classification of this measure as an export restriction. However, in terms of its economic effect, restricting raw material production is identical to an export quota, that is, it limits the overall supply of the commodity.

The government can also intervene indirectly in the export market through currency exchange rates determined by bilateral arrangements, which generally require that export earnings be received in certain specific currencies or that recipients of foreign currency sell the proceeds to the authorities within a determined period of time and at a specified rate of exchange. Such currency restrictions lead to differential pricing of commodities exported without directly interfering in the quantities sold or in nominal prices. In real terms the government's intervention constitutes a loss to consumers that can be expressed as the difference between the real and the nominal rate of exchange they have to pay.

Export quotas are implemented through licensing systems that sever the relationship between quantity supplied and prices. In such a case an implicit tax revenue is generated by the artificially created scarcity, which may remain with the recipients of the quota allocation or with the government. In terms of its economic impact, the effect of an export quota is identical to that of an export tax. A quota imposes physical limits beyond which no additional exports are permitted, while an export tax does not directly restrict the volume exported. In the short-term an export quota will lead to higher prices per unit, the same effect generated by an export tax.

The feasibility of the measure depends on the position and shape of domestic and foreign demand and supply curves. Brazil, for example, imposed in 1973 quotas on the export of green coffee in order to maintain prices on foreign markets. The measure was, to a large degree, successful since Brazil supplied then 23 percent of world coffee exports (see Appendix B), and the impact on the world market was great, although other coffee producers could have provided the necessary supply. Obviously, if the measure is coordinated among all or most producing countries the effect on prices is immediate. Quotas have also been imposed, inter alia, by Canada on wheat, by the US on sugar, and by Japan on nickel, rice, and wheat. Not only developing countries impose export restricting measures. For example, Canada - a net exporter of raw materials - amended its Export-Import Permits Act in May 1974 explicitly to authorize export controls, and made clear its intention to use such controls, if necessary, as part of Canada's overall economic policy.

The export embargo is the extreme form of the export quota. In this case the quantitative limit on exports is total and causes a direct reduction in the export receipts of the country adopting the embargo. In many cases, the embargo imposed on the exports of commodities in their raw form, while the sale of goods processed from such commodities is left unrestricted. For example, almost every country forbids the export of ferrous scrap or at least imposes quantitative restrictions on such exports, in order to guarantee domestic supply (for recycling processes) at prices below those prevailing on international markets. Curiously, among all commodities, the greatest frequency of embargoes is on hides and skins, presumably because many countries have their own leather manufacturing industry for which they wish to ensure domestic supply of raw materials. Some authors have stated that an embargo is largely a very short-term measure, useful over a limited period of time.$^1$ Yet, although an embargo reduces the country's inflow of foreign currency in the short-run, it also serves to guarantee the supply of inputs for the processing industry. The immediate loss of foreign receipts must thus be compared with the currency gains derived from the exports of processed goods.

In terms of economic welfare analysis (except where monopolistic conditions prevail), the effect of an export tax is equivalent to that of an import tariff. The resulting changes in domestic and foreign prices, production and consumption, and the volume of exports depend on the position and shape of domestic and foreign demand curves.

The best example of export taxes are the measures adopted by OPEC and other cartels. The arbitrary decision to raise supply prices is equivalent to an export tax since the change in prices does not occur according to shifts in supply or demand, as in the case of a free market. Similar measures were also imposed by the International Bauxite Association (IBA), which controls more than 70 percent of world bauxite production and can be considered as successful a cartel as OPEC.[2] Jamaica, Guayana, Surinam, Haiti, the Dominican Republic and Ghana imposed taxes on bauxite exports and this increased their foreign currency earnings. In 1974 Jamaica forced consumers to pay a 7.5 percent tax on ingot. Jamaica's tax revenue increased from $ 25 million to $ 170 million, leading other IBA members to adopt similar measures in a joint action on a minimum pricing policy.

Similar attempts by producers' associations of such commodities as copper, cocoa, tin, and coffee were less successful, either because the members could not agree on a joint action or because their market power was not strong enough to impose higher prices.

Export licensing and administrative documentation appear to be more institutional than economic measures, yet there are special licensing systems that, by regulating the flow of exportables, enable the government to impose controls on quantities and prices of raw materials.

Many developed countries including Australia (minerals), the US (soybeans), Finland and Norway (raw timber, wood) have introduced the licensing system either to reinforce their economic policy or to control the exports of raw material. Developing countries such as Brazil, Colombia, Venezuela, Zambia, Malaysia, and Thailand have adopted the licensing measure in order to control and strengthen their foreign trade policy.

Finally, we must note that, especially in the case of agricultural exports (e.g., cocoa, coffee, meat), there are hygiene and quality controls that also prevent foreign trade from being completely free. Such measures are often intended to protect the consumers from losses due to low quality standards but may serve as an indirect method of controlling the flow and prices of the commodity.[4]

## MOTIVES FOR IMPOSING EXPORT RESTRICTIONS

In table 2.2 we present the motives of developing and developed countries for imposing import controls. The most frequent motive of LDCs is the desire to increase export earnings, followed by the desire to improve the processing industries. Both are standard targets of LDCs: to improve their terms of trade - or to prevent their deterioration - and to promote and diversify the domestic industry (infant industry argument).

Table 2.2  Frequency of Motives for Imposing Export Restrictions*

|  | L D Cs | | Countries<br>D Cs<br>Commodities | | T o t a l<br>Agricul- |
|---|---|---|---|---|---|
|  | Agricultural<br>products | Min-<br>erals | Agricultural<br>products | Min-<br>erals | tural and<br>mineral |
| Continuity of<br>domestic supply | 11 | 3 | 17 | 5 | 36 |
| Stabilization of<br>domestic prices | 4 | 2 | 21 | 1 | 28 |
| Fight against<br>inflation caused<br>by balance of<br>payments surplus | 7 | 4 | 0 | 2 | 13 |
| Protection of pro-<br>cessing industries | 34 | 15 | 0 | 1 | 50 |
| Raising of domestic<br>prices to world<br>level | 12 | 2 | 4 | 0 | 18 |
| Conservation of<br>domestic supply | 16 | 4 | 0 | 2 | 22 |
| Compliance with<br>international<br>agreements | 3 | 0 | 0 | 0 | 3 |
| Alignment with<br>world market<br>prices | 22 | 10 | 4 | 0 | 36 |
| Generation of<br>export earnings | 40 | 17 | 1 | 2 | 60 |
| Response to re-<br>strictions in<br>other markets | 0 | 0 | 5 | 0 | 7 |
| Subtotal | 149 | 59 | 52 | 13 | 273 |
| Total |  | 208 |  | 65 | 273 |

Source:  See Classification (Appendix A).
*Mainly during the period 1973-1977.

The developed countries, on the other hand, generally impose restrictions in order to guarantee the continuity of domestic supply and to stabilize prices in domestic markets. Both motives apply largely to agricultural markets. In the mineral sector, where controls are far less frequently applied in developed countries, they are most often imposed in order to guarantee continuous domestic supply or to prevent either unemployment or higher raw material input costs.[5]

In the following section we discuss the motives behind export controls and draw conclusions on their implications.

## Assurance of Continuity of Domestic Supply: Prevention of Shortages Caused by Abnormal Foreign Demand

Under free market conditions, the demand for a specific commodity is composed of foreign and domestic demand. Whenever foreign demand rises more than domestic demand, a supply shift from domestic to foreign markets occurs. In the case of raw materials, we are dealing with resources that are not available on any market nor is substitution possible in the short run. As we have shown, the majority of countries that imposed restrictions in order to prevent abnormal foreign demand from affecting their domestic market, are developed economies that are also the largest consumers of world commodity production. In some cases these countries may be the main commodity producers (for example, the US in oil and soybeans; Canada in logs and wood; Australia in Bauxite and iron ore), but their domestic comsumption rises above their domestic supply, necessitating additional imports. Since in market economies domestic supply is affected by fluctuations of foreign demand, an important motive in adopting the restrictive measure is to protect domestic supply from foreign demand changes (see appendix B, tables 2.A.2 and 2.A.3 for comparison). For example, one can see in table 2.A.2 (Appendix B) that the US is the largest producer of 25 selected commodities (10.72 percent of total world output), followed by the USSR (9.99 percent) and Brazil (5.66 percent) - all countries with large domestic markets.

The US, a major producer of hides and skins, is still attempting to protect its domestic market by imposing controls on the export of this commodity in order to avoid external demand effects. Similarly, the UK imposed controls on tin and nickel exports and Japan imposed controls on nickel and foodstuffs. Net exporters of raw materials (e.g. Indonesia and Malaysia, which produce 24.5 percent and 44.8 percent, respectively, of world rubber; see table 2.A.3, appendix B) usually have additional motives for imposing export controls that go beyond the wish to prevent domestic shortages. These include stabilization of export earnings and the promotion of processing industries (discussed below).

## Stabilization of Export Earnings and Protection Against Fluctuations in Commodity Supply

Another motive behind the adoption of export restriction measures is the desire to cope with uneven fluctuations between foreign demand for and domestic supply of the raw material.

If demand elasticity for a commodity is low, small changes in aggregate supply cause wide fluctuations in market prices and producers' revenue. The same effect occurs in the case of low supply elasticity and changes in aggregate demand. The attempt to regulate exports is therefore aimed at stabilizing producers'

earnings by blunting the effects of changes in aggregate demand or supply on commodity prices.
Since demand, especially foreign demand, is not in the hands of the exporting country, the attempt is made to keep supply of the commodity at a constant rate and thus avoid losses in periods of low demand. Further advantages of controls concern risk averse producers in developing countries. Their expectations (through stabilization) affects investment in supply capacity, either in the agricultural sectors, where gestation periods are long, or in mineral production, where significant investment in capital equipment is required. In addition, the commodity producing countries are concerned with the stabilization of prices in their internal markets. Any fluctuation of commodity prices on world markets creates instability of domestic prices and may lead to inflationary pressures. Thus, developed economies that are also commodity producers (see appendix B, table 2.A.2) impose export controls in order to protect their domestic supply from price fluctuations occurring on world markets. Australia, Canada, the US, and the EEC countries have imposed export controls on foodstuffs, whose prices are more subject to fluctuations than those of minerals.[6] Developing countries such as Indonesia (rubber, hides); the Philippines (copra, bananas); and Turkey (wood, molasses) have imposed controls to stabilize export earnings in the long-run.

To sum up, we have two cases. In the first, more typical of developed countries, the aim is to stabilize domestic prices; in the second, typical of net commodity exporting developing countries, the aim is to guarantee constant export earnings.[7]

## Fight Against Inflation Caused by Balance of Payment Surplus or by Increases in World Prices of Commodities

Worldwide inflation has led many countries to introduce export restrictions in order to relieve the pressure of exogenous shocks on domestic prices. The use of export restrictions in response to an aggregate balance of payments surplus is rare. Yet, as indicated by Morgan (1979), many of the oil exporting countries suffer from increased price levels generated by feedback effects of accumulated export earning surpluses. Export restrictions have also been adopted, in some instances, either as a substitute for or as a complement to major economic targets in developed economies. For example, 1968 West Germany used export taxes in order to reduce the size of its balance of payments surplus and avoid speculative pressures on the Deutsche Mark. Uruguay, Pakistan, and the Philippines are among the developing countries that have imposed export controls in order to regulate domestic prices.

The US imposed quotas on soybean exports in order to control the price of its domestic supply.[8] In this case the purpose of the measure was to shift the burden of inflation caused by foreign demand. The outcome was price discrimination between home and foreign markets, with prices abroad higher than those charged to domestic consumers.[9]

Promotion of Industrial Processing in Order to Increase Export Earnings from Sale of Processed Commodities

One of the objectives of UNCTAD IV was "to diversify production in developing countries, including food production, and to expand processing of primary products in LDCs with a view to promote their industrialization and increase export earnings."[10]

During the period between 1974 and 1976, the developing countries' share in total world exports (including oil) was 24 percent.[11] Their share in total world exports of 33 core commodities was 70 percent, while their share of processed goods was only 9.8 percent (appendix B table 3.A.3). Fifty eight percent of the OECD countries' imports from developing countries were imports of comodities in their raw form and 22 percent were imports of fully processed products. These figures indicate that the developed countries' imports from LDCs were much more concentrated in raw materials than in processed goods, in spite of the fact that the developed countries themselves are main producers of commodities (63 percent of total world output in a weighted average of 25 commodities); (appendix B, table 2A.2). Since the commodity production of these developed countries is insufficient to satisfy domestic needs they are dependent on imports of raw commodities and prefer them to imports of processed commodities. Thus, many commodity importing countries tend to impose low tariffs on raw materials and higher duties on processed primary products.

Table 2.4 indicates that the processing activity in the importing country is effectively protected by the difference between the two tariffs, i.e., the duty imposed on processed imports is higher than the tariff imposed on raw materials, which in many cases is almost zero.[12] Export earnings of commodity exporting countries are low due to the effective protection policy of importing countries. This would probably not be so if processed goods could be exported at the same conditions as raw materials.

Table 2.3 Developing Countries Share of World Commodity Exports* and Total World Exports

| Period | Share in Total World Exports (in percent) | Share in World Commodity Exports (in percent) |
| --- | --- | --- |
| 1970-1972 | 16.7 | 67.0 |
| 1974-1976 | 24.2 | 69.0 |
| 1975-1977 | 23.5 | 69.6 |
| 1979-1981 | 28.3 | 69.3 |

*Based on 33 core commodities

Source: Commodity Trade and Price Trends (Washington, D.C.: The World Bank, 1975, 1978, 1979, 1983).

Table 2.4: Structure of Nominal and Effective Tariff Protection in Developed Market Economies on Selected Primary and Processed Goods Imported from Developing Countries*; LDC Export Taxes on Selected Commodities**

| SITC Heading by stage of processing | LDCs Export tax | US Nominal | US Effective | DCs EEC Nominal | DCs EEC Effective | Japan Nominal | Japan Effective |
|---|---|---|---|---|---|---|---|
| **Meat** | | | | | | | |
| 011 Fresh and frozen | NA | 4.6 | 4.6 | 17.8 | 17.8 | 6.2 | 6.2 |
| 013 Meat preparations | NA | 4.7 | 5.6 | 19.5 | 44.3 | 16.4 | 47.3 |
| **Cocoa** | | | | | | | |
| 072.1 Cocoa beans | 26.5 | 0 | 0 | 3.2 | 3.2 | 3.0 | 3.0 |
| 072.2 Cocoa powder butter | 5.6 | 1.6 | 11.6 | 18.2 | 126.6 | 12.2 | 98.3 |
| **Leather** | | | | | | | |
| 211 Hides and skins | 23.4 | 1.1 | 1.1 | 0 | 0 | 0 | 0 |
| 611 Leather | 13.3 | 4.7 | 12.0 | 4.8 | 12.3 | 11.6 | 34.7 |
| **Copra** | | | | | | | |
| 221.1 Copra | 6.0 | 0 | 0 | 0 | 0 | 0 | 0 |
| Ex422.3 Coconut oil | 4.0 | 24.1 | -13.8 | 7.5 | 92.5 | 20.3 | 27.5 |
| **Rubber** | | | | | | | |
| 231.1 Natural rubber | 6.3 | 0 | 0 | 0 | 0 | 0 | 0 |
| 629 Rubber products | 0 | 4.6 | 6.6 | 7.9 | 16.3 | 6.4 | 10.3 |
| **Cotton** | | | | | | | |
| 263.1 Raw cotton | 11.9 | 6.2 | 6.2 | 0 | 0 | 0 | 0 |
| 651.3 Cotton yarn | 0 | 10.5 | 25.0 | 10.0 | 32.9 | 2.8 | 6.8 |

Table 2.4 (Continued)

| SITC Heading by stage of processing | | LDCs Export tax | US | | DCs EEC | | Japan | |
|---|---|---|---|---|---|---|---|---|
| | | | Nominal | Effective | Nominal | Effective | Nominal | Effective |
| Jute | | | | | | | | |
| 264 | Jute, raw | NA | 0 | 0 | 0 | 0 | 0 | 0 |
| 653.4 | Jute fabric | NA | 0 | -0.6 | 19.6 | 53.3 | 20.0 | 54.4 |
| Sisal | | | | | | | | |
| 265.4 | Sisal henequen | NA | 0 | 0 | 0 | 0 | 0 | 0 |
| 655.6 | Cordage | NA | 3.6 | 10.3 | 10.3 | 30.6 | 9.6 | 28.1 |
| Copper*** | | | | | | | | |
| 283.1 | Copper ore concentrates | NA | 0 | 0 | 0 | 0 | 0 | 0 |
| 682.1 | Copper unwrought | NA | 2.3 | 11.2 | 0 | -5.6 | 7.0 | 43.1 |
| Aluminium | | | | | | | | |
| 283.3 | Bauxite | 7.5*** | 0 | 0 | 0 | 0 | 0 | 0 |
| 513.6 | Alumina | NA | 0 | 0 | 5.6 | 11.1 | 0 | 0 |
| 684.1 | Aluminium unwrought | NA | 4.0 | 6.0 | 5.8 | 5.6 | 10.4 | 11.4 |
| 684.2 | Aluminium wrought | NA | 5.9 | 11.5 | 12.8 | 29.3 | 13.6 | 29.0 |
| Zinc | | | | | | | | |
| Ex283.5 | Zinc ore concentrates | NA | 12.0 | 0 | 0 | 0 | 0 | 0 |
| | Zinc unwrought | NA | 6.6 | 2.5 | 5.8 | 13.4 | 6.5 | 14.8 |

Sources:
* UNCTAD V. The Processing Before Exports of Primary Commodities: Areas for Further Cooperation. May 1979, 18 f.
** S.S. Golub and J.M. Finger. The Processing of Primary Commodities; Effects of Developed Country Tariff Escalation and Developing-Country Export Taxes. Journal of Political Economy 87:
*** Eight Mineral Cartels. Metal Week, USA 1975, IBA members imposed this tax in 1974.

The Tokyo Round on Multilateral Trade Negotiations (MTN) was hoping to reduce import restrictions in developed economies. Under a recently achieved formula, the developed countries agreed on an average tariff reduction of 33 to 38 percent. However, as Balassa (1980) shows, tariff cuts are smaller on industrial products that are of special interest for developing countries.

An important question is whether the exporting countries are better off in terms of economic welfare by producing the raw or the processed commodity. In our classification the commodities most frequently restricted for processing reasons are coffee (instant, soluble coffee); cocoa (soluble cocoa); hides and skins (leather products); phosphates (fertilizers); raw wood (plywood, furniture); and bauxite (aluminium). Most of the countries that impose export quotas or taxes are developing countries that are interested in promoting their domestic processing industries.[13] In some cases (coffee, cocoa) the exporting countries hold sufficient monopolistic power to improve their processing industries through coordinated action. Similarly, the main exporters of bauxite, organized in the IBA, succeeded by joint action in developing their own domestic aluminium production for exports.[14] The Association decided: (1) "to promote the orderly and rational development of the bauxite industry" and (2) "to secure for member countries fair and reasonable returns from the exploitation, processing and marketing of bauxite and its products, for the economic and social development of their people, bearing in mind the recognized interest of comsumers."[15]

The success of export restricting measures in promoting processing industries in LDCs depends upon the relative scarcity of the commodity on world markets; the degree of dependence of importing countries on the raw material, which affects their capacity for retaliation to export restrictions by means of tariffs on processed goods; and the feasibility of selling raw materials on the domestic market (inputs to processing industries) at prices below those prevailing on the world market (see (4) table 2.2). This means that domestic sales of raw materials must be as profitable as sales abroad. Such an objective can be achieved either by a direct subsidy to the processing industry or by imposing taxes on the exports of raw materials. Both measures should facilitate for domestic producers to achieve the necessary scales of production to enable them to begin or increase the export of processed goods to world markets. Quantitative controls such as quotas or embargo have similar effects. Since the domestic supply of the commodity increases as a result of the restrictions, prices at home adjust to a lower level than those abroad. The motives behind the quantitative restrictions imposed by LDCs, therefore, often include the desire to encourage local industry to process natural resources (see appendix A).[16]

Conservation of Non-renewable Resources

Current exploitation of raw materials may not reflect the future profit foregone as a result of current sales. The so-called "future exhaustion cost" has lead many countries to adopt measures designed to regulate domestic production and/or exports according to constant growth rates. Abnormal rates of exhaustion have been increasingly used to justify restriction on the exports of, for example, saw logs, timber (Malaysia, Panama, the Philippines), phosphates (Morocco, Spain) and, of course, petroleum.

The optimal rate of production depends on the rate of domestic consumption of each exporting country; on the estimated reserves of its resources; on its need for foreign currency earnings to finance imports; and on the expected rate of world price changes and interest rates. In practice, any attempt to determine an optimal rate of exports of resources involves a large degree of uncertainty regarding future world demand and supply conditions. Again we must distinguish between the implications of the measure as adopted by developing and developed countries. Developed countries that protect their economies from current excessive supply of exhaustible commodities are interested in securing a well-established processing industry against future physical shortages in order to maintain economic activity and prevent unemployment. For developing countries, the export of raw materials is usually the sole, or near sole, source of foreign currency (appendix B, table 2.A.3). A further complication derives from the fact that the companies that are unwilling to sacrifice current profits to ensure future supply may fear expropriation at a later date. Moreover, those LDCs that depend on commodity exports for their foreign currency earnings are severely limited in their efforts to conserve natural resources if they have to import basic consumer goods not produced domestically.

## Compliance with International Agreements

International contracts, such as bilateral agreements, may lead producers to adapt export prices or quantities to the conditions agreed upon in such accords. Furthermore, the possible future consequences of distortions caused by interventions in commodity markets may motivate producers to enter bilateral agreements rather than to take the risks of fluctuating export earnings. None of the countries in our classification specifically imposed restrictions in order to comply with international agreements; the many commodity exporters that did enter into such contracts (e.g., the cases of tin, sugar, coffee) did so to stabilize export earnings.

## Alignment of Export Prices with World Market Prices

The alignment of export prices with world market prices has occurred mainly during periods of commodity price booms. The question why almost all raw material prices rise at the same time during a boom is an interesting one. Is such a phenomenon a result of cyclical changes in consumption and production, or are there additional structural factors affecting such booms? Are export controls a cause or a consequence of commodity price increases? The evidence suggests that export controls represent both a cause and an effect. When producers have the necessary monopolistic power to impose higher prices, export controls cause commodity prices to rise; on the other hand, export controls are applied when countries want to protect their domestic commodity markets from world inflation.

During periods of rising world inflation, commodity exporters strive to adjust their export prices so as to maintain the real price of their good. Where possible, that is, where demand elasticity is relatively low or where exporting countries are able to exert monopolistic power, they try to improve real gains. Monopolistic power may be exerted by countries (mostly LDCs) that are both major world producers and world exporters of commodities (e.g., exporters of coffee, cocoa, bauxite, phosphates, manganese (compare appendix B, table 2.A.1, 2.A.2). Moreover, when prices of essential materials, such as oil, rise, the countries whose main source of foreign currency earnings are commodity exports try to compensate for the higher costs of their imports. They do that raising the prices of their own commodities, thereby preventing a deterioration in their terms of trade.

Increase in Export Earnings

The desire to increase export earnings is closely related to the alignment of export prices with world market prices, yet its roots are deeper than the problem of rising oil prices. Prebisch held that there is a general tendency towards a deterioration in the terms of trade of LDCs. This led UNCTAD IV to decide that proposals should be elaborated in order to "improve and sustain the real income of individual developing countries through increased export earnings, and to protect them from fluctuations in export earnings especially from commodities."[17]

This issue is related to the basic demand by LDCs for indexation of commodity prices to world inflation and changing monetary situations. According to LDCs, indexation should also take into account changes in the prices of manufactured goods imported by the LDCs. This demand, known as the terms of trade argument, was originally formulated by Prebisch.[18]

Many doubts may be cast on Prebisch's hypothesis, but in fact, as we have noted, this is one of the central motives for LDCs in applying export controls.[19] Developing countries also claim that the decline in their terms of trade result from low price and income elasticities of primary commodity demand. Furthermore, since LDCs are assumed to be limited in their ability to transfer labor from primary production to other economic activities, technological improvement in primary production tends to lead to lower commodity prices rather than to higher wage rates. Developed economies with capital intensive industries, on the other hand, can pay higher wage rates as a result of technological improvements.

From table 2.5 we realize that the terms of trade of industrial countries slightly deteriorated between 1968 and 1978, while the figures for developing countries including oil exporting countries indicate a change in their favor, particularly since 1973. However, a different picture emerges for developing countries that are net commodity exporters but not oil exporting countries. Their terms of trade deteriorated significantly in 1974 and 1975 and started to improve again only in 1976, after they had absorbed the effects of the oil price shock.

The worst-off countries are LDCs that have neither reached developed industrialized standards, nor are net exporters of commodities. Thus the terms of trade of individual countries that are mainly commodity exporters might differ from those shown in table 2.5.

Table 2.6 shows that most of the selected countries enjoyed an improvement of their terms of trade in 1972 and 1973. These were two years when export restrictions were at their peak. Nevertheless, 1974 and 1975 were years of deterioration in the terms of trade of most LDCs listed in this table. This deterioration has to be partly attributed to the hike in oil prices. Moreover, it seems that the advantages enjoyed by commodity exporters were of short duration because the rise in commodity prices led the industrialized countries to adjust the price of manufactures to the higher input costs, which in turn led to higher costs of imports of manufactures for the net commodity exporters and had a negative influence on their terms of trade.[20]

We know that trade flows depend on relative prices. In a long-run equilibrium analysis it does not matter theoretically whether relative price changes result from import or export controls. According to the Lerner symmetry theorem (1936), a tax on imports or exports affects the relative price in the same way. Therefore, a foreign trade tax drives a margin between the domestic and the world price ratio. A decline in domestic production due to a tax, combined with increased world demand, reduces overall foreign supply, resulting in a loss in world welfare. But the gains of the individual country in this case depend upon the terms of trade effect. The terms of trade improve when (1) domestic import demand elasticity is larger than one and (2) the country's supply curve has a finite elasticity larger than one.

We have already mentioned that many countries are unable to improve their trade position because of their dependence on imports of basic essential commodities (e.g., oil), whose domestic import demand elasticity is less than one. Condition (2) above depends on the supply curve of each commodity. The supply elasticity depends on structural conditions and on the capacity of each commodity producer to adapt his supply curve to changing demand. Thus, the condition obviously differs according to the type of raw materials, i.e., whether they are minerals, agricultural goods, or semi-final goods. We know that cyclical changes in commodity demand create supply surpluses with consequent losses to producers and to export earnings.

To sum up, countries that have a sufficient share of world production of a specific commodity can increase their export earnings by adopting export restrictions. Their real terms of

Table 2.5 Annual Rates of Change of Terms of Trade (in Percent) (1976=100)

| Country group | 1968 | 1969 | 1970 | 1971 | 1972 | 1973 | 1974 | 1975 | 1976 | 1977 | 1978 | 1979 | 1980 | 1981 | 1982 |
|---|---|---|---|---|---|---|---|---|---|---|---|---|---|---|---|
| Industrial | 0.0 | -0.9 | 1.8 | -0.9 | 0.9 | -0.9 | -11.8 | 3.1 | -1.0 | -1.0 | 2.0 | -2.0 | -8.2 | -1.1 | 2.2 |
| LDC, including oil exporters | 0.0 | 1.4 | -1.4 | 1.4 | 1.4 | 9.6 | 38.8 | -9.9 | 5.0 | 0.9 | -5.7 | 9.0 | 13.8 | 3.2 | -0.8 |
| LDC, excluding oil exporters | 4.6 | 6.2 | 0.0 | -7.5 | 0.9 | 7.1 | -9.2 | -8.2 | 6.0 | 13.2 | -5.5 | -0.9 | -6.5 | -7.0 | NA |

Source: Calculation based on data from IMF Yearbook 1983 and Commodity Trade and Price Trends 1983.

Table 2.6: Annual Rates of Change of Terms of Trade of Commodity Exporting Countries (in percent)

| Country | 1968 | 1969 | 1970 | 1971 | 1972 | 1973 | 1974 | 1975 | 1976 | 1977 | 1978 | 1979 | 1980 | 1981 |
|---|---|---|---|---|---|---|---|---|---|---|---|---|---|---|
| **Latin America** | | | | | | | | | | | | | | |
| Brazil | -1.9 | 4.9 | 10.3 | -8.4 | 7.4 | 7.8 | -17.6 | -2.9 | 12.0 | 17.9 | -14.4 | -8.0 | -17.3 | -15.1 |
| Colombia | NA | NA | NA | -5.1 | 3.2 | 8.3 | 2.9 | -6.5 | 40.0 | -3.5 | -23.7 | 10.1 | -16.9 | NA |
| El Salvador | 4.0 | 1.9 | 16.6 | -5.0 | 0.8 | 7.9 | -13.0 | -6.5 | 50.0 | 31.3 | -24.7 | 1.3 | -18.5 | -1.6 |
| Jamaica | NA | NA | 0.0 | 0.0 | -10.2 | -25.0 | 21.9 | -21.9 | -5.0 | -19.4 | 10.7 | NA | NA | NA |
| Mexico | -3.5 | 0.0 | -1.2 | -2.4 | 3.7 | 7.2 | 3.3 | 8.6 | NA | 6.9 | 1.8 | NA | NA | NA |
| Panama | 12.4 | -0.8 | 0.0 | -0.8 | 0.0 | -1.7 | -17.5 | 6.3 | -10.0 | -1.0 | -9.3 | NA | NA | NA |
| **Africa** | | | | | | | | | | | | | | |
| Ivory Coast | NA | NA | NA | NA | 12.3 | 23.4 | -7.5 | -18.0 | 30.0 | 46.1 | -20.0 | -3.7 | -3.0 | -23.9 |
| Kenya | 2.4 | -2.4 | 6.6 | -1.5 | 3.1 | -6.1 | -10.5 | -9.0 | 16.0 | 32.7 | -19.7 | -7.4 | -8.8 | NA |
| Morocco | -1.2 | -5.0 | 0.0 | -2.6 | -8.1 | -4.4 | 43.0 | 7.5 | -21.0 | -8.4 | 0.0 | NA | NA | NA |
| Tanzania | 3.3 | 0.0 | -3.2 | -18.6 | 4.0 | 10.2 | -6.1 | -6.5 | NA | 20.2 | -17.3 | -11.4 | 2.4 | NA |
| Tunisia | 1.6 | 4.6 | -2.9 | -1.5 | 6.2 | 8.8 | 50.0 | -9.9 | -6.0 | 0.0 | 3.2 | 22.7 | NA | NA |
| Zambia | 8.8 | 30.1 | -15.4 | -27.3 | -4.1 | 32.5 | -4.2 | -50.7 | 9.0 | -5.5 | -3.9 | NA | NA | NA |
| **Asia** | | | | | | | | | | | | | | |
| India | -0.7 | 2.2 | 0.7 | 3.5 | 3.4 | -6.6 | -23.4 | -7.4 | 0.0 | 23.0 | -2.5 | -7.6 | -20.9 | NA |
| Malasia | -8.9 | 14.6 | -6.4 | -11.4 | -12.0 | 25.5 | -0.7 | -21.8 | 16.0 | 11.2 | 3.9 | 22.3 | -2.1 | -14.7 |
| Pakistan | NA | NA | NA | -1.6 | 9.6 | -27.2 | 29.3 | -21.8 | 13.0 | 16.8 | -5.3 | 7.3 | -16.5 | -13.5 |
| Philippines | -0.6 | -2.1 | -2.8 | -7.4 | -9.6 | 14.1 | 1.5 | -23.6 | -11.0 | -8.9 | 11.1 | 4.5 | -16.1 | -11.5 |

Sources: International Financial Statistics (Washington, D.C.: IMF, 1983) and UN Statistical Yearbook, New York: UN, 1973, 1974, 1975, 1976, 1977, 1983).

trade improve, however, only if domestic import demand elasticity for other raw materials or final goods is greater than one, and their export supply curve is elastic enough to adjust in periods of low demand.

Restrictions in Other Markets

Export restrictions in one country often lead to the imposition of controls in other exporting countries. The latter wish to protect their domestic markets from the shift in demand caused by the quotas imposed by the first country. For example, Canada imposed controls on the export of logs, plywood, soya, beef, and pork because of controls adopted by the US.

Another case where a country may be motivated to impose restrictions because of the adoption of controls in another is the so-called "set an example" case. As we have mentioned, OPEC's success in implementing their price policy led many countries to follow that example and to attempt to cartelize commodity exports.

Summary

Table 2.7 indicates the type of export restrictions that were adopted for the various motives. The most frequent cases are export taxes imposed by LCDs in order to increase export earnings and to guarantee domestic prices below those prevailing on world markets to promote the processing industries. The motive of LDCs seeking to align commodity export prices to world market levels is also important. Export embargoes, quotas, and licensing are most often imposed to guarantee domestic supply in developed countries, although LDCs also used these measures to promote domestic processing.

We can, then, say that in general the main objectives of export restrictions appear to be: (1) the achievement of a shift of world income from the developed to the developing commodity exporting countries; (2) the improvement of local processing industries in LDCs and the concomitant benefits to employment and development in those countries; (3) the prevention of unemployment and welfare losses in developed countries.

Not all of these targets can be fulfilled simultaneously. Furthermore, it remains unclear whether losses in world welfare are greater in the absence of export controls. Alternative sources of redistribution (such as foreign aid, direct subsidies to production in LDCs, etc.) can contribute towards helping LDCs develop and at the same time prevent adverse effects such as higher prices of inputs (raw materials), successive cost-push inflation, and stagflation in the importing countries.

THE IMPACT OF CHANGES IN COMMODITY SUPPLY

The impact of export restrictions on the commodity importing countries depends on the power of the exporters to achieve higher prices. The consumers' situation depends on the respective demand elasticities for the various types of commodities. Agricultural

Table 2.7  Measures/Motives Matrix Frequency Controls on Commodity Exports by Country

| Motives | State trading | Export quota | Export embargo | Export taxes | Export licensing | Total |
|---|---|---|---|---|---|---|
| Continuity of domestic supply | 2 | 6 | 11 | 0 | 11 | 30 |
| Stabilization of domestic prices | 1 | 3 | 3 | 2 | 5 | 14 |
| Fight against inflation caused by balance of payments surplus | 0 | 0 | 2 | 2 | 1 | 5 |
| Protection of processing industries | 1 | 4 | 7 | 10 | 4 | 26 |
| Raising of domestic prices to world level | 2 | 3 | 1 | 2 | 2 | 10 |
| Conservation of domestic supply | 0 | 0 | 4 | 1 | 4 | 9 |
| Compliance with international agreements | 0 | 0 | 0 | 1 | 0 | 1 |
| Alignment with world market prices | 5 | 0 | 1 | 9 | 1 | 16 |
| Generation of export earnings | 10 | 1 | 1 | 12 | 4 | 28 |
| Response to restrictions in other markets | 0 | 1 | 2 | 0 | 0 | 3 |
| Subtotal LDC | 19 | 7 | | 35 | 10 | 92 |
| Subtotal DC | 2 | 11 | | 4 | 22 | 50 |
| Total | 21 | 18 | | 39 | 32 | 142 |

Source:  Appendix 2.A; see also table 2.1

commodities can be considered to be intermediate-final goods while minerals can be identified as inputs. Demand behavior **varies** according to the attributes of each commodity.

In the short-run, agricultural commodities can be substituted when prices rise sharply. In this case, consumers tend to cease purchasing the high priced products and alter their preferences in favor of other commodities. Supply derived shocks like those that occurred in 1973 in the agricultural markets may also shift comparative advantages of traditional exporters and constitute an

Table 2.8  Annual Rate of Change of Commodity Prices (in percent).

| Commodities | 1972 | 1973 | 1974 | 1975 | 1976 | 1977 | 1978 | 1979 | 1980 |
|---|---|---|---|---|---|---|---|---|---|
| Agricultural commodities | | | | | | | | | |
| Cocoa | 19.4 | 75.9 | 37.8 | -30.1 | 64.2 | 85.3 | -10.1 | -8.3 | -23.9 |
| Coffee | 12.2 | 23.4 | 9.3 | 6.6 | 95.9 | 61.3 | -32.3 | 8.8 | 8.9 |
| Rice | 14.0 | 142.6 | 64.0 | -33.0 | -29.9 | 6.9 | 34.9 | -18.5 | 19.9 |
| Bananas | 15.1 | 1.9 | 11.7 | 32.9 | 5.3 | 5.5 | 5.3 | 13.6 | 15.2 |
| Copra | -25.2 | 150.5 | 87.3 | 61.2 | 7.3 | 46.3 | 16.8 | 42.9 | -32.6 |
| Soybeans | 10.9 | 108 | -4.8 | -20.5 | 5.0 | 20.7 | -3.9 | 10.8 | 0.0 |
| Fishmeal | 42.1 | 127.2 | -31.3 | -34.0 | 53.3 | 20.4 | -9.5 | -3.6 | 27.8 |
| Cotton | 23.9 | 63.4 | 3.2 | -22.1 | 50.8 | -9.4 | -6.5 | 7.8 | 30.9 |
| Jute | 4.2 | -3.4 | 22.6 | 6.6 | -20.5 | 8.1 | 24.4 | -3.2 | -18.5 |
| Sisal | 40.9 | 119.8 | 100.3 | -45.0 | -19.2 | 9.4 | -4.5 | 44.2 | 8.3 |
| Rubber | 0.4 | 94.5 | 13.0 | -24.8 | 32.4 | 5.0 | 20.2 | 28.4 | 14.5 |
| Timber | -4.8 | 66.8 | 19.2 | -17.4 | 36.3 | -2.4 | 2.2 | 56.4 | 11.2 |
| Hides and skins | 104.1 | 15.9 | -31.1 | -1.2 | 44.2 | 10.1 | 27.5 | 55.1 | -37.3 |
| Tobacco | 8.8 | 4.4 | 14.2 | 8.6 | 1.9 | 8.8 | 7.75 | 8.6 | 5.8 |
| Sugar | 6.5 | 13.3 | 186 | -23.6 | -40.8 | -16.8 | NA | 19.9 | 23.0 |
| Minerals | | | | | | | | | |
| Aluminium | -5.6 | 1.4 | 27.6 | 13.5 | 2.5 | 28.4 | 15.7 | 17.0 | 21.6 |
| Bauxite | 7.6 | 13.8 | 18.5 | 46.4 | 11.4 | 14.9 | NA | 10.2 | 39.2 |
| Copper | -1.1 | 66.7 | 15.1 | -39.9 | 13.9 | -6.5 | 3.9 | 45.6 | 10.3 |
| Nickel | 5.1 | 9.4 | 13.4 | 18.6 | 9.6 | 4.6 | -11.4 | 29.8 | 24.8 |
| Tin | 7.4 | 28.0 | 70.0 | -16.4 | 11.5 | 41.2 | 18.9 | 20.3 | 8.9 |
| Lead | 19.0 | 42.4 | 37.7 | -30.4 | 9.2 | 37.4 | 6.4 | 80.5 | -24.3 |
| Zinc | 34.4 | 104.6 | 45.6 | -39.8 | -4.5 | -16.7 | -1.2 | 25.7 | 2.5 |
| Iron Ore | -4.9 | 33.8 | 10.9 | 20.0 | -3.6 | -1.7 | -10.2 | 20.9 | 13.9 |
| Manganese | 1.0 | 18.0 | 50.0 | 22.5 | 5.2 | 2.0 | -4.0 | -3.0 | 10.9 |
| Phosphates | 2.3 | 19.8 | 296.0 | 21.1 | -46.7 | -14.2 | -5.4 | 13.6 | 36.2 |

Source: International Financial Statistics Yearbook 1979 (Washington, D.C.: IMF, 1983).

Table 2.9 Developing Countries' Exports of Principal Commodities: Relative Annual Quantity Change (in percent).

| Commodities | 1972 | 1973 | 1974 | 1975 | 1976 | 1977 | 1978 | 1979 | 1980 |
|---|---|---|---|---|---|---|---|---|---|
| Agricultural commodities | | | | | | | | | |
| Cocoa | 5.0 | -11.4 | 5.9 | -2.7 | -1.2 | -15.6 | 11.2 | -5.4 | 6.5 |
| Coffee | 7.5 | 5.2 | -11.5 | 5.9 | 1.5 | -21.3 | 18.6 | 10.5 | -1.9 |
| Rice | -3.7 | -24.4 | -11.7 | -2.4 | 80.1 | 41.2 | -30.8 | 47.2 | 2.9 |
| Bananas | 3.5 | 0.4 | -2.4 | -2.5 | 2.6 | 2.6 | 4.7 | 1.8 | -0.8 |
| Copra | 27.4 | -23.1 | -49.1 | 105.0 | 3.7 | -23.7 | -32.1 | -33.8 | 0.7 |
| Soybeans | 356.9 | 73.3 | 50.3 | 21.6 | 13.9 | -12.4 | -16.56 | 32.66 | 17.44 |
| Fishmeal | -6.8 | -66.2 | 41.8 | 14.0 | -7.3 | -15.9 | -0.20 | 8.58 | 7.75 |
| Cotton | 11.5 | -5.4 | -28.6 | 20.6 | -7.1 | -10.5 | 21.70 | -10.83 | 4.19 |
| Jute | -0.8 | 11.5 | 2.8 | -41.0 | 19.1 | -11.1 | -16.96 | 10.00 | -9.67 |
| Sisal | -4.6 | -5.8 | -8.4 | -34.4 | 2.2 | -3.4 | -9.93 | -4.49 | -2.99 |
| Rubber | -1.3 | 17.7 | -6.9 | -4.0 | 6.1 | 2.1 | 0.83 | 3.14 | -2.84 |
| Timber | 6.1 | 20.6 | -12.9 | -12.8 | 24.4 | 0.5 | 2.94 | 5.37 | -7.58 |
| Hides and skins | -2.1 | -28.6 | -9.9 | -0.3 | 15.0 | 0.0 | 1.95 | 4.31 | 0.46 |
| Tobacco | 9.1 | 0.2 | 21.4 | -1.5 | 5.2 | -5.2 | 9.79 | 7.38 | 7.38 |
| Sugar | 12.5 | 6.8 | 0.0 | -12.6 | 6.7 | 22.8 | -28.44 | 9.83 | 1.85 |
| Minerals | | | | | | | | | |
| Aluminium | 40.0 | 12.0 | 13.3 | -20.5 | 19.6 | 3.4 | 5.85 | 35.77 | -3.23 |
| Bauxite | -6.1 | 2.6 | 22.6 | -10.8 | 6.9 | 5.2 | -2.60 | -4.26 | 12.11 |
| Copper | 10.3 | 5.1 | 13.0 | -11.3 | 14.2 | 4.0 | -5.98 | 1.34 | 4.99 |
| Nickel | -17.5 | 11.3 | 13.6 | 0.5 | -1.7 | 4.8 | -10.98 | 38.36 | -2.48 |
| Tin | 1.4 | -6.7 | 5.4 | -8.5 | 1.1 | 4.0 | 1.20 | 2.37 | -0.58 |
| Lead | -5.2 | -19.8 | -8.2 | 0.5 | 2.1 | 3.3 | 14.88 | -8.69 | -3.98 |
| Zinc | 10.5 | -15.4 | 11.4 | -2.5 | 13.5 | -2.6 | 1.02 | -2.02 | -2.02 |
| Iron Ore | -3.6 | 19.5 | 14.3 | -5.0 | -6.6 | -9.8 | 3.25 | 10.06 | 1.71 |
| Manganese | -10.8 | -15.6 | 18.5 | 0.5 | -13.0 | -20.2 | 16.13 | 6.37 | -11.59 |
| Phosphates | 7.1 | 21.9 | 19.1 | -26.8 | -0.1 | 14.1 | 10.28 | 2.35 | -3.80 |

Source: International Financial Statistics Yearbook 1979 (Washington, D.C.: IMF, 1983).

Table 2.10  Developing Countries' Exports of Principal Commodities: Relative Annual Value Change (in percent)

| Commodities | 1972 | 1973 | 1974 | 1975 | 1976 | 1977 | 1978 | 1979 | 1980 |
|---|---|---|---|---|---|---|---|---|---|
| Agricultural commodities | | | | | | | | | |
| Cocoa | -8.5 | 24.8 | 58.0 | -9.3 | 1.0 | 56.4 | 13.55 | 2.24 | -14.40 |
| Coffee | 13.8 | 25.0 | -12.1 | -7.3 | -3.9 | 38.8 | -23.88 | -2.78 | 5.79 |
| Rice | 3.1 | 19.1 | 83.6 | 27.1 | 17.2 | 32.7 | 32.76 | -4.26 | 18.83 |
| Bananas | 5.2 | -0.8 | -8.2 | 15.9 | 0.7 | 9.29 | 4.7 | 11.44 | 9.40 |
| Copra | 1.8 | -16.5 | 12.2 | -11.9 | -29.5 | 28.4 | 17.29 | 56.00 | -30.11 |
| Soybeans | 389.5 | 276.3 | 9.0 | 9.2 | 13.6 | 11.1 | -15.23 | 8.17 | -7.91 |
| Fishmeal | -13.7 | -22.8 | 12.3 | -33.4 | 28.0 | -0.6 | -0.13 | -9.33 | 30.31 |
| Cotton | 18.2 | 7.1 | -0.2 | -15.0 | 0.2 | 4.5 | -5.06 | 2.72 | 6.29 |
| Jute | 10.2 | -6.2 | -11.5 | -39.4 | 21.2 | -6.4 | 19.69 | 14.13 | 2.25 |
| Sisal | 16.3 | 90.7 | 93.3 | -66.5 | -30.9 | 0.5 | 5.23 | 26.43 | 20.68 |
| Rubber | -11.6 | 107.1 | 10.4 | -37.6 | 40.3 | 5.1 | 15.60 | 29.26 | 11.10 |
| Timber | 11.6 | 82.8 | -4.3 | -35.2 | 45.8 | 0.0 | 4.76 | 52.45 | 10.89 |
| Hides and skins | 36.7 | 9.5 | -25.0 | -15.6 | -0.9 | -5.4 | 5.49 | 16.66 | -16.98 |
| Tobacco | 35.1 | -12.4 | 36.0 | 5.9 | 6.1 | 4.2 | 8.28 | 1.24 | 3.19 |
| Sugar | 13.2 | 18.9 | 126.3 | 4.5 | -48.0 | -10.1 | -0.93 | 7.74 | 96.18 |
| Minerals | | | | | | | | | |
| Aluminium | 23.7 | -0.1 | 45.3 | -17.6 | 99.5 | 11.8 | 4.30 | -7.15 | 82.46 |
| Bauxite | -5.1 | -3.7 | 47.1 | -1.2 | 20.7 | 1.8 | 1.28 | 15.19 | 1.83 |
| Copper | 6.3 | 50.9 | 24.9 | -50.9 | 19.6 | -4.6 | 4.58 | 42.41 | 7.91 |
| Nickel | -17.1 | 15.5 | 21.9 | 10.7 | -8.2 | 4.2 | -14.64 | 34.53 | 43.50 |
| Tin | 3.6 | 7.9 | 62.0 | -27.0 | 7.1 | 29.1 | 22.44 | 18.33 | 13.41 |
| Lead | 14.7 | 4.1 | 54.1 | -40.1 | -6.6 | 26.6 | 8.29 | 54.77 | -13.19 |
| Zinc | 21.6 | 24.2 | 67.6 | -12.4 | 15.5 | 7.5 | -8.97 | 16.28 | 4.71 |
| Iron Ore | -5.6 | 16.6 | 30.2 | 13.6 | -1.1 | -13.3 | -4.71 | 12.95 | 14.01 |
| Manganese | -9.3 | -5.9 | 61.8 | 23.8 | -4.2 | -23.4 | -26.48 | 27.68 | 11.95 |
| Phosphates | 13.1 | 25.6 | 397.3 | -17.0 | 46.9 | -7.8 | -2.27 | 3.65 | 46.47 |

Source: International Financial Statistics Yearbook 1979 (Washington, D.C.: IMF, 1983).

incentive for importing countries to produce their own agricultural commodities or search for alternative sources of supply.[21] Furthermore, agricultural exports react rapidly to higher prices because their output is not subject to large processing activities and consumers' welfare is affected directly, i.e., prices rise or fall.

Minerals are much easier to conserve and stock than agricultural products, and they are thus less sensitive to short-run impacts of embargoes, quotas, or price increase. On the other hand, they cannot be substituted in the short-run. Demand for minerals is determined primarily by the needs of the processing industries. The structural adaptation to higher input costs is not immediate in this sector, since the composition of production factors cannot be altered in the short-run. Furthermore, a switch to alternative sources of supply is not possible because mineral production has natural constraints. Contractual obligations to supply industrial consumer goods must also be fulfilled. The mineral users' market reacts to higher prices at a later stage, i.e., the shift in purchased quantities occurs at a later period. This lagged behavior can be observed in tables 2.8, 2.9, and 2.10. The impact of a supply shock may simultaneously cause a reduction of output and employment in the processing industries and higher prices of final consumer goods. The fall in demand for minerals following the 1973/74 supply shock led many exporting countries to reduce mining investment. Shortages of mineral inputs during periods when world industrial output revives from the recession are the consequence and once again lead to higher prices.[22]

APPENDIX A
Classification of Export Restrictions in Commodity Markets

| Region/ country | Commodity | Type of measure (1)-(5) | Motive (6)-(16) | Effect (17)-(21) | GATT regulations (22)-(27) | Period of notification |
|---|---|---|---|---|---|---|
| **I. South America** | | | | | | |
| Argentina | Hides and skins | (3) | (14) | (17)-(18) | (22) | June 1977 |
| | Wheat, grain, corn | (4) | (10) | (20) | (22) | 1972/1975 |
| Bolivia | Coffee | (4) | (14) | (20),(18) | (26) | 1974 |
| | Tin | (1) (4) | (14) | (18) | (26) | 1971 |
| Brazil | Sisal | (1) | (14) | (19) | (22) | |
| | Green coffee | (2) | (9) | (18),(20) | (22) | 1973 |
| | Leather, tin, copper, nickel aluminium, wood, magnesium, zinc | (3) | (9) | (20),(17), (18) | (22) | |
| | Iron ore | (5) | (14) | (17),(18) | (22) | |
| Chile | Copper | (4) | (14) | (18) | (22) | 1971/1973 |
| Colombia | Molases, fertilizers | (1) | (14) | (20),(18) | (22) | |
| | Hides, skins, wood, timber | (3) | (9),(6), (11) | (17) | (22) | |
| | Platinum | (5) | (9),(14) | (17),(18), (20) | (22) | |
| Ecuador | Molasses | (2) | (14) | (18) | (22) | |
| | Hides, bananas, coffee | (4) | (9),(14) | (17),(22) | (22) | |
| Guyana | Bauxite, timber, molasses | (4) | (9),(13), (14) | (17),(19), (20),(21) | (22) | 1974 |
| Peru | Copper, iron ore, silver, zinc | (1),(4) | (14) | (17),(20) | (22) | 1975 |
| | Fish, coffee | (1) | (9),(14) | (17),(20) | (22) | 1975 |
| Uruguay | Hides and skins | (4) | (9) | (17) | (22) | 1977 |
| Venezuela | Hides | (3) | (9) | (19),(20) | (22) | |
| | Fertilizers | (5) | (9) | (17),(18) | (22) | |

Table continued

| Region/country | Commodity | Type of measure (1)-(5) | Motive (6)-(16) | Effect (17)-(21) | GATT regulations (22)-(27) | Period of notification |
|---|---|---|---|---|---|---|
| **II. Central America** | | | | | | |
| Dominican Republic | Raw hides | (3) | (13) | (17) | (22) | 1977 |
| | coffee | (4) | (14) | (18) | (22) | 1975 |
| | Sugar, cocoa, tobacco | (4) | (14) | (18) | (22) | 1975 |
| Guatemala | Leather, soles, sawn wood, molasses | (5) | - | - | (26) | |
| Haiti | Coffee | (1) | (14) | (18) | (22) | |
| | Bauxite, sisal, molasses | (4) | (13),(14) | (17),(18),(21) | (22) | 1977 |
| Honduras | Corn, rice, beans, potatoes, lumber | (1) | (13),(14) | (18) | (22) | 1975 |
| Jamaica | Bauxite | (4) | (9),(8),(13),(14),(15) | (17),(19),(20),(21) | (22) | 1973 |
| Mexico | Hides and skins | (3) | (9) | (17) | (26) | |
| Nicaragua | Molasses | (3) | (6),(9) | (17),(20) | (23) | |
| Panama | Hides, raw coffee | (2) | (9),(10) | (17),(18) | (26) | |
| | Bananas | (4) | (13),(14) | (18) | (26) | |
| **III. Africa** | | | | | | |
| Cameroon | Cocoa | (4) | (9),(14) | (17) | | 1975/1976 |
| Gabon | Manganese, coffee | (4) | (9),(12) | (17) | (22) | |
| Ghana | Logs, lumber | (4) | (9),(12) | (17) | (22) | |
| | Cocoa | (4) | (14) | (18) | (22) | 1975/1976 |
| Ivory Coast | Cocoa | (4) | (13),(14) | (18) | | 1975/1976 |
| Morocco | Citrus fruit | (1) | (13),(14) | (18) | | 1975 |
| | Phosphates | (1),(4) | (13) | (18) | | |
| Nigeria | Cocoa | (4) | (13),(14) | (18) | | till 1974 |

Table continued

| Region/ country | Commodity | Type of measure (1)-(5) | Motive (6)-(16) | Effect (17)-(21) | GATT reg- ulations (22)-(27) | Period of notifica- tion |
|---|---|---|---|---|---|---|
| Togo | Cocoa | (4) | (9),(13) (14) | (17),(18) | | 1973 |
| | Phosphates | (1) | (13),(14) | (17),(18) | | 1975 |
| Tanzania | Sisal, coffee | (4) | (9),(13) (14) | (17),(18) | (22) | 1973/1977 |
| Tunisia | Iron ore, phosphates | (1),(4) | (9),(13) (14) | (17) | (22) | 1973/1977 |
| Zambia | Copper | (5) | (13),(14) | (17) | | 1975 |

IV. Asia

| Region/ country | Commodity | Type of measure | Motive | Effect | GATT reg- ulations | Period of notifica- tion |
|---|---|---|---|---|---|---|
| India | Jute, hides and skins | (1) | (14) | (18) | (22) | |
| Indonesia | Rubber, hides | (3) | (6),(7) (9) | (17) | (23) | |
| Malaysia | Saw logs | (2) | (6),(9) (10),(11) | (18) | (23) | 1973/1977 |
| | Fertilizers | (5) | (6),(10), (11) | (18) | (23),(25) | 1973/1977 |
| | Timber | (4) | (9),(10), (11) | (17),(20) | (23),(25) | |
| Pakistan | Fertilizers, hides and skins, bamboo, timber | (3) | (6),(8), (9),(10), (11) | (17),(18), (20) | (22) | |
| Philippines | Logs | (2) | (6),(9) (10) | (17) | (24),(25) | |
| | Chromium ore, abaca, molasses, iron, copra, bananas | (4) | (7),(8), (9),(13) | (18) | (22) | |
| Thailand | Logs, fertilizers Hides and skins, rubber, molasses | (5) (4) | (6),(9) (9),(10), (13),(14) | (17),(18) (17),(18) | (26) (26) | |

Table continued

| Region/country | Commodity | Type of measure (1)-(5) | Motive (6)-(16) | Effect (17)-(21) | GATT regulations (22)-(27) | Period of notification |
|---|---|---|---|---|---|---|
| **V. Others** | | | | | | |
| Australia | Molasses, minerals, fertilizers | (5) | (6),(14) | (17),(18),(20) | | 1973 |
| | Wheat | (1) | (7),(10) | (18),(20) | (22) | |
| | Soya, oil aliments | (5) | (6),(7) | (18),(20) | (22) | 1973 |
| New Zealand | Fertilizers, forest products | (5) | (6),(11) | (17),(18) | (22) | 1966,1973 |
| | Fish | (5) | (6) | (7) | (22) | 1937 |
| | Potatoes | (3) | (6) | (7) | (22) | 1953 |
| Japan | Minerals from tungsten | (3) | (6),(11) | (17),(18),(20) | (22) | 1949 |
| | Nickel | (2) | (6) | (18) | (22) | 1966 |
| | Rice, wheat | (2) | (6) | (18) | (22) | 1950 |
| | Farine of fish and other foodstuffs | (3) | (6),11) | (18) | (22) | 1950 |
| **VI. North America** | | | | | | |
| Canada | Wheat | (1) | (10) | (18),(20) | (22) | 1973 |
| | Mineral ores | (3),(4) | (9) | (17) | (22) | |
| | Logs and pulpwood | (3) | (6),(11),(15) | (17),(18),(20) | (22) | |
| | Soya | (3) | (6),(7),(15) | (17),(18),(20) | (22) | 1973 |
| | Beef and pork | (2) | (6),(7),(15) | (17),(18),(20) | (22) | 1973 |
| U S | Sugar | (2) | (6),(7) | (17),(18),(20) | (22) | 1963/1964 |
| | Leather | (2),(5) | (6) | (17),(18),(20) | (22) | 1966/1972 |
| | Nickel | (5) | (6),(7) | (17),(18),(20) | (22) | 1967/1970 |
| | Soybeans, cotton grains | (3),(5) | (6),(7),(8) | (17),(18),(20) | (22) | 1973 |
| | 41 other commodities | (3),(5) | (6),(7) | | (22) | 1973 |

Table continued

| Region/ country | Commodity | Type of measure (1)-(5) | Motive (6)-(16) | Effect (17)-(21) | GATT reg- ulations (22)-(27) | Period of notification |
|---|---|---|---|---|---|---|

## VII. Europe

| Region/ country | Commodity | Type of measure (1)-(5) | Motive (6)-(16) | Effect (17)-(21) | GATT reg- ulations (22)-(27) | Period of notification |
|---|---|---|---|---|---|---|
| EEC, exclusive of UK | Wheat | (4) | (7) | (20) | (22) | 1973/1975 |
| | | (3) | (6) | (20) | (22) | 1973 |
| | Cereals | (2),(4) | (6),(7),(13) | (20) | (22) | 1973 |
| | Farine grain | (3) | (6) | (20),(18) | (22) | 1973 |
| | Rice | (2) | (6),(13) | | (22) | 1973 |
| | Sugar | (2) | (6),(7),(13) | | | 1973 |
| | Olive oil | (2) | (7),(13) | | | 1972 |
| Finland | Raw timber | (5) | (6),(11) | (17),(20) | (22) | |
| Ireland | Timber | (5) | (6),(7) | (17),(20) | (22) | |
| Norway | Wood | (5) | (6),(7) | (17),(20) | (22) | 1973 |
| | Potatoes | (5) | (6) | | | 1973 |
| Spain | Fertilizers, phosphates | (5) | (6),(11) | (17) | (22) | 1973 |
| | Fish, bananas, rice, olive oil | (5) | (6),(7) | (17),(18) | (22) | 1973 |
| Sweden | Barley, malt | (5) | (6) | | (24) | |
| | Various foodstuff | (2) | (6),(7) | | | 1973 |
| Turkey | Hides and skins | (2) | (9),(10) | (17),(18),(20) | (22) | 1972 |
| | Meerschaum | (5) | (9),(10) | (17),(18) | (22) | 1972 |
| | Wood | (2),(5) | (7) | (17) | (22) | 1973 |
| | Molasses | (5) | (6),(7) | (17),(18) | (22) | 1973 |
| U K | Tin, nickel | (3) | (6) | (18) | | |

Notes to Appendix A:

Type of Measure
(1) State trading; cartelisation; differential pricing
(2) Export quota
(3) Export embargo
(4) Export taxes
(5) Export licensing and administrative documentation

Motives
(6) Continuity of domestic supply; prevention of shortages caused by abnormal foreign demand
(7) Stabilization of export earnings and protection against fluctuations of commodity supply
(8) Fight against inflation caused by balance of payments surplus or increased world prices
(9) Promotion of industrial processing in order to increase export earnings from sale of processed commodities
(10) Ensurance of domestic supply at prices below those in world markets
(11) Conservation of non-renewable resources
(13) Alignment of export prices with world market prices
(14) Increase of export earnings
(15) Restrictions in other markets
(16) Others

Effect
(17) Higher input costs of further processed good in importing countries; inflationary pressures
(18) Higher supply prices of commodities; shortages in world market; price fluctuations; and possible shortages in consumption and production
(19) Diversification of raw material substitutes
(20) Demand pressures on other commodity exporting countries, inflationary pressures and distortion of supply-demand relationship
(21) Total dependency of importing country on commodity supply leading to production supply shortages

Consistency with GATT regulations
(22) Not consistent with GATT Regulations Article XI
(23) Consistent with GATT Regulations Article XIII 1-5
(24) Consistent with GATT Regulations Article XX
(25) Consistent with GATT Regulations Article XXXVI
(26) The country is not a member of GATT
(27) Undefined in GATT agreement

Appendix B. Table 2.A.1 Selected Developing Countries' Share of World Commodity Exports. Average 1974-76 (percents).

| Region/country | Cocoa | Coffee | Rice | Wheat | Sugar | Bananas | Copra | Fish-meal | Cotton | Jute | Sisal | Rubber | Timber | Hides and skins | Tobacco |
|---|---|---|---|---|---|---|---|---|---|---|---|---|---|---|---|
| I. South America | | | | | | | | | | | | | | | |
| Argentina | | | 0.6 | 3.4 | 1.8 | | | | 0.8 | | | | | 1.1 | 0.8 |
| Bolivia | | | | | 0.3 | | | | 0.3 | | | | | 0.8 | 5.3 |
| Brazil | 13 | 23.1 | 0.3 | | 9.9 | 3.0 | | | 1.4 | 0.3 | 33.2 | | 0.2 | 0.1 | |
| Chile | | | | | 0.2 | | | | | | | 0.1 | 0.9 | | 0.8 |
| Colombia | | | 1.3 | | 0.7 | 4.5 | | | 1.1 | | | | 0.2 | | |
| Ecuador | 3.6 | 2.0 | 0.1 | | 0.2 | 16.6 | | | | | | | 0.1 | | |
| Guyana | | | 1.0 | | 1.4 | | | | | | 1.6 | | | | |
| Peru | | 1.1 | 0.7 | | 1.8 | | | | 1.8 | | | | | 0.1 | |
| Uruguay | | | 0.9 | 0.1 | | | | | | | | | | 0.8 | |
| Venezuela | 0.9 | 0.5 | 0.4 | | 0.1 | 0.1 | | | | | 0.5 | | | | 0.1 |
| II. Central America | | | | | | | | | | | | | | | |
| Dominican Republic | 1.9 | 1.1 | | | 4.1 | 0.2 | | | | | | | | | 1.4 |
| Guatemala | | 0.6 | | | 1.0 | 2.4 | | | 1.6 | | | | | | |
| Haiti | | | | | | | | | | | | | 0.4 | | |
| Honduras | | | | | | 9.2 | | | 0.1 | | | | | | 0.2 |
| Jamaica | 0.1 | 1.2 | | | 1.1 | 1.8 | | | | | | | | | |
| Mexico | 0.5 | 0.1 | | 0.1 | 1.2 | 0.1 | | | 3.1 | | 1.6 | 0.2 | | | 1.1 |
| Nicaragua | | 4.3 | | | 0.4 | 0.6 | | | 2.5 | | | | | | 0.2 |
| Panama | | 1.3 | | | 0.4 | 7.2 | | | | | | | 0.2 | | |

Table continued

Appendix B. Table 2.A.1

| Region/country | Cocoa | Coffee | Rice | Wheat | Sugar | Bananas | Copra | Fish-meal | Cotton | Jute | Sisal | Rubber | Timber | Hides and skins | Tobacco |
|---|---|---|---|---|---|---|---|---|---|---|---|---|---|---|---|
| III. Africa | | | | | | | | | | | | | | | |
| Cameroon | 6.9 | 2.3 | | | | 2.3 | | | | | | | 0.5 | 0.1 | 0.1 |
| Gabon | 0.1 | | | | | | | | | | | | 1.0 | | |
| Ghana | 27.9 | | | | | | | | | | | | 0.8 | | |
| Ivory Coast | 15.6 | 6.6 | 0.1 | | | 1.8 | 0.5 | | | | | 0.5 | 2.5 | | |
| Morocco | | | | | | | | | 0.1 | | | | | | |
| Nigeria | 18.0 | | | | | | | | 0.5 | | | | | | |
| Togo | 1.7 | 0.2 | | | | | 0.1 | | | | | | | | |
| Tanzania | | 1.6 | | | 0.1 | | | | 1.3 | | 24.8 | | | 0.4 | 0.9 |
| Tunisia | | | | | 0.1 | | | | | | | | | 0.1 | 0.3 |
| Zambia | | | | | | | | | | | | | | | |
| IV. Asia | | | | | | | | | | | | | | | |
| India | | 1.7 | 0.6 | | 4.0 | | | 0.1 | 0.6 | 7.7 | | 21.9 | 6.5 | 0.6 | 4.2 |
| Indonesia | 0.9 | 2.6 | | | | | | 0.2 | | | | 52.2 | 6.8 | | 1.3 |
| Malasia | | | | | 0.4 | 0.2 | 2.5 | 0.3 | 2.1 | | | | | 0.2 | 0.4 |
| Pakistan | | | | | | | | | | | | | | | |
| Philippines | | | 12.8 | | 6.3 | 8.2 | 62.6 | 1.0 | | 22.1 | | 10.0 | 2.1 | | 1.2 |
| Thailand | | | 33.7 | 3.6 | 2.3 | | | | | | | | 0.3 | | 1.1 |
| Total LDCs | 97.7 | 92.8 | 33.7 | 3.6 | 51.2 | 93.0 | 98.4 | 42.2 | 46.6 | 95.9 | 97.9 | 95.8 | 25.4 | 13.9 | 28.3 |
| Other | 2.3 | 7.2 | 66.3 | 96.4 | 48.8 | 7.0 | 1.6 | 57.8 | 53.4 | 4.1 | 2.1 | 4.2 | 74.6 | 86.1 | 71.7 |

Table 2.A.1  Part 2

| Region/country | Petro-leum | Bauxite | Copper | Tin | Lead | Zinc | Iron | Manga-nese | Phos-phate | Total Comm. | Other Comm. | Total Export |
|---|---|---|---|---|---|---|---|---|---|---|---|---|
| I. South America | | | | | | | | | | | | |
| Argentina | | | | | | | | | | | | |
| Bolivia | 0.1 | | 0.1 | 16.4 | 1.0 | 1.8 | | | | | | |
| Brazil | 0.1 | 0.1 | | 1.5 | | | 16.1 | 17.3 | | | | |
| Chile | | | 16.7 | | | | 2.6 | | | | | |
| Colombia | | | | | | | | | | | | |
| Ecuador | 0.5 | | | | | | | | | | | |
| Guyana | | 14.4 | | | | | | | | | | |
| Peru | | | 3.3 | | 7.2 | 6.5 | 1.1 | | | | | |
| Uruguay | | | | | | | | | | | | |
| Venezuela | 4.9 | | | | | | 5.0 | | | | | |
| II. Central America | | | | | | | | | | | | |
| Dominican Republic | | 3.1 | | | | | | | | | | |
| Guatemala | | | | | | | | | | | | |
| Haiti | | 2.2 | | | | | | | | | | |
| Honduras | | | | | 0.7 | 0.5 | | | | | | |
| Jamaica | | 24.5 | | | | | | | | | | |
| Mexico | 0.3 | | 0.2 | 5.9 | 5.4 | | | 1.7 | | | | |
| Nicaragua | | | | | | | | | | | | |
| Panama | | | | | | | | | | | | |

Table 2.A.1  Part 2 Continued

| Region/country | Petroleum | Bauxite | Copper | Tin | Lead | Zinc | Iron | Manganese | Phosphate | Total Comm. | Other Comm. | Total Export |
|---|---|---|---|---|---|---|---|---|---|---|---|---|
| **III. Africa** | | | | | | | | | | | | |
| Cameroon | 0.7 | | | | | | | | | | | |
| Gabon | | | | | | | | 20 | | | | |
| Ghana | | | | | | | | 3.4 | | | | |
| Ivory Coast | | | | | | | | | | | | |
| Morocco | | | | | 2.8 | 0.3 | 0.2 | 2.3 | 37.9 | | | |
| Nigeria | 6.9 | | | | | | | | | | | |
| Togo | | | | | | | | | 4.7 | | | |
| Tanzania | | | | | | | | | 4.0 | | | |
| Tunisia | 0.3 | | | | 1.3 | 0.1 | 0.1 | | | | | |
| Zambia | | | 13.6 | | 1.1 | 1.8 | | | | | | |
| **IV. Asia** | | | | | | | | | | | | |
| India | | | | | | | | 4.2 | | | | |
| Indonesia | 4.1 | 0.1 | 1.2 | 10.4 | | | | | | | | |
| Malasia | 0.4 | 1.2 | | 44.2 | | | | | | | | |
| Pakistan | | 0.9 | | | | | | | | | | |
| Philippines | | | 3.9 | | | | | | | | | |
| Thailand | | | | 10.5 | 0.1 | 0.2 | | | | | | |
| Total LDCs | 91.2 | 77.4 | 52.8 | 88.9 | 23.6 | 20.5 | 40.2 | 50.2 | 68.7 | 30.0 | 90.2 | 75.8 |
| Other | 8.8 | 22.6 | 47.2 | 11.1 | 76.4 | 79.5 | 59.8 | 49.8 | 31.3 | | | |

Appendix B. Table 2.A.2 World Commodity Production: Share by Country. Average 1974-76 (percents)

| Region/country | Cocoa | Coffee | Bananas | Soy-beans | Rice | Wheat | Cotton | Jute | Sugar | Alumin-ium | Bauxite | Iron ore | Copper |
|---|---|---|---|---|---|---|---|---|---|---|---|---|---|
| I. South America | | | | | | | | | | | | | |
| Argentina | | | | 0.9 | 1.4 | 2.0 | 1.1 | | | | | | |
| Bolivia | | | | 0.7 | | | | | | | | | |
| Brazil | 17.2 | 29.9 | 16.2 | 17.7 | 2.2 | | 3.7 | | 2.4 | 8.5 | | 9.6 | |
| Chile | | | | | | | | | | | | 1.2 | 12.6 |
| Colombia | 1.6 | 11.6 | 3.1 | 0.2 | | | 1.0 | | | | | | |
| Ecuador | 4.7 | | 7.3 | | | | | | | | | | |
| Guyana | | | | | | | | | | | 3.9 | | |
| Surinam | | | | | | | | | | | 7.9 | | |
| Peru | | | | | | | | | 0.1 | | | | |
| Venezuela | 1.1 | | 2.5 | | | | | | | | | 2.6 | 2.7 |
| II. Central America | | | | | | | | | | | | | |
| Dominican Republic | 1.9 | | 0.9 | | | | | | | | | | |
| Guatemala | | 3.2 | 1.5 | | | | | | | | | | |
| Haiti | | | | | | | | | | | | | |
| Honduras | | | 2.9 | | | | | | | | | | |
| Jamaica | | | 0.4 | | | | | | | | 16.0 | | |
| Mexico | | 5.2 | 3.4 | 0.7 | | | 2.5 | | | | | | 1.1 |
| Nicaragua | | | 0.4 | | | | | | | | | | |
| Panama | | | 2.8 | | | | | | | | | | |

Table continued

Table 2.A.2  Continued

| Region/country | Cocoa | Coffee | Bananas | Soy-beans | Rice | Wheat | Cotton | Jute | Sugar | Aluminium | Bauxite | Iron ore | Copper |
|---|---|---|---|---|---|---|---|---|---|---|---|---|---|
| **III. Africa** | | | | | | | | | | | | | |
| Cameroon | 7.2 | 2.0 | 0.3 | | | | | | | | | | |
| Gabon | 24.9 | | | | | | | | | 0.2 | | | |
| Ghana | | | | | | | | | | | | | |
| Guinea | | | | | | | | | | | 11.7 | | |
| Ivory Coast | 15.6 | 5.9 | 0.4 | | | | | | | | | | |
| Morocco | | | | | | | | | | | | | |
| Nigeria | 14.3 | | | | | | | | | | | | |
| Tanzania | | | 2.2 | | | | | | | | | | |
| Togo | | | | | | | | | | | | | |
| Tunisia | | | | | | | | | | | | | |
| Zambia | | | | | | | | | | | | | 9.6 |
| **IV. Asia** | | | | | | | | | | | | | |
| India | 2.1 | 10.6 | | | 19.8 | 6.6 | 9.2 | 34.4 | 6.7 | | | 4.5 | |
| Indonesia | 3.8 | 8.7 | | 0.9 | 6.6 | | | 0.4 | 1.2 | | | | |
| Malasia | | | | | | | | | | | | 1.0 | |
| Pakistan | | | | | 2.2 | 4.6 | | | | | | | |
| Philippines | | 3.7 | | | 1.7 | | | | | | | | |
| Thailand | | 4.1 | | 0.2 | 4.4 | | 6.4 | | 3.3 | | | | 3.1 |
| **VI. OECD** | | | | | | | | | | | | | |
| Australia | | | | 0.5 | | 3.3 | | | 3.5 | 0.7 | 27.9 | 10.7 | 3.2 |
| Canada | | | | | | 4.3 | | | | 3.4 | | 5.8 | 10.6 |
| Finland | | | | | | | | | | | | | 0.5 |
| France | | | | | | 4.8 | | | 3.4 | 1.5 | 3.4 | 5.5 | |
| Japan | | | | 0.2 | 4.7 | | | | | 4.0 | | | 1.2 |
| Italy | | | | | | 2.6 | | | | 0.8 | | | |
| Norway | | | | | | | | | | 2.5 | | | |
| Spain | | | | | | 1.2 | | | | 0.8 | | 0.9 | |
| U K | | | | | | 1.4 | | | | 1.2 | | 0.5 | |
| U S | | | | 59.4 | 1.5 | 14.2 | 18.3 | | 10.4 | 15.6 | 2.5 | 9.2 | 19.3 |
| Turkey | | | | | | 2.6 | 4.0 | | | | | | |
| Germany | | | | | | 2.0 | | | | 2.7 | | 0.4 | 2.9 |
| U S S R | | | | 0.9 | | 24.1 | 19.2 | 1.2 | 6.0 | 5.6 | 25.8 | 10.6 | |

Table 2.A.2    Part 2

| Region/country | Hides and skins | Manganese | Molasses | Rubber | Tin | Tobacco | Tungsten | Phosphate | Zinc | Petroleum | Copra | Weighted average |
|---|---|---|---|---|---|---|---|---|---|---|---|---|
| I. South America | | | | | | | | | | | | |
| Argentina | 6.3 | | 2.2 | | | | 0.2 | | | | 0.7 | 0.6 |
| Bolivia | | 7.9 | | | 12.9 | | 6.5 | | | | | -0.8 |
| Brazil | 6.2 | | 9.2 | 2.2 | | | 2.8 | | | | | 5.7 |
| Chile | | 0.1 | | 0.6 | | 4.9 | | 0.4 | | | | 0.6 |
| Colombia | | | | | | | | | | | | 0.7 |
| Ecuador | | | | | | | | | | | | 0.5 |
| Guyana | | | | | | | | | | | | 0.2 |
| Surinam | | | | | | | | | | | | 0.3 |
| Peru | | | | | | | | | 1.2 | | | 0.2 |
| Venezuela | | | | | | | | | | 4.5 | | 0.2 |
| II. Central America | | | | | | | | | | | | |
| Dominican Republic | | | | | | | | | | | | 0.1 |
| Guatemala | | | | | | | | | | | | 0.2 |
| Haiti | | | | | | | | | | | | 0.1 |
| Honduras | | | | | | | | | | | | 0.7 |
| Jamaica | | | | | | | | | | | | |
| Mexico | 2.3 | 1.8 | 4.6 | | | | | | 2.9 | 1.4 | | 1.0 |
| Nicaragua | | | | | | | | | | | | 0.2 |
| Panama | | | | | | | | | | | | 0.1 |

Table continued

Table 2.A.2   Part 2 Continued

| Region/country | Hides and skins | Manga-nese | Mo-lasses | Rubber | Tin | Tobacco | Tungsten | Phos-phate | Zinc | Petro-leum | Copra | Weighted average |
|---|---|---|---|---|---|---|---|---|---|---|---|---|
| **III. Africa** | | | | | | | | | | | | |
| Cameroon | | 9.1 | | | | | | | | | | 0.4 |
| Gabon | | 1.4 | | | | | | | | | | 0.4 |
| Ghana | | | | | | | | | | | | 1.1 |
| Guinea | | | | | | | | | | | | 0.5 |
| Ivory Coast | 0.6 | | | | | | | | | | | 0.9 |
| Morocco | | | | | | | | 15.1 | | | | 0.6 |
| Nigeria | | | | | 2.0 | | | | | | | 0.8 |
| Tanzania | | | | | | | | | | 3.5 | | 0.1 |
| Togo | | | | | | | | 1.8 | | | | 0.1 |
| Tunisia | | | | | | | | 3.3 | | | | 0.1 |
| Zambia | | | | | | | | | | | | 0.4 |
| **IV. Asia** | | | | | | | | | | | | |
| India | | 6.7 | 7.0 | 4.0 | | 7.5 | | | | | | 4.8 |
| Indonesia | | | | 24.5 | 10.5 | 1.5 | | | | 2.5 | 2.9 | 2.5 |
| Malasia | | | | 44.8 | 28.7 | | | | | | 0.9 | 3.0 |
| Pakistan | | | 3.6 | 1.4 | | 1.3 | | | | | | 0.3 |
| Philippines | | | | 11.0 | | 1.5 | | | | | 66.0 | 3.4 |
| Thailand | | | | | 8.4 | | 4.7 | | | | | 1.6 |
| **VI. OECD** | | | | | | | | | | | | |
| Australia | 4.2 | 7.3 | 2.2 | | 4.4 | | 4.9 | | 4.4 | | | 3.1 |
| Canada | 2.3 | | | | | | 3.5 | | 3.5 | | | 1.5 |
| Finland | 4.1 | | | | | | | | | | | 0.0 |
| France | | | 4.2 | | | 1.1 | | | 4.3 | | | 1.8 |
| Japan | | 0.6 | | | | 3.1 | 2.0 | | 14.2 | | | 1.2 |
| Italy | 2.6 | | 1.1 | | | 2.0 | | | 3.5 | | | 0.5 |
| Norway | | | | | | | | | 1.2 | | | 0.1 |
| Spain | | | | | | | 0.8 | | | | | 0.4 |
| U K | 2.2 | | 1.0 | | | | | | 1.1 | | | 0.4 |
| U S | 22.8 | | 6.2 | | 1.6 | 12.8 | | | 8.4 | 15.1 | | 10.7 |
| Turkey | 1.4 | | | | | 4.5 | | 40.2 | | | | 0.5 |
| Germany | 2.9 | | 2.7 | | | | | | 8.7 | | | 0.9 |
| U S S R | 19.8 | 35.2 | 10.3 | | 13. | | 19.9 | 1.9 | 13.0 | | | 10.0 |

Appendix B  Table 2.A.3  Commodities' Shares of Country Total Exports.
Average 1974-76 (percents)

| Region/ country | Cocoa | Coffee | Bananas | Soy- beans | Sugar | Cotton | Jute | Rubber | Hides and skins | Tobacco |
|---|---|---|---|---|---|---|---|---|---|---|
| **I. South America** | | | | | | | | | | |
| Argentina | | | | | 4.6 | 1.1 | | | 0.5 | 0.5 |
| Bolivia | | 1.7 | | | 5.4 | 3.0 | | 0.3 | | |
| Brazil | 2.4 | 14.5 | 0.3 | | 10.2 | 0.7 | | | 0.1 | 1.5 |
| Chile | | | | | 0.7 | | | | | |
| Colombia | | 49.1 | 2.3 | | 4.1 | 3.6 | | | | 1.3 |
| Ecuador | 5.7 | 10.9 | 12.4 | | 1.5 | 0.1 | | | | |
| Guyana | | | | | 43.8 | | | | 0.1 | 0.4 |
| Peru | | 4.4 | | | 11.9 | 6.0 | | | 0.1 | 0.1 |
| Surinam | | | 1.2 | | | | | | | |
| Venezuela | 0.2 | 0.3 | | | | | | | | |
| **II. Central America** | | | | | | | | | | |
| Dominican Republic | 4.2 | 8.3 | 0.3 | | 50.7 | | | | | 4.9 |
| Guatemala | 0.1 | 27.3 | 2.9 | | 13.9 | 11.5 | | | | 0.8 |
| Haiti | 0.7 | 34.4 | | | 4.8 | 0.1 | | | | 1.7 |
| Honduras | | 21.3 | 23.1 | | 1.4 | 1.4 | | | 0.2 | 0.1 |
| Jamaica | 0.2 | 0.5 | 2.0 | | 13.7 | | | | | |
| Mexico | 0.2 | 7.4 | | | 3.5 | 4.6 | | 0.1 | | 0.9 |
| Nicaragua | 0.1 | 16.5 | | | 8.4 | 27.9 | | | 0.1 | 1.0 |
| Panama | 0.3 | 1.0 | 23.6 | | 14.5 | | | | 0.2 | 0.1 |
| **III. Africa** | | | | | | | | | | |
| Cameroon | 22.9 | 26.0 | 3.6 | | 0.1 | 2.0 | | 2.0 | 0.6 | 0.4 |
| Gabon | 0.2 | | | | | | | | 0.2 | |
| Ghana | 64.1 | 0.4 | | | | | | | | 0.1 |
| Guinea | | 3.4 | 0.3 | | | | | | | |
| Ivory Coast | 19.4 | 27.5 | 1.1 | | | 1.6 | | 0.8 | 2.5 | |
| Morocco | | | | | | 0.4 | | | | |
| Nigeria | 3.2 | | | | | | | 0.3 | | |
| Tanzania | 0.3 | 22.6 | | | 1.4 | 15.5 | | | 1.5 | 5.5 |
| Togo | 18.9 | 7.3 | | | | 1.5 | | | | |
| Tunisia | | | | | 0.9 | 0.1 | | | 0.2 | |
| Zambia | | | | | | | | | | 0.7 |
| **IV. Asia** | | | | | | | | | | |
| India | | 2.0 | | | 8.0 | 0.6 | 0.3 | | | 2.4 |
| Indonesia | | 1.9 | | | | | | 5.9 | 0.1 | 0.4 |
| Malasia | 0.3 | | | | 0.7 | | | 22.6 | | |
| Pakistan | | | | | | | | | 0.2 | 1.0 |
| Philippines | | 0.1 | 2.6 | | 23.0 | | | | | 1.2 |
| Thailand | | | | | 10.3 | | 1.5 | 8.0 | 0.1 | 1.1 |
| Total developed | 0.8 | 2.4 | 0.3 | | 2.2 | 1.0 | 0.1 | 0.9 | 0.1 | 0.3 |
| Other | 0.0 | 0.0 | 0.0 | | 0.7 | 0.4 | 0.0 | 0.0 | 0.2 | 0.3 |
| World Gross | 0.2 | 0.6 | 0.1 | | 1.0 | 0.5 | 0.0 | 0.2 | 0.2 | 0.3 |

Table 2.A.3    Continued

| Region/country | Petro-leum | Alumin-ium | Bauxite | Copper | Tin | Zinc | Iron ore | Manga-nese | Phos-phate | Total commodity export |
|---|---|---|---|---|---|---|---|---|---|---|
| **I. South America** | | | | | | | | | | |
| Argentina | | | | | | | | | | 41.4 |
| Bolivia | 23.3 | | | 1.9 | 39.8 | 7.1 | | | | 87.5 |
| Brazil | 1.4 | | | | 0.2 | | 9.3 | 0.8 | | 46.4 |
| Chile | | | | 59.3 | | | 6.5 | | | 69.7 |
| Colombia | 0.1 | | | | | | | | | 65.1 |
| Ecuador | 56.1 | | | | | | | | | 88.4 |
| Guyana | | 26.0 | | | | | | | | 80.7 |
| Peru | 0.9 | | | 17.5 | | 9.7 | | | | 72.2 |
| Surinam | | 20.6 | | | | | 4.2 | | | 30.5 |
| Venezuela | 63.7 | | | | | | 2.7 | | | 67.0 |
| **II. Central America** | | | | | | | | | | |
| Dominican Republic | | 2.2 | | | | | | | | 71.6 |
| Guatemala | | | | | | | | | | 59.9 |
| Haiti | | 12.8 | | | | | | | | 57.4 |
| Honduras | | | | | | 3.1 | | | | 74.6 |
| Jamaica | | 18.4 | | | | | | | | 34.9 |
| Mexico | 10.4 | | | 0.5 | | 3.5 | | 0.2 | | 34.0 |
| Nicaragua | | | | 0.8 | | | | | | 64.5 |
| Panama | | | | | | | | | | 41.6 |
| **III. Africa** | | | | | | | | | | |
| Cameroon | | | | | | | | | | 69.5 |
| Gabon | | | | | | | | 8.0 | | 96.7 |
| Ghana | | 0.5 | | | | | | 2.0 | | 79.0 |
| Guinea | | 70.2 | | | | | | | | 77.4 |
| Ivory Coast | | | | | | | | | | 73.6 |
| Morocco | | | | 0.2 | | 0.4 | 0.7 | 0.6 | 52.0 | 56.5 |
| Nigeria | 93.0 | | | | 0.3 | | | | | 97.3 |
| Tanzania | 5.1 | | | | | | | | | 67.1 |
| Togo | | | | | | | | | 66.3 | 94.3 |
| Tunisia | 38.9 | | | | | 0.2 | 0.4 | | 9.6 | 51.9 |
| Zambia | | | | 92.1 | | 3.6 | | | | 98.1 |
| **IV. Asia** | | | | | | | | | | |
| India | | | | | | | 5.1 | 0.4 | | 27.4 |
| Indonesia | 66.2 | 0.1 | | 1.1 | 1.8 | | | | | 89.1 |
| Malasia | 9.4 | 0.1 | | | 12.0 | | | | | 70.7 |
| Pakistan | 1.0 | | | | | | | | | 32.0 |
| Philippines | 1.2 | | | 11.3 | | 0.1 | 0.4 | | | 65.2 |
| Thailand | | | | | 5.3 | | | | | 53.7 |
| Total developed | 52.4 | 0.2 | | 1.8 | 0.5 | 0.2 | 1.0 | 0.1 | 0.7 | 69.2 |
| Other | 1.6 | 0.0 | | 0.5 | 0.0 | 0.2 | 0.5 | 0.0 | 0.1 | 9.4 |
| World Gross | 13.9 | 0.1 | | 0.8 | 0.1 | 0.2 | 0.6 | 0.0 | 0.2 | 23.9 |

NOTES

1. Bergsten 1975, 118 argues that demand elasticities are low in the short but higher in the long-run, hence such measures should be adopted for a limited time. But something must be said about demand elasticities of processed goods in order to get a precise figure.

2. In the case of bauxite for example, the US, a main producer of aluminium, depends on imports for 90 percent of its bauxite consumption. In 1973 the ten members of IBA mined 80 percent of world bauxite and produced only 5 percent of world aluminium output. The US, on the other hand, mined only 3 percent of world bauxite but produced 41 percent of world aluminium. (Eight Mineral Cartels 1975, 118; Commodity Yearbook 1979.

3. See Kiel Discussion Papers No. 36, 1974, 24.

4. Often the restrictions are actually imposed by the importing countries, whose standards of demand are higher than those of the exporting (developing) countries.

5. Note that developed countries are not necessarily main exporters of minerals, hence the frequency is lower in this case.

6. Prices of agricultural commodities tend to react faster to quantitative restrictions than minerals prices.

7. The common interest of producers and consumers to guarantee both constant export earnings and free access to supplies was a primary motive for the proposals on an Integrated Programme for Commodities prepared at UNCTAD IV in Nairobi in 1976, and the attempt to create buffer stocks in order to avoid price fluctuations. For a controversial discussion on gains and losses associated with buffer stocks see Behrman 1977 and Johnson 1977.

8. This occurred in 1973 after the collapse of the Bretton Woods System. The US dollar was devaluated, causing an increase in foreign demand for US commodities.

9. It must be noted, however, that the very imposition of controls on exportables may have adverse effects on the balance of payments. For instance, in the case of quotas, the results could be a decline in the balance of payments (or an increase deficit) and a consequent depreciation of the country's currency. In the absence of compensating monetary and fiscal policies this process increases the costs of imports and reduce the relative prices of exportables (through depreciation), adding again to inflationary pressures.

10. Final Resolution of UNCTAD IV, 1976.

11. During the period from 1979 to 1981 this figure was 28.3 percent. Relative to the period from 1970 to 1972 (16.7 percent share) an expansion of almost 12 percent took place. Yet, during the same period (1970 to 1981) no significant change in the developing countries' share of world commodity exports occurred, i.e., expansion was in the manufacturing sector.

12. The effective rate of protection is defined as $E_j = (V'_j - V_j)/V_j$, $E_j$ is the percentage difference between the industry's value added per unit of output under protection $(V'_j)$ and its

value added in the absence of protection ($V_j$). The nominal tariff rate concerns the duty on the product itself (see Yeats 1974, 31 f.).

13. The argument most frequently used in support of restrictions aimed at encouraging processing is related to the claim for protection of infant industries, i.e. the temporary protection of an industry requiring a learning period in order to become competitive. It seems that some developing countries believe in the restricting mechanism as an effective means to promote processing.

14. A good example is a smelter to be built in Guyana, owned and financed also by Jamaica and Trinidad-Tobago (Eight Mineral Cartels 1975, 215).

15. Eight Mineral Cartels 1975, 124.

16. Note that this case is different from the motive of the fight against inflation, balance of payments distortions, or increased world prices. Here, the issues is the subsidization of domestic processing through lower input prices and not protection against exogenous shocks as in the previous cases.

17. UNCTAD IV 1976.

18. For a controversial discussion, see Cuddy 1978.

19. For a critique of Prebisch, see Flanders, 1964.

20. This process became effective after 1974 (see table 2.6) when the initial shock had been absorbed by commodity importing countries and was neutralized in real terms by higher domestic and world inflation rates. Nevertheless, the higher oil prices affected all net petroleum importers, which led net exporters of commodities to use export restrictions to prevent a further deterioration of their terms of trade.

21. For example, Argentina became a major exporter of soybeans after the US imposed an embargo on soybeans.

22. Kaldor (1976) assumes further that there is a general tendency in the industrial sector of developed economies not to reduce prices of their products in periods during which raw material prices fluctuate downwards. This process can also be caused by unions that have higher inflationary expectations. For controversial views, see Finger and DeRosa (1978) or Baron (1978).

REFERENCES

Balassa, B. 1980. The Tokyo Round and the Developing Countries. Journal of World Trade Law 14: 93-118.

Baron, S. 1978. Weniger Inflation Durch Rohstoffpreisstabiliesierung? Die Weltwirtschaft 1:47-55.

Behrman, J.R. 1977. International Commodity Agreements: An Evaluation of the UNCTAD Integrated Commodity Programme. Washington, D.C.: ODC, NIEO Series, Monograph No. 9.

Bergsten, F.C. 1976. A New OPEC in Bauxite. Challenge 19: 12-20.

———— 1975. Toward a New International Economic Order: 1972-74. Selected Papers of C. Fred Bergsten, 1972-1974 London, Lexington Books.

Commodity Yearbook 1979. New York: Commodity Research Bureau Inc.
Commodity Trade and Price Trends 1975, 1978, 1979. Washington, D.C.: World Bank.
The Economist Intelligence Unit, Ltd. 1978. World Commodity Outlook 1978/79. London.
Eight Mineral Cartels: The New Challenge to Industrialised Nations. 1975 Metal Week, New York.
Finger, V.M., DeRosa, D. 1978. Commodity Price Stabilisation and the Ratchet-Effect. The World Economy, edited by _____ vol. 1, London.
Flanders, M.J. 1964. Prebisch on Protectionism: An Evaluation. The Economic Journal 74: 307-326.
Food and Agriculture Organisation of the United Nations (FAO). 1976. FAO Production Yearbook. Rome.
General Agreement of Tariffs and Trade (GATT). 1969. Basic Instruments and Selected Documents. In Text of the General Agreement, vol. IV. Geneva.
Golub, S.A., Finger, J.M. 1979. The Processing of Primary Commodities: Effects of Developed Country Tariff Escalation and Developing Country Export Taxes. Journal of Political Economy 87: 559-77.
International Monetary Fund (IMF) 1975. Eighth Annual Report of Exchange Restrictions. Washington, D.C.
_____ 1979. International Financial Statistics Yearbook, Washington, D.C.
Johnson, H.G. 1977. Commodities: Less Developed Countries' Demands and Developed Countries' Responses. In The New International Economic Order: The North-South Debate, edited by J.N. Bhagwati, 240-51. Boston: MIT.
Kaldor, N. 1976. Inflation and Recession in the World Economy. The Economic Journal 86: 703-14.
Lerner, A.D. 1936. The Symmetry Between Import and Export Taxes. Economica 3: 306-13.
Morgan, D. 1979. Fiscal Policy in Oil Exporting Countries, 1972-78. Finance and Development 16: 14-17.
Organisation for Economic Cooperation and Development (OECD). 1974. Export Restrictions Inventory TC/ (74) 12-21/6/74 Scale 2, Paris.
UNCTAD IV. 1976. Resolution Adopted by the Conference: Integrated Programme for Commodities. TD/MES/93/ (IV). Geneva.
UNCTAD V. 1979. The Processing Before Exports of Primary Commodities: Areas for Further International Cooperation. TD/229/SUPP2/ Item 10(a) - Supporting Paper Manila, May.
United Nations (UN) 1973, 1974, 1975, 1976, 1977. Statistical Yearbook. New York.
Weltrohstoff Versorgung: Konflikt Oder Kooperation? 1974. Kiel Discussion Papers, No. 36.
Yeats, A. 1976. Effective Protection for Processed Agricultural Commodities: A Comparison of Industrial Countries. Journal of Economics and Business 29: 31-39.

# 3
# Commodity Export Taxes as a Means of Promoting Internal Processing Industries— A General Equilibrium Model

*Horst Keppler*

INTRODUCTION

By introducing an export tax on raw material exports any country or group of countries may cause a divergence between domestic and world market prices for the commodity concerned. Taken alone, the resulting (relative) drop in raw material prices within the group of supplying countries has the effect of subsidizing domestic further processing industries. If, additionally, the group controls a large enough share of total world supply - thus being confronted with a price inelastic commodity import demand in countries outside the group - then taxing raw material exports is also a means of raising export revenues. Under specific conditions it thus seems to pay for commodity exporting developing countries to join together in a supply cartel, restrict their commodity exports, and **simultaneously** realize the two goals of intensifying the processing of raw materials before export and raising export receipts.
However, concentrating the analysis only on the market of the restricted commodity does harbour the danger of misrepresenting the ultimate effects of export restrictions, since possible repercussions in other markets are ignored. For instance, the extent to which interventions in raw material trade serve to promote processing industries will depend on the world wide demand and supply conditions in the branches of industry concerned. Additional side effects may be expected from the possible initial increase in the income of the cartel member countries, which will be used to finance higher imports of goods and services. Depending on the structure of this demand, different multiplier effects will occur within and outside the cartel. Thus the only way to gain a more complete picture is to take into account adjustment reactions outside the directly affected raw material market. The present chapter provides answers to the following two questions:
- Is it really possible to simultaneously achieve the two goals of promoting a raw material processing industry and attaining higher income from commodity exports by imposing a tax on them?

- What determines the degree of promotion of the processing industry?

The answers to the above questions are drawn from a general equilibrium model.[1] Thus, all allocative effects are determined by changes in relative product prices and real incomes within a hypothetical raw material supply cartel and outside of it. From this it follows that the model analysis is best suited to cases where a group of commodity exporting developing countries has already built up a significant processing industry for its raw material supply, which is able to react to price incentives. Specifically, the investigation in this paper concentrates on situations where the cartel group considered is already a net exporter not only of the raw material but also of the related processed good. Since problems of cartel formation itself are completely left out of the analysis, all algebraic results represent the most favourable case for the raw material supplying developing countries.

The first section of the chapter outlines the basic assumptions and the structure of the model. Because of the complex of production, consumption, and total equilibrium conditions, this is undertaken step by step. The second section contains the equilibrium solutions for the more important endogenous variables, the results being expressed in terms of elasticities. An analysis of the results in the light of the above two questions follows in the third section.

## STRUCTURE OF THE GENERAL EQUILIBRIUM MODEL

### Basic Assumptions

The effects of the export taxes on raw materials are analysed in a comparative static framework. Two groups are considered: the cartel group, comprising some or all of the commodity exporters, and the group of non-cartel countries, comprising all other countries whether they be net exporters or net importers of the commodity. Three traded goods are incorporated: good number 1, the raw material which is subject to the export restriction; good number 3, the related further processed product; and good number 2, defined as the bundle of all cartel group imports. The cartel group countries are specialized in the production of goods numbers 1 and 3 and export both. The countries outside the cartel produce all three commodities. In order to keep the input-output ratios simple, raw material number 1 is defined as a pure intermediate good, while products number 2 and 3 are consumer goods. Furthermore, the intermediate good is only used in the production of good number 3; good number 2 is not involved in any input-output relationship.[2] Perfect competition prevails on all markets, and no trade barriers exist prior to the adoption of the export restrictions considered here. Transport costs need not be taken into account.

In the interest of lucid results it is further assumed that the production of the raw material (good number 1) in the group of non-cartel countries is practicaly independent of price movements occurring on the market of product number 2.[3] Only allocative effects between goods number 1 and 3 and number 2 and 3 exist in this non-cartel group. All variables concerning the non-cartel countries are indicated by an asterisk.

The Production Side of the Model

The following relations exist between net (X) and gross (Z) output:

cartel members  non-cartel countries

$$Z_1 = Z_1 + b_{13}Z_3 \qquad Z_1^* = X_1^* + b_{13}^* Z_3^*$$

$$Z_2^* = X_2^* \qquad (3.1)$$

$$Z_3 = X_3 \qquad Z_3^* = X_3^*$$

where $b_{13}$ and $b_{13}^*$ represent the quantity of good number 1 needed to produce one unit of product number 3. It is important to note that for the intermediate good, net output is equal to exports (E) or imports (I) respectively. For cartel member countries exporting product number 1, one has

$$X_1 = E_1 \qquad X_1^* = I_1^* \ . \qquad (3.1a)$$

Under the assumption of perfect competition the net outputs are determined by relative prices. Thus, for every possible combination of product prices, $p_1$, $p_3$ within the cartel and $p_1^*$, $p_2^*$, $p_3^*$ outside, there is exactly one combination of net produced quantities (4):

$$X_1 = X_1(p_1, p_3) \qquad X_1^* = X_1^*(p_1^*, p_2^*, p_3^*)$$

$$X_2^* = X_2^*(p_1^*, p_2^*, p_3^*) \qquad (3.2)$$

$$X_3 = X_3(p_1, p_3) \qquad X_3^* = X_3^*(p_1^*, p_2^*, p_3^*) \ .$$

Equation system (3.2) has -- under the assumption made -- the convenient property of a symmetric matrix of substitution terms, thus from the total differential form of equation 3.2

$$dX_1 = \frac{\delta X_1}{\delta p_1} \, dp_1 + \frac{\delta X_1}{\delta p_3} \, dp_3 \qquad dX_1^* = \frac{\delta X_1^*}{\delta d_1^*} \, dp_1^* + \frac{\delta X_1^*}{\delta p_2^*} \, dp_2^* + \frac{\delta X_1^*}{\delta p_3^*} \, dp_3^*$$

$$dX_2^* = \frac{\delta X_2^*}{\delta p_1^*} \, dp_1^* + \frac{\delta X_2^*}{\delta p_2^*} \, dp_2^* + \frac{\delta X_2^*}{\delta p_3^*} \, dp_3^*$$

$$(3.2a)$$

$$dX_3 = \frac{\delta X_3}{\delta p_1} \, dp_1 + \frac{\delta X_3}{\delta p_3} \, dp_3 \qquad dX_3^* = \frac{\delta X_3^*}{\delta d_1^*} \, dp_1^* + \frac{\delta X_3^*}{\delta p_2^*} \, dp_2^* + \frac{\delta X_3^*}{\delta p_3^*} \, dp_3^*$$

one has (5)

$$\frac{\delta X_i}{\delta p_j} = \frac{\delta X_j}{\delta p_i} \quad (i,j = 1,3) \qquad \frac{\delta X_i^*}{\delta p_j^*} = \frac{\delta X_j^*}{\delta p_i^*} \quad (i,j = 1,2,3) \quad (3.2b)$$

If producers have no money illusion, equations (3.2) are homogeneous of degree zero, which means, e.g.,

$$\frac{\delta X_1}{\delta p_1} p_1 + \frac{\delta X_1}{\delta p_3} p_3 = 0 \qquad \frac{\delta X_1^*}{\delta p_1^*} p_1^* + \frac{\delta X_1^*}{\delta p_2^*} p_2^* + \frac{\delta X_1^*}{\delta p_3^*} p_3^* = 0$$

$$\frac{\delta X_2^*}{\delta p_1^*} p_1^* + \frac{\delta X_2^*}{\delta p_2^*} p_2^* + \frac{\delta X_2^*}{\delta p_3^*} p_3^* = 0$$

(3.2c)

$$\frac{\delta X_3}{\delta p_1} p_1 + \frac{\delta X_3}{\delta p_3} p_3 = 0 \qquad \frac{\delta X_3^*}{\delta p_1^*} p_1^* + \frac{\delta X_3^*}{\delta p_2^*} p_2^* + \frac{\delta X_3^*}{\delta p_3^*} p_3^* = 0$$

or equivalently (using equations (3.2a) and the symmetry conditions (3.2b):

$$dX_1 p_1 + dX_3 p_3 = 0 \qquad dX_1 p_1 + dX_2 p_2 + dX_3 p_3 = 0$$

## The Demand Side of the Model

Under the assumption of perfect competition on the product markets, the demand functions for the two final products will be

$$D_2 = D_2(p_2, p_3, y) \qquad D_2^* = D_2^*(p_2^*, p_3^*, y^*)$$

$$D_3 = D_3(p_2, p_3, y) \qquad D_3^* = D_3^*(p_2^*, p_3^*, y^*)$$

(3.3)

where $y$ and $y^*$ represent real incomes within and outside the cartel respectively. The corresponding differential equations are:

$$dD_2 = \frac{\delta D_2}{\delta p_2} dp_2 + \frac{\delta D_2}{\delta p_3} dp_3 + \frac{\delta D_2}{\delta y} dy \qquad dD_2^* = \frac{\delta D_2^*}{\delta p_2^*} dp_2^* + \frac{\delta D_2^*}{\delta p_3^*} dp_3^* + \frac{\delta D_2^*}{\delta y^*} dy^*$$

$$dD_2 = \frac{\delta D_3}{\delta p_2} dp_2 + \frac{\delta D_3}{\delta p_3} dp_3 + \frac{\delta D_3}{\delta y} dy \qquad dD_3^* = \frac{\delta D_3^*}{\delta p_2^*} dp_2^* + \frac{\delta D_3^*}{\delta p_3^*} dp_3^* + \frac{\delta D_3^*}{\delta y^*} dy^* \quad (3.3a)$$

## Determination of Changes in Real National Incomes

Since the ultimate goal of export restriction policies is to increase the consumption possibilities of the cartel countries, changes in real national incomes within and outside the supply cartel (dy and dy$^*$) may be defined as changes in consumed quantities, appropriately weighted with price indices. Here, real incomes are measured in terms of product number 2. It is admissible to use the price of "one" product as income deflator instead of incorporating all three products into an index, since product number 2 has been defined very broadly as being a bundle of all goods produced outside the cartel except numbers 1 and 3. Using $p_1$ and $p_2^*$ as price deflators, one has for changes in real national incomes:

$$dy = dD_2 + \frac{p_3}{p_2} dD_3 \qquad dy^* = dD_2^* + \frac{p_3^*}{p_2^*} dD_3^* \quad . \qquad (3.4)$$

Although according to (3.4) on the demand side pure price changes are irrelevant to real national income, prices (terms of trade) matter a lot on the supply side, since they determine the conditions under which the cartel member countries are able to exchange their export production for imported goods (especially good number 2). This can be best seen by excluding possible temporary current account deficits from the analysis. Under this restriction, in each country group total real expenditure on consumption is always equal to total real national product:

$$D_2 + \frac{p_3}{p_2} D_3 = \frac{p_1}{p_2} X_1(1+t_1) + \frac{p_3}{p_2} X_3 \qquad D_2^* + \frac{p_3^*}{p_2^*} D_3^* = \frac{p_1^*}{p_2^*} X_1^* + X_2^* + \frac{p_3^*}{p_2^*} X_3^*$$

The possible income from cartel export taxation at the rate $t_1$ has already been included in system (3.5), this system being valid both before and after export restriction measures.[6]

Relations Between Prices Within and Outside the Supply Cartel

After describing separately the supply and demand conditions for the cartel and non-cartel economies, the changes are made comparable by introducing relations between prices within and outside the supply cartel. If the export tax is the only disturbance in the price mechanism, and product number 2 is used as a numeraire, one has

$$p_1^* = p_1(1+t_1)$$

$$p_2^* = p_2 = 1 \qquad (3.6)$$

$$p_3^* = p_3$$

or (assuming the initial export tax to be zero):

$$dp_1^* = p_1^* dt_1 + dp_1$$

$$dp_2^* = dp_2^* = 0 \qquad (3.6a)$$

$$dp_3^* = dp_3^*$$

Equilibrium Conditions

Finally, equilibrium conditions are introduced into the model. Since a closed system is considered, according to Walras' Law only two equilibrium conditions are needed for the three product markets:[7]

$$E_1 = -E_1^*[= I_1^*] \qquad (3.7)$$

$$E_3 = -E_3^*[= I_3^*]$$

where (recognizing property (3.1a) for the first equation):

$$E_1 = X_1 \qquad\qquad E_1^* = X_1^* \qquad (3.8)$$

$$E_3 = X_3 - D_3 \qquad\qquad E_3^* = X_3^* - D_3^*$$

From equation (3.8) and (3.7) one gets for the differential form of the equilibrium conditions:

$$dE_1 + dE_1^* = dX_1 + dX_1^* = 0 \qquad (3.7a)$$

$$dE_3 + dE_3^* = [dX_3 - dD_3] + [dX_3^* - dD_3^*] = 0 \ .$$

## COMPARATIVE STATIC SOLUTION OF THE MODEL

The model developed in the previous section can be solved in such a way that changes in the endogenous variables appear as a function of the change in the export tax. The analysis of the model is undertaken in two stages. In the next paragraph the number of available equations will be reduced, and in the following paragraph the results will be given in terms of elasticities.

### Elimination of Two Redundant Equations

The above system (equations (3.2) through (3.8)) contains twenty-one endogenous variables:

$$X_1, X_3, X_1^*, X_2^*, X_3^*$$

$$D_2, D_3, D_2^*, D_3^*$$

$$P_1, P_2, P_3, P_1^*, P_2^*, P_3^*$$

$$y, y^*$$

$$E_1, E_1^*, E_3, E_3^*,$$

while twenty-three equations are available. It can be shown, however, that two equations are linearly dependent on the others, thus making the model complete.

Firstly, if the equilibrium position is reached, the budget constraint for the non-cartel countries can easily be transformed into one for the cartel countries. From equation (3.5) one has for the countries outside the cartel

$$0 = \frac{p_3^*}{p_2^*} (X_3^* - D_3^*) + (X_2^* - D_2^*) + \frac{p_1^*}{p_2^*} X_1^* \quad .$$

Inserting equations (3.6), (3.7) and (3.8) and remembering that according to Walras' Law the market for the second product is also in equilibrium, i.e.

$$D_2 = X_2^* - D_2^* \quad ,$$

one has budget constraint (3.5) for the cartel members.

Secondly, according to the special definitions of real income changes in equation (3.4), total world income $dy + dy^*$ (in terms of product number 2) will not change in this model as a consequence of export taxation. This can be seen in the following: from equation (3.4) together with the price equations one has

$$dy + dy^* = (dD_2 + dD_2^*) + \frac{p_3^*}{p_2^*} (dD_3 + dD_3^*) \quad .$$

With the equilibrium conditions (3.7a) and in recognition of the fact that the market for the second product is also in equilibrium, this becomes:

$$dy + dy^* = \frac{1}{p_2^*} (-p_1^* dX_1^* - p_1 dX_1) = 0$$

or

$$dy = dy^* \quad ,$$

which is precisely the assertion made above.

It may seem rather restrictive to work with a model which only covers pure distributive effects and which does not measure overall welfare decreases as a consequence of interventions in initially optimal allocation patterns. However, <u>relative</u> gains and losses occuring for different countries – these being of great importance in the international discussions on export controls – are indeed covered and the relative degree of subsidization for the raw material processing industry in the cartel member countries can be measured.[8]

## Solution of the Model in Terms of Elasticities

In order to solve the above model the equation system (3.7a) may be directly filled with the supply equations (3.2a). In order to cover the demand changes, the expressions for dy and dy* have to be somewhat modified before they can be inserted into equation (3.3a). We start by differentiating equation (3.5) while observing equation (3.6a) and equation (3.6) and remembering that $t_1 = 0$ at initial equilibrium. The resulting equations are:

$$X_1(dp_1^* - p_1^* dt_1) + p_1 dX_1^* + p_1^* X_1 dt_1 \qquad X_1^* dp_1^* + p_1^* dX_1^* + dX_2^* + X_3^* dp_3^*  \qquad (3.5a)$$

$$+ X_3 dp_3^* + p_3^* dX_3 \qquad\qquad\qquad + p_3^* dX_3^*$$

$$= dD_2 + D_3 dp_3^* + p_3^* dD_3 \qquad\qquad = dD_2^* + D_3^* dp_3^* + p_3^* dD_3^*$$

Combining equation (3.5a) with equation (3.4a) one finally has for the changes in real national incomes:

$$dy = X_1 dp_1^* + p_1^* dX_1 + p_3^* dX_3 \qquad dy^* = X_1^* dp_1^* + p_1^* dX_1^* + dX_2^* \qquad (3.9a)$$

$$+ (X_3 - D_3) dp_3^* \qquad\qquad\qquad + p_3^* dX_3^* + (X_3^* - D_3^*) dp_3^* .$$

Equations (3.9a) may be further simplified by using proportions (3.2c) and inserting the definition for exports of product number 3:

$$dy = X_1 dp_1^* + E_3 dp_3^* \qquad\qquad dy^* = X_1^* dp_1^* + E_3^* dp_3^* . \qquad (3.10a)$$

Equations (3.10a) are used to describe the demand for final goods (equations (3.3a)) under consideration of price equations (3.6a):

$$dD_2 = \frac{\delta D_2}{\delta p_3} dp_3 + \qquad\qquad dD_2^* = \frac{\delta D_2^*}{\delta p_3^*} dp_3^* +$$

$$\qquad\qquad\qquad\qquad\qquad\qquad\qquad\qquad\qquad (3.11a)$$

$$+ \frac{\delta D_2}{\delta y} (X_1 dp_1^* + E_3 dp_3^*) \qquad + \frac{\delta D_2^*}{\delta y} (X_1^* dp_1^* + E_3^* dp_3^*)$$

$$dD_3 = \frac{\delta D_3}{\delta p_3} dp_3^* + \qquad\qquad dD_3^* = \frac{\delta D_3^*}{\delta p_3^*} dp_3^* +$$

$$+ \frac{\delta D_3}{\delta y}(X_1 dp_1^* + E_3 dp_3^*) \qquad\qquad + \frac{\delta D_3^*}{\delta y}(X_1^* dp_1^* + E_3^* dp_3^*) \;.$$

Inserting equation (3.2a) into the first line of (3.7a) and equations (3.2a) and (3.11a) into the second line of equation (3.7a) gives:

$$\left(\frac{\delta X_1}{\delta p_1} + \frac{\delta X_1^*}{\delta p_1^*}\right) dp_1^* + \left(\frac{\delta X_1}{\delta p_3} + \frac{\delta X_1^*}{\delta p_3^*}\right) dp_3^* = \frac{\delta X_1}{\delta p_1} p_1 \, dt_1 \qquad (3.12a)$$

$$\left[\left(\frac{\delta X_3}{\delta p_1} - \frac{\delta D_3}{\delta y} X_1\right) + \left(\frac{\delta X_3^*}{\delta p_1^*} - \frac{\delta D_3^*}{\delta y} X_1^*\right)\right] dp_1 + \left[\left(\frac{\delta X_3}{\delta p_3} - \frac{\delta D_3}{\delta p_3} - \frac{\delta D_3}{\delta y}\right) E_3\right.$$

$$\left. + \left(\frac{\delta X_3^*}{\delta p_3^*} - \frac{\delta D_3^*}{\delta p_3^*} - \frac{\delta D_3^*}{\delta y} E_3^*\right)\right] dp_3^* = \frac{\delta X_3}{\delta p_1} p_1 \, dt_1 \;.$$

Recognizing the property of a symmetric matrix of substitution terms and the absence of money illusion on the producers' side, and introducing the above assumption that no direct connection exists between the production of good number 2 and the price of the raw material, i.e.

$$\frac{\delta X_1^*}{\delta p_2^*} = 0 \;,$$

equation (3.12a) may be reformulated as:

$$\left(\frac{\delta X_1}{\delta p_1}p_1 + \frac{\delta X_1^*}{\delta p_1^*}p_1^*\right)\frac{dp_1^*}{p_1^*} - \left(\frac{\delta X_1}{\delta p_1}p_1^* + \frac{\delta X_1^*}{\delta p_1^*}p_1^*\right)\frac{dp_3^*}{p_3^*} = \frac{\delta X_1}{\delta p_1}p_1\, dt_1$$

$$\left\{\left(\frac{\delta X_1}{\delta p_1}p_1 + \frac{\delta X_1^*}{\delta p_1}p_1^*\right) + \left(\frac{\delta D_3}{\delta y}p_3 X_1 + \frac{\delta D_3^*}{\delta y}p_3^* X_1^*\right)\right\}\frac{dp_1^*}{p_1^*} - \quad (3.13a)$$

$$\frac{p_3^*}{p_1^*}\left\{\left(\frac{\delta X_3}{\delta p_3} - \frac{\delta D_3}{\delta p_3}\right)p_3 + \left(\frac{\delta X_3^*}{\delta p_3^*} - \frac{\delta D_3^*}{\delta p_3^*}\right)p_3^*\right.$$

$$\left. - \left(\frac{\delta D_3}{\delta y}p_3 E_3 + \frac{\delta D_3^*}{\delta y}p_3^* E_3^*\right)\right\}\frac{dp_3^*}{p_3^*} = \frac{\delta X_1}{\delta p_1}p_1\, dt_1 .$$

Observing equation (3.8) and using direct price elasticities of export supply $\mu_1$ and $\mu_3$ of the countries within the cartel and $\mu_1^*$ and $\mu_3^*$ for non-cartel countries as well as $c_3$ and $c_3^*$ as abbreviations for the marginal propensities to consume product number 3 one has for equation (3.13a):

$$E_1[\mu_1-\mu_1^*]\frac{dp_1^*}{p_1^*} - E_1[\mu_1-\mu_1^*]\frac{dp_3^*}{p_3^*} = E_1\mu_1 dt_1$$

(3.14a)

$$E_1[(\mu_1-\mu_1^*) + (c_3-c_3^*)]\frac{dp_1^*}{p_1^*} - E_3\frac{p_3^*}{p_1^*}[(\mu_3-\mu_3^*)-(c_3-c_3^*)]\frac{dp_3^*}{p_3^*} = E_1\mu_1 dt_1.$$

Solving equation (3.14a) for the endogenous outside the cartel gives:

$$\frac{dp_1^*}{p_1^*} = \frac{1 - \dfrac{(c_3 - c_3^*)E_3 p_3^*}{(\mu_3 - \mu_3^*)E_3 p_3^* - (\mu_1 - \mu_1^*)E_1 p_1^*}}{1 - \dfrac{\mu_1^*}{\mu_1}\left[1 - \dfrac{(c_3 - c_3^*)(E_1 p_1^* + E_3 p_3^*)}{(\mu_3 - \mu_3^*)E_3 p_3^* - (\mu_1 - \mu_1^*)E_1 p_1^*}\right]} dt_1 \quad . \qquad (3.15a)$$

$$\frac{dp_3^*}{p_3^*} = \frac{1 - \dfrac{(c_3 - c_3^*)E_1 p_1^*}{(\mu_3 - \mu_3^*)E_3 p_3^* - (\mu_1 - \mu_1^*)E_1 p_1^*}}{1 - \dfrac{\mu_1^*}{\mu_1}\left[1 - \dfrac{(c_3 - c_3^*)(E_1 p_1^* + E_3 p_3^*)}{(\mu_3 - \mu_3^*)E_3 p_3^* - (\mu_1 - \mu_1^*)E_1 p_1^*}\right]} dt_1 \quad . \qquad (3.16a)$$

For the price changes within the cartel one has from equation (3.6a):

$$\frac{dp_1}{p_1} = \frac{dp_1^*}{p_1^*} - dt_1$$

$$\frac{dp_3}{p_3} = \frac{dp_3^*}{p_3^*} \quad .$$

Inserting equations (3.15a) and (3.16a) into the first equation leads to a direct relationship between $p_1$ and $p_3$:

$$\frac{dp_1}{p_1} = \frac{dp_3}{p_3} + \frac{\mu_1^*}{\mu_1} \frac{1}{1 - \dfrac{\mu_1^*}{\mu_1}} dt_1 \quad . \qquad (3.17a)$$

The changes in real production within and outside the cartel are determined simultaneously with the price movements. Since producers have no money illusion (condition (3.2b)) from (3.2a) one has for the relative production changes of goods number 1 (the raw material) and number 3 (the related processed product):

$$\frac{dX_1}{X_1} = \frac{\delta X_1}{\delta p_1} \frac{p_1}{X_1} \frac{dp_1}{p_1} - \frac{\delta X_1}{\delta p_1} \frac{p_1}{X_1} \frac{dp_3}{p_3} \qquad \frac{dX_1^*}{X_1^*} = \frac{\delta X_1^*}{\delta p_1^*} \frac{p_1^*}{X_1^*} \frac{dp_1^*}{p_1^*} - \frac{\delta X_1^*}{\delta p_1^*} \frac{p_1}{X_1^*} \frac{dp_3^*}{p_3^*}$$

(3.18a)

$$\frac{dX_3}{X_3} = \frac{\delta X_3}{\delta p_3} \frac{p_3}{X_3} \frac{dp_1}{p_1} - \frac{\delta X_3}{\delta p_3} \frac{p_3}{X_3} \frac{dp_3}{p_3} \qquad \frac{dX_3^*}{X_3^*} = \frac{\delta X_3^*}{\delta p_3^*} \frac{p_3^*}{X_3^*} \frac{dp_1^*}{p_1^*} - \frac{\delta X_3^*}{\delta p_3^*} \frac{p_3^*}{X_3^*} \frac{dp_3^*}{p_3^*}$$

Introducing price elasticities of supply, the equation system (3.18a) may be simplified to:

$$\frac{dX_1}{X_1} = \varepsilon_1 \left( \frac{dp_1}{p_1} - \frac{dp_3}{p_3} \right) \qquad \frac{dX_1^*}{X_1^*} = \varepsilon_1^* \left( \frac{dp_1^*}{p_1^*} - \frac{dp_3^*}{p_3^*} \right)$$

(3.19a)

$$\frac{dX_3}{X_3} = \varepsilon_3 \left( \frac{dp_3}{p_3} - \frac{dp_1}{p_1} \right) \qquad \frac{dX_3^*}{X_3^*} = \varepsilon_3^* \left( \frac{dp_3^*}{p_3^*} - \frac{dp_1^*}{p_1^*} \right),$$

with

$$\varepsilon_1 = \frac{\delta X_1}{\delta p_1} \cdot \frac{p_1}{X_1} = \mu_1 > 0 \qquad \varepsilon_1^* = \frac{\delta X_1^*}{\delta p_1^*} \cdot \frac{p_1^*}{X_1^*} = -\mu_1^* > 0$$

$$\varepsilon_3 = \frac{\delta X_3}{\delta p_3} \frac{p_3}{X_3} > 0 \qquad \varepsilon_3^* = \frac{\delta X_3^*}{\delta p_3^*} \frac{p_3^*}{X_3^*} > 0 \; .$$

Inserting the price changes within and outside the cartel one finally has for the relative changes in production quantities:

$$\frac{dX_1}{X_1} = \frac{1}{1 - \frac{\mu_1^*}{\mu_1}} \mu_1^* \, dt_1 \qquad \frac{dX_1^*}{X_1^*} = -\frac{1}{1 - \frac{\mu_1^*}{\mu_1}} \mu_1^* \, dt_1$$

(3.20a)

$$\frac{dX_3}{X_3} = -\left(\frac{1}{1 - \frac{\mu_1^*}{\mu_1}} \frac{\mu_1^*}{\mu_1}\right) \varepsilon_3 \, dt_1 \qquad \frac{dX_3^*}{X_3^*} = -\left(\frac{1}{1 - \frac{\mu_1^*}{\mu_1}}\right) \varepsilon_3^* \, dt_1 \, .$$

## INTERPRETATION OF THE RESULTS

### Interpretations Within the Model Framework

Taking into consideration the changes in endogenous variables as a result of common export tax levied by the supply cartel as given in equations (3.15a), (3.16a) and (3.20a), it becomes clear that all results can be split into two multiplicative factors. The first factor

$$\frac{1}{1 - \frac{\mu_1^*}{\mu_1}}$$

is included in all equations, and is exactly equal to the expression gained for endogenous changes in the world market price when the effect of an infinitesimal export tax in the partial model is calculated on the basis of raw material number 1 alone.[10] If the supply cartel is a net exporter of the commodity and is able to vary its supply, then $\mu_1^* < 0$ and $\mu_1 > 0$. Under the realistic assumption that the cartel is faced with a not completely price elastic import demand function, then it is further true that $-\infty < \mu_1^*$ and thus:

$$\frac{1}{1 - \frac{\mu_1^*}{\mu_1}} > 0 \, . \qquad (3.21)$$

The initial effects stemming from direct reactions on the raw material market are modified by repercussions from other markets, which are covered through relatively complicated second multiplicative factors for the changes in product prices (equations (3.15a) and (3.16a). However, if the focus is on situations in which the cartel group is already a significant exporter not only of the commodity but also of the related processed good, the model results are stable and the direction of changes in the endogenous variables clear-cut.[11]

The summary of results given in table 3.1 shows that a supply cartel formed by raw material exporting countries can increase its production of the related processed product through commodity export restrictions. According to the equations system (3.20a) the necessary conditions for this outcome are a commodity import demand of countries outside the cartel which is not completely price elastic ($-\infty < \mu_1^*$), and an internal processing industry, which is flexible enough to show a positive price elasticity of supply ($\varepsilon_3 > 0$).

The distribution of production within the processing industry over various countries is influenced by three effects. Firstly, the export tax on the raw material causes the price of the restricted commodity outside the supply cartel to rise ($dp_1^* > 0$) and within the cartel to fall ($dp_1 < 0$). The processing industry of the non-cartel countries thus sustains higher raw material costs per unit of production than the processing industry of the cartel countries. As shown in table 3.1, this situation still holds after completion of all adjustment processes. The processing industry within the cartel is in a relatively more favourable position than that outside the cartel.

Secondly, curbing raw material production in the cartel countries as a result of export taxation causes resources to be liberated. Thus, aided by sinking factor prices, value-added costs in other branches of the economy (such as in the processing industry) also sink. The consequence of this is higher sales within the cartel group as increased net exports. The countries outside the supply cartel attempt to elude part of the increase in raw material prices by increasing their own production of the good. This requires the withdrawal of additional resources from other branches, at higher cost. On the whole the change in factor prices has a favourable effect on the processing industry within the cartel and an unfavourable impact on the processing industry of countries outside the cartel.

Thirdly, it is possible that the price of good number 3 itself alters. As shown in table 3.1, the price remains constant if the marginal propensity to consume good number 3 within the cartel is the same as outside it ($c_3 = c_3^*$), it increases if $c_3 > c_3^*$, and falls if $c_3 < c_3^*$. Since in the model used it was assumed that trade in processed good number 3 is not in any way restricted, a change in $p_3^* (=p_3)$ will have the same effect in countries within and outside the cartel.

Table 3.1 Direction of Changes in Endogenous Variables Depending on the Marginal Propensities to Consume Product Number 3.

| Endogenous variables | | Marginal propensities to consume product number 3 within the cartel (c3) and outside of it | | |
|---|---|---|---|---|
| | | $c_3 < c_3^*$ | $c_3 = c_3^*$ | $c_3 > c_3^*$ |
| **Cartel member countries** | | | | |
| Price of the raw material | $p_1$ | | decrease | |
| Price of the related processed good | $p_3$ | decrease | no change | increase |
| Production of the raw material | $X_1$ | | decrease | |
| Production of the related processed good | $X_3$ | | increase | |
| **Countries outside the cartel** | | | | |
| Price of the raw material | $p_1^*$ | | increase | |
| Price of the related processed good | $p_3^*$ | decrease | no change | increase |
| Production of the raw material | $X_1^*$ | | increase | |
| Production of the related processed good | $X_3^*$ | | decrease | |

Although the overall conclusion to be drawn from the results of the general equilibrium model is that the levying of a common commodity export tax by a supply cartel will in all cases have the effect of promoting the processing industry within the cartel, this result should not be misinterpreted as being a signal for most developing countries to restrict their raw material exports. As was pointed out at the beginning of the chapter, developing countries want to reach the goals of more domestic processing and higher incomes from commodity exports simultaneously. However, even in the world of the perfect competition model, which assumes favourable conditions for the developing country suppliers, this outcome is only possible for very powerful cartel groups facing an inelastic commodity import demand from outside ($-1 < \mu_1^*$). Empirical evidence shows[12] that this condition is only fulfilled for very few raw materials. Thus, in most cases developing country suppliers are faced with a trade-off between the goal of promoting the internal commodity processing industry and the goal of increasing their foreign exchange receipts from commodity exports.

But even if the relevant elasticity condition for the raw material market is given ($-1 < \mu_1^*$), allowing the cartel members to simultaneously pursue their goals of processing industry promotion and export income increases, their success will only be moderate: According to the results of equation system (3.20a) an inelastic commodity import demand outside the cartel is equivalent to relatively small incentives for the internal processing industry. This is intuitively clear, since an inelastic demand for the commodity means that countries outside the cartel are unwilling to abandon processing lines to other countries, even if their input prices rise.

Finally, one should keep in mind that according to (3.20a) an additional condition for the successful promotion of processing is a comparably high price elasticity $_3$ of the industry's supply within the cartel.

## Limitations on the Applicability of the Model Results

The results of the general equilibrium model used here imply that it may sometimes be to the advantage of cartels comprising raw material exporting developing countries to restrict their raw materials exports and instead to export processed goods. These results however are not completely in line with those of empirical studies dealing with the difficulties faced by raw material processing industries in developing countries. It is this which leads an UNCTAD study to make the general statement: "There is... no overriding economic reason for each developing country to process the totality of its crude material output before export."[13]

One should certainly take care in trying to apply the results gained in the present work without modifications to real economic situations. The analysis of the effects of export taxes as

carried out here involves a series of assumptions, some of which may stand open to debate.[14] More technical assumptions will not be discussed here. Of greater significance are the problems which give rise to the fact that:
- producers, traders and consumers do not behave as price takers;
- the transport of raw materials and related processed goods involves time and costs;
- a considerable role is played by indivisibilities, expecially in the field of raw materials processing.

Any digression from the situation of perfect competition is caused in the first place by the official trade policy of the raw material importing countries. In many cases effective protection increases with the degree of raw material processing.[15] Although the effects of tariff protection have been mitigated to a certain extent by the General System of Preferences and special trade agreements (such as the Lome-Convention), they nevertheless present an obstacle to the building up of export oriented processing industries in developing countries. Regulative non-tariff restrictions, declaration obligations, etc., are easier to enforce with processed products than with raw materials. The situation of perfect competition is disturbed in the second place by the important role of restrictive business practices in raw material trade, as engaged in by multinational corporations.[16] However, the cost-minimizing distribution of various activities within affiliated multinationals should not necessarily be seen as harmful to the production structure in developing countries. Thirdly, in view of the high level of unemployment in raw material importing countries it is not to be expected that these countries will willingly hand over production lines to other countries: unilateral export taxes can give occasion to retaliation measures.

Transport problems have not been dealt with in the model used above, and in this sense the model has been greatly simplified. Transport costs are often used as an argument in favour of raw material processing in the country of origin. Nevertheless, detailed studies on the problem have shown that this is only valid for a few products. For other products, either the savings are minimal or they are more than cancelled out by loss in quality during transport of the end product.[17] These effects cannot be adequately handled in a general study.

In determining infinitesimal changes in the endogenous variables it was assumed that individual magnitudes could be divided at discretion. Precisely in the raw material processing branch, technical necessity forces production to be highly investment intensive per unit. Such high investment outlays are only economically profitable if either sufficient quantities of the processed good can be exported or if the domestic market is large enough in the developing country concerned. In the case of exports, one again comes up against the type of restrictions outlined above.

In summary, one can say that the model developed in this chapter gives an idea of the effects of export taxes on further processing industries. As with all studies of a general nature, the advantage of general validity is set against the disadvantage of extensive simplification. Specific product studies would be able to provide additional results.

NOTES

1. The model used is based on one published by Suzuki 1978, 55-69. The base has been modified to obtain results compatible with the quantitative analysis of export controls.
2. The latter assumption is more restrictive than the one used by Suzuki in his model. Suzuki assumed the intermediate good to be used in the production of both consumer goods (cf. Suzuki 1978, 56). The more restrictive assumption is not unrealistic, since some products may be closely related to a specific raw material (number 3) while others (number 2) are hardly influenced by changes in the market of the raw product under consideration.
3. This additional assumption was not made by Suzuki. However, in order to make the model manageable for practical purposes it is unavoidable.
4. A formal and complete set of conditions for this is given in Khang and Uekawa 1973, 283-90.
5. The proof of this symmetry is illustrated in Silberberg 1974, 734-41. Cf. also Samuelson 1947, 63.
6. According to equation (3.1a)

$$\frac{P_1}{P_2} X_1(1 + t_1) = \frac{P_1}{P_2} E_1(1 + t_1)$$

is the export income of the cartel group (including tax income). The same argument applies for the import payments of the non-cartel group.
7. The introduction of (negative) net exports (e) into equation (3.7) instead of using imports (I) is purely for reasons of symmetry. The following calculations will be made with the symbols $E_1$ and $E_3$.
8. In principle it would appear possible to enlarge the model above for measuring world allocative losses. However, studies undertaken by the present author in this direction gave rise to a model structure much more complicated than the one described here.
9.

$$\mu_1 = \frac{\delta E_1}{\delta p_1} \frac{\delta p_1}{\delta E_1} > 0 \qquad \mu_1^* = \frac{\delta E_1^*}{\delta p_1^*} \frac{\delta p_1^*}{\delta E_1^*} < 0$$

$$\mu_3 = \frac{\delta E_3}{\delta p_3} \frac{\delta p_3}{\delta E_3} > 0 \qquad \mu_3^* = \frac{\delta E_3^*}{\delta p_3^*} \frac{\delta p_3^*}{\delta E_3^*} < 0$$

$$c_3 = \frac{\delta D_3}{\delta y} \; p_3 > 0 \qquad\qquad c_3^* = \frac{\delta D_3^*}{\delta y^*} \; p_3^* > 0 \; .$$

10. See for instance equation (4.13) in chapter 4.
11. The most important stability condition may be directly derived from equation (3.16a):

$$(\mu_3 - \mu_3^*)E_3 p_3^* - (\mu_1 - \mu_1^*)E_1 p_1^* > 0 \; .$$

12. See the results of chapter 4.
13. UNCTAD 1976, 44.
14. See section 3.1.1.
15. See UNCTAD 1979, 16.
16. See Wall (1980).
17. A survey of such studies is provided by Roemer (1979).

REFERENCES

Khang, Chulsoon and Yasuo, Uekawa. 1973. The production Possibility Set in a Model Allowing Interindustry Flows: The Necessary and Sufficient Conditions for its Strict Convexity. Journal of International Economics 3: 283-90.

Roemer, Michael. 1973. Resource-Based Industrialization in the Developing Countries. Journal of Development Economics 6: 163-202.

Samuelson, Paul A. 1947. Foundations of Economic Analysis. Cambridge, Mass:

Silberberg, Eugene. 1974. The Theory of the Firm in the Long-Run Equilibrium. American Economic Review 64: 734-41.

Suzuki, Katsuhiko. 1978. The Welfare Effects of an Export Tax Levied on an Intermediate Good. Quarterly Journal of Economics 92: 55-69.

UNCTAD. 1976. Processing of Primary Products in Developing Countries: Problems and Prospects, Report by the UNCTAD Secretariat, UNCTAD/MD/79, GE. 76-64124.

UNCTAD. 1979. The Processing Before Export of Primary Commodities: Areas for Further International Co-operation. Report by the UNCTAD Secretariat, UNCTAD TD/229/Supp. 2, GE. 79-51483.

Wall, David. 1980. Industrial Processing of Natural Resources. World Development 8:303-16.

# 4
# Free Access to Supplies Versus Restrictive Supply Policies: The Ability of LDCs to Control Commodity Markets

*Horst Keppler*

INTRODUCTION AND SUMMARY OF EMPIRICAL FINDINGS

The last few years have witnessed the appearance of a new threat to international trade relations that could well, in the opinion of many trade politicians, endanger global economic growth. This threat is embodied in the export restrictions adopted by many countries in recent years in their attempt to achieve specific national policy objectives. The most spectacular control measure to date has been the restriction on oil exports imposed at the end of 1973 made by the OPEC cartel. Further examples are the temporary restrictions on soybeans and uranium exports adopted by the US and Canada, the US ban on wheat exports to the USSR, and the latest attempts by the US government to reduce the volume of high technology exports to socialist countries. The oil crisis and the subsequent pressure on the petroleum market caused both suppliers and consumers to become newly aware of the possibilities and dangers involved in control policies of this nature.

In the field of raw material trade it is for the most part developing countries that are interested in introducing export restrictions with the aim of increasing their export revenues and promoting their own raw material processing industries. With the help of a simple equilibrium model it is possible to examine whether unilateral export restrictions do in fact lead to increased export revenues and profits for developing countries. The empirical calculations in the present work show that -- assuming favorable conditions for the developing countries -- this is principally possible for 5 of the 10 UNCTAD core commodities, namely: cocoa, tea, sisal, rubber and tin. In the cases of coffee and jute the results are heavily dependent on the composition of the export cartel. However, the increases in export earnings caused by unilateral export restrictions will be relatively small. Even if all developing countries exporting the products concerned were to join together to form supply cartels and cause price increases of 10 percent on world markets, then the total revenue of the export cartels would increase by no more than

6 percent per year ($ 5 billion in 1977 prices for the five core commodities or roughly $ 1 billion for the seven commodities). The structure of the chapter is as follows:
The first section provides a survey of the range of objectives underlying export restrictions, whereby particular attention is paid to the possible interest of developing countries in such market interventions. The quantitative significance of export controls for international trade today is illustrated with the help of empirical data. The analysis covers only those export restrictions that constitute governmental interventions in the markets of single products. General measures aimed at modifying the overall export pattern of any one country and private market agreements are thus excluded from the investigation. In the next section a partial equilibrium model is developed that enables the measurement of changes in both the export revenues and the profits of developing country suppliers that attempt to raise export taxes on their commodity exports. Based on this model analysis, empirical estimates are made in the third section for revenue and profit changes resulting from export restrictions adopted by alternative cartel constructions. Since the empirical results diverge greatly from those obtained in other studies, an extensive comparison is made of the methods of measurement and the empirical data (the precise calculations in this respect may be found in Appendix 4.C).

OBJECTIVES OF EXPORT RESTRICTION MEASURES

General Objectives

Government export controls may be broadly classified into those adopted mainly for political reasons and those aimed primarily at economic goals, although, of course, the effects of restrictive measures will be felt in both spheres.[1]
Since the Second World War politically motivated export restrictions imposed on key products have been aimed primarily at limiting the economic and military potential of other states.[2] Outstanding examples of this are the export controls applied by the US and its allies during the Cold War period in order to hamper development in the USSR and other socialist countries. Such restrictions were not well harmonized amongst the group of supplying countries, their application being left to each country's political initiative. It has happened for instance in the case of strategically important tube exports, that one country (West Germany) has refused to deliver the materials whilst another (Great Britain) has continued its supply. More recent examples of export controls with the purpose of limiting the economic and military potential of demanding countries are the restrictions applied by some countries on trade with South Africa and Israel.
The second reason for politically motivated export controls may be seen in the attempt to force other countries to change their political behavior. Most prominent in this respect are the temporary supply boycotts for petroleum applied by the Arab oil producing countries to the Netherlands and the US during the

Israeli-Arab war in late 1973. Other examples are the trade embargo imposed on Rhodesia (Zimbabwe) after its unilateral declaration of independence from Great Britain and the refusal of the US to deliver grain to the USSR after the political change in Afghanistan. However, as in the tube export case above, not all suppliers respected the boycotts on a long-term basis, rendering them ineffective.

There exist only very limited possibilities for handling politically motivated export controls with the normal economic tools. Economists are not able to compare the costs of such trade restrictions with their potential gains, since no numeraire exists to weigh military, ideological, and moral gains against losses in production. Accordingly, the political objectives of export restrictions will not be explicitly dealt with here. The following analysis of economic effects, however, serves to make politicians aware of the economic costs involved in export control policies.

Economically motivated export restrictions may be conveniently classified according to their underlying goals, as shown in Table 4.1. As can be seen, export controls affect the achievement of all important economic goals.

By restricting the export of certain products a country can assure a stable level of employment and growth in the short-run, since (short-run) physical supply shortages are thereby avoided. Such shortages can occur if for instance total domestic supply remains constant and export demand from abroad increases sharply, or if export demand remains inelastic when domestic production suffers a dropback. By diverting part of the supply to the domestic market through export controls, it is possible to prevent sudden decreases in employment and growth in those sectors where the controlled export is an input. Examples of export restrictions of this kind are the prohibition imposed by Japan on sales of petroleum-based synthetics to other East Asian countries during the oil crisis and the control of metal scrap exports (especially copper scrap) applied by European countries from time to time.[3]

In market economies, the goal of ensuring short-run supply of specific goods is always combined with a second objective of export controls, namely a reduction in the internal supply prices of the restricted product. Low internal supply prices may serve to reach anti-inflationary, distributive and growth/employment targets. This strategy provides perfect complementarity with the avoidance of (short-run) supply shortages argument insofar as restricted exports keep the domestic product price temporarily low. In fact, in this case it seems to be impossible to distinguish between the two objectives. Accordingly, the prohibition of soybean exports from the United States in mid-1973 and the following temporary quantitative restrictions could be attributed to reasons of price control as well as to ensuring uninterrupted supply.[4]

A special aspect of anti-inflationary objectives can be seen in the need to combine internal price contols for certain products in market economies with export restrictions, in order to prevent

Table 4.1. Specific Goals of Economically Motivated Export Restrictions

| | | | | | |
|---|---|---|---|---|---|
| Immediately observable effects of export restrictions | Short-term diversion of supply away from export and towards the domestic market | Revenues through export taxation | Reduction of internal supply price | Increase in world market price | Longrun reduction of supply delivered to the world market |
| Underlying economic goals | Stabilization of economic environment by avoiding "critical" supply shortages in the domestic economy | Distributional effects of keeping certain commodity prices low | Growth and employment effects through subsidizing of domestic further processing | Balance of payments and growth effects through increased export income | Longrun growth effects through secure raw material reserves, which can be tapped off later |

suppliers from exporting their products at higher prices thus causing supply deficits at home.

The anti-inflationary aspect of export controls is not, of course, necessarily limited to the respective product under consideration. Depending on the weight the product has in different price indices, a lower price for the restricted good will lower the index. However, it seems improbable that diverting supply of one or two products from external to internal demanders will be successful in the long run as an anti-inflationary measure. This is because no sole product is likely to carry sufficient weight to be able to affect general price indices. One exception to this may perhaps be crude petroleum.

Long-term reduction of internal supply prices by export controls on a commodity is usually aimed at influencing internal distribution and growth patterns. The distributional aspects of keeping certain commodity prices low are most obvious in cases of food price increases, where domestic private consumers are subsidized. In countries where the public fiscal system is underdeveloped, export taxes or export licences sold to competing buyers may be used to raise government revenue, thus distributing money away from the private to the public sector. An example of this kind of export control is the longstanding tax on rice exports in Thailand.

Growth and employment are the underlying economic objectives when export restrictions are used to promote domestic processing industries through reduced input prices. Depending on the state of domestic development, this means either a subsidization of already existing industries in order to reduce the impact of foreign competition in the field of finished goods or a promotion of small or even initially non-existent industrial branches at home in analogy to the infant industry argument on the import side. Examples of export controls of the latter type are the taxes on raw coffee exports adopted by Brazil since 1965 or Pakistan's quantitative restrictions on leather exports in the 1960s. Subsidies to existing industries were effectively provided by Spain's export controls on raw leather exports in 1972. Present-day complaints from processing industries throughout different branches about the underpricing of raw materials abroad due to export restrictions point to the actuality of the problem.[5]

So far all economic objectives mentioned have been analyzed in terms of the internal economy of the restricting country. No mention has been made of possible effects outside the economy under consideration. One could consider handling the theme within a national welfare maximizing framework. However, this is only possible under special circumstances: the country adopting export controls for specific products must be a marginal supplier on the world market in the sense that its share in world supply is negligible or that other supplying countries are able to react very elastically, thus being able to fill any gap stemming from export controls of the home country.

In many cases, however, exports are restricted by non-marginal suppliers. These countries may well recognize the above-mentioned objectives as side effects of their specific trade control policy, but their main interest lies in international redistribution of income through export restrictions. The two main variants of this goal are possible increases in commodity terms of trade for the restricting country or -- under special circumstances -- in income terms of trade. Whenever a country or group of countries faces a demand curve for its exports that is not totally elastic with respect to export prices, then any restriction on exports will increase the unit price of the export good. If, in addition, the price elasticity of demand is less than unity, total export revenue will be increased as a result of restrictions. These price and revenue increases lead to improvements in the commodity terms of trade or in the income terms of trade, respectively, if for the country considered there are no or only relatively loose connections between export prices and the import price index. Past experience shows that export restrictions with the aim of changing the international income distribution are primarily to be expected in the field of raw materials.

The terms of trade argument is presented on two time planes, on the one hand the immediate increase in import capacity of the country in question and on the other hand the role of long-term considerations. Reflections on the depletion of natural resources as formulated in the first Report to the Club of Rome belong to the latter time plane.[6] The underlying economic argument for adopting export controls in the case of limited natural resources rests on the assumption that the country in question is not in a position to build up a diversified export production before the raw material shortage actually occurs. Moreover, the country is mistrustful of the real value of money assets over time and of their true worth as future reserves. If these two assumptions hold, then the country might be better off in the future if it stretches exploitation of its important natural resources over a longer period.[7]

## Special Interests of Developing Countries

Export tax income does not play a significant role in the central government budget of any industrial member countries of the IMF.[8] Even in developing countries, by far the greatest share of state revenues from taxes on international trade come from import duties. However, the majority of developing countries levy export duties too, either in the form of general taxes or product-specific duties. Since in this essay export restrictions on individual goods are investigated, table 4.2 lists all developing countries in which revenues from product-specific export duties contribute at least 5 percent of the central government budget. The fact that so few countries appear in the table is a result of the fact that many levy only general export taxes (on all goods). However, in quite a number of cases exports are so strongly concentrated on a reduced number of products that in effect tax revenues stem from one or a few exported raw materials. The percentage share of export tax revenues in the central government budget is nevertheless representative for all cases.[9]

Table 4.2 IMF Member Contries in Which at Least 5 Percent of Central Government Revenue Stems from Product Specific Export Duties.

| Country | Period of measurement | Share of specific export duties in Central Government Revenue (percent) | Tax income stemming mainly from exports of |
|---|---|---|---|
| Swaziland | 1975-1977 | 22.5 | sugar |
| Guatemala | 1976-1978 | 20.7 | coffee |
| Burundi | 1975-1977 | 20.2 | coffee |
| Sri Lanka | 1976-1978 | 19.7 | tea, rubber, coconuts |
| Malaysia | 1976-1978 | 16.4 | rubber, tin, palm oil |
| Dominican Republic | 1975-1977 | 14.9 | sugar, coffee cocoa |
| Sierra Leone | 1976-1978 | 14.5 | coffee, cocoa, diamonds |
| Zaire | 1975-1977 | 13.1 | minerals, animals, plants |
| Peru | 1977-1979 | 12.4 | "traditional" goods |
| Colombia | 1976-1978 | 9.9 | coffee |
| Tanzania | 1977-1979 | 9.2 | coffee, cotton, sisal |
| Honduras | 1974-1976 | 8.4 | bananas, coffee |
| Ecuador | 1977-1979 | 7.3 | coffee |

Source: Calculated from IMF, 1980.

The developing countries listed in table 4.2 will at least in the medium-run be interested in maintaining their traditional budget financing, which includes financing from export taxes. However, one can assume that the goal of state revenues through

export taxation will gradually lose significance in the developing countries as their tax system becomes more diversified.
The fact that developing countries are dissatisfied with the existing world trade system gives rise to the possibility that they might introduce additional export controls. The dissatisfaction has been clearly documented in the two basic resolutions in the UN Assembly on the creation of a New International Economic Order.[10] One important part of the proposed new scheme would be a modified raw material distribution framework to replace the principles of the Havana Charter of 1948, which relied on the view "... that the free working of commodity markets would result in an optimal allocation of the world's resources as well as providing a stimulus to the economic development of the underdeveloped countries."[11] According to the charter, market interventions should primarily be limited to the control of excessive short run price fluctuations.[12] Although the mentioned UN Resolution was formulated as a call for common action among all nations, in cases of economic conflict some specific parts of the resolution could serve to justify unilateral export restrictions in raw material trade. The particular claims in this respect are:
- To ensure "full permanent sovereignty of every State over its natural resources and all economic activities."
- "To facilitate the functioning and to further the aims of producers' associations, including... improvement in the export income of producing developing countries and in their terms of trade..."
- "To evolve a just and equitable relationship between the prices of raw materials, primary commodities, manufactured and semi-manufactured goods..."
- "To take measures to promote the processing of raw materials in the producer developing countries."[13]

As is clear from the UN General Assembly Resolution, the terms of trade objective and the goal of subsidizing domestic processing industries through export controls on raw materials are of decisive importance for the developing countries in their attempt to achieve higher raw material prices through supply controls. Negotiations for raw material agreements within the framework of UNCTAD show, on the one hand, the desire of all affected trade partners to avoid unilateral measures restricting raw material exports; the length of the discussions, on the other hand, shows that the solutions are not always free of conflict.

## The Present Day Significance of Export Restrictions

Several studies were dedicated to the influence of export restrictions on present-day world trade.[14] The data base for the analysis of this problem is unreliable and inexact for three reasons. Firstly, a whole series of government measures exists for controlling exports whereby it is not clearly stated whether their purpose is to restrict exports. State monopolies and export licensing practices fall, for instance, in this category. In both cases there is a lack of concrete information on the behavior of government agencies. Secondly, statistics on export controls are for the most part provided by the controlling country itself.[15] This means that the data are presented in such a form as to make it appear that there is no direct over-stepping of the (very generous) GATT restrictions or controvention of the general interests of trading partners. General export taxes pose a particular problem in this connection since they are levied by many countries whose exports are highly concentrated on one or two raw materials, the general tax thus having the effect of a specific one. Thirdly, there are a number of export quotas which are at least from time to time ineffective since the actually exported quantities fall below the quota level. The quota ceiling is nevertheless retained as a security measure. If the available data base is interpreted without qualifications, the first and the third of the above reasons would tend to indicate that the significance of export restrictions for present-day world trade has been over-estimated. The second reason would lead one to believe that the problem has been underestimated.

On the basis of the given restrictions, the following can be concluded from Schenkel's analysis for 1975:[16]
- Barely one third of the given restrictions, of all IMF member countries impose embargoes or quotas for quantitative regulation of the exports of individual products.
- Barely one fifth of all IMF member-countries levy export taxes on individual goods.
- Both quantitative control measures and export taxes are almost exclusively applied by developing countries.

In interpreting the estimates one should recall that countries restricting the exports of only one product have also been considered. Account has not been taken of the significance of exports of this product for the total trade of the country.

How heavily trade in individual goods is affected by export controls or restrictions can only be approximately assessed. Schenkel's study shows that:
- Among agricultural products, control is exerted on the export particularly of those products which UNCTAD hopes to cover with international raw material agreements (cocoa, coffee, tea, jute, rubber).
- In the case of non-agricultural raw materials, export controls exist mainly for crude petroleum and crude petroleum products, metal ores and scrap.
- Industrial exports are very rarely subject to controls.

World trade flows have adapted themselves to the respective export restrictions; only in the case of crude petroleum are the effects of these measures to be clearly seen at the present time. Although most national economies are to a certain extent flexible, the more intensive and possibly more coordinated application of export restrictions (as in the cartel case) for the purpose of achieving national goals would provoke disturbances in world trade.

## THE EFFECT OF COMMON EXPORT TAXES ON THE REVENUES AND PROFITS OF EXPORT CARTELS: PARTIAL EQUILIBRIUM ANALYSIS

One of the main aims of developing countries in discussions on a re-ordering of international raw material trade is to increase the prices of their exported raw materials (improvement of commodity terms of trade) and to achieve higher export incomes (improvement of income terms of trade).[17] Formulated in such a way, it is not clear whether the ultimate goal is the maximization of export incomes or of export profits. The optimum level of export restrictions is different for each specific good. In order not to be pinned down by inflexible statements, both **variations** of the goal will be looked at in this essay.

In general, no one country has a large enough share in world exports of a single commodity to be able to induce a significant effect on prices within the world market by adopting export restriction measures. A necessary condition for reaching the objective of terms of trade improvement is thus cartelization of the supply side. In practice, many obstacles stand in the way of efficient longer run price and quantity controls by major groups of suppliers, and it is difficult to bring such obstacles into an abstract model. To study them properly requires a detailed product market analysis. For the purposes of a general analysis it is more convenient to set aside the problems involved in cartel formation and to assume the existence of a newly formed export cartel which pursues a common policy of restrictions. The argument in the present chapter will begin from this standpoint, though in doing so it should be made clear from the outset that a very favorable constellation is assumed for the export restricting countries, and that all empirical calculations must be accordingly qualified.

Effects of export restrictions will be analyzed in a comparative static framework dealing with two groups of countries, the cartel group and the "rest of the world", comprising net exporters of the commodity in question remaining outside the supply cartel, and net importers. All algebraic expressions relating to the "rest of the world" group will be indicated throughout the remainder of the essay by an asterisk. The partial equilibrium analysis of the world market situation for each respective commodity is built on the following assumptions:
- cross-price elasticities between the product considered and other goods are negligible, i.e., price movements on the market of the restricted export good do not influence other product prices;
- the "rest of the world" demand curve for exports of the restricted product is given, implying absence of any retaliation policies as a consequence of the cartel's export restrictions;
- private and social production costs for the product are equal within the cartel;
- the demand pattern within the cartel is given, implying given tastes and income distribution.

Although not essential to the analysis, it is assumed for convenience that prior to the adoption of the export restriction no significant trade barriers existed for the respective product and that perfect competition prevailed on the product market.

For reasons of algebraic simplicity only export taxes are considered. In the geometrical analysis taxes may be easily substituted by quantitative restrictions.

Figure 4.1 shows the initial equilibrium situation, $e_o$, in which export quantity $E_o$ is exchanged between the cartel and the "rest of the world" at price $p_o$. Since no trade barriers exist $p_o = p_o^*$.

Figure 4.1 Price and Quantity Changes Resulting from an Export Tax.

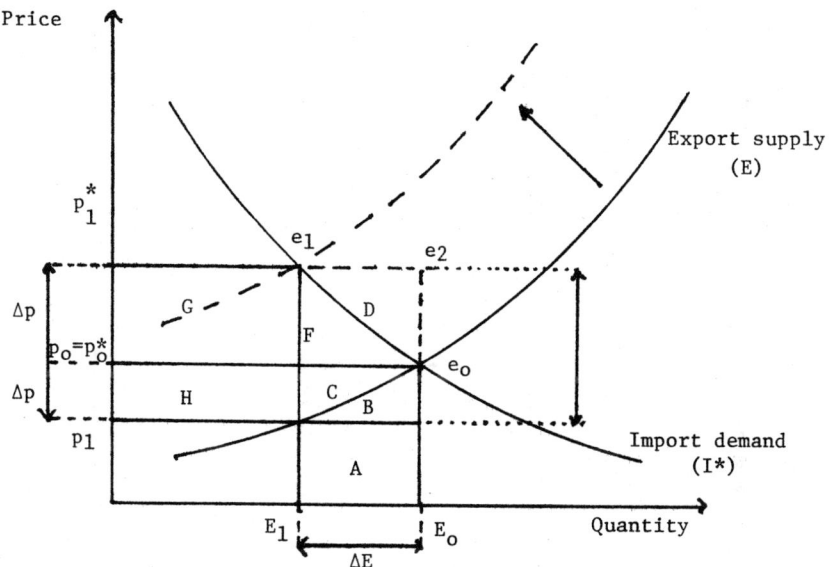

Subsequent to all adjustments after the levying of a common export tax t by the cartel, the new equilibrium settles at $e_1$ and the price of the product outside the cartel rises by $\Delta p^*$. The traded quantity in the new equilibrium situation falls by $\Delta E$ and the price of the product within the cartel is $\Delta p$ lower than previously.

Table 4.3 shows the changes in revenues and profits both for the cartel group and the non-cartel group as a result of export taxation. It can be seen that a shift from situation $e_o$ to situation $e_1$ causes the export revenues of the producer cartel to change by

$$\Delta Ex = + G - (A + B) - C \,.  \tag{4.1}$$

Table 4.3. Changes in Revenues and Profits Resulting from Export Taxation

| Shift from situation $e_o$ to... | Measured changes | Total | Producer side (cartel members) Private production | Producer side Public sector | Total | Consumer side (non-cartel members) Private Production | Consumer side Public sector | Net change in world efficiency |
|---|---|---|---|---|---|---|---|---|
| Situation $e_1$ | Changes in net foreign exchange position | + G <br> − (A + B) <br> − C | − H <br> − (A + B) <br> − C | + G + H | − G <br> + (A + B) <br> + C | − G <br> + (A + B) <br> + C | No change | Not relevant |
| | Changes in producers' & consumers' surpluses | + G <br> − C | − H <br> − C | + G + H | − F <br> − G | − F <br> − G | No change | − F <br> − C |
| Situation $e_2$ | Changes in net foreign exchange position | + (D + F) <br> + G | No change | + (D + F) <br> + G | − (D + F) <br> − G | No change | − (D + F) <br> − G | Not relevant |
| | Changes in producers' & consumers' surpluses | + (D + F) <br> + G | No change | + (D + F) <br> + G | − (D + F) <br> − G | No change | − (D + F) <br> − G | No change |

Source: Figure 4.1

The value of the absolute change in import expenditures of the non-cartel countries is the same as equation (4.1). Export revenues of the producers only increase if:

$G > A + B + C.$

It is worth noting that in any case the public authorities in export restricting countries achieve higher receipts from tax income [+ G + H] whereas private producers in these countries always receive less [- H - (A + B) - C]. On the side of the net importing countrygroup the public authorities are not affected at all, and the total burden of adjustment to higher export prices falls on the private sector.

The resulting changes in production profits (measured at producers' surplus) are:

$$\Delta Ps = + G - C \qquad (4.2)$$

They are greater than changes in revenue by [A + B], since the production dropback as against the initial situation also caused costs to go down. Profits increase if:

$G > C.$

The welfare position of the countries outside the cartel undoubtedly worsens since their consumers' surplus is reduced by [- F - G]. The above statements are valid for the distribution of gains and losses between private producers or consumers and the public sector, and it is only the magnitude of the changes that alters.

The transition from situation $e_0$ perfect competition to $e_1$ (export taxation) signifies a loss in efficiency of [- F - C] for the world as a whole. This loss originates in the intervention into the factor allocation mechanism both within and outside the cartel, with the aim of altering distribution. Table 4.3 also examines an alternative path, namely a shift from $e_0$ to $e_2$, whereby transactions between public sectors lead to a transfer of income from the net importing to the net exporting countries. The transfer is determined in such a way that it is equivalent to a price increase of the commodity under consideration to the value of the price in situation $e_1$, the trade quantities being however unchanged. As can be seen, if there are no changes for private producers and consumers, then world efficiency also remains unaltered. A pure transfer regulation - with possibly smaller agreed transfers than in the situation $e_1$ - thus represents a favorable alternative to pugnacious attempts at redistribution within the allocation mechanism.

Expressing the areas in table 4.3 in terms of the price and quantity values of figure (4.1), we have:[18]

$G = (E_o + \Delta E) \cdot \Delta p^*$

$-(A + B + C) = \Delta E \cdot p_o^* \; .$

Assuming the export supply curve in the relevant zone to be approximately linear, we also have:[19]

$$- C \approx - \frac{1}{2} \cdot \Delta E \cdot \Delta p \ .$$

Using three equations, for the export revenue changes $\Delta E$ and producers' surplus changes $\Delta Ps$ in the cartel as given in equations (4.1) and (4.2) we have:

$$\Delta Ex = E_o \cdot \Delta p^* + \Delta E \cdot p_o^* + \Delta E \cdot \Delta p^* \qquad (4.3)$$

or

$$\Delta Ps \approx E_o \cdot \Delta p^* + \Delta E \cdot \Delta p^* - \frac{1}{2} \Delta E \cdot \Delta p \ . \qquad (4.4)$$

The difference between equations (4.4) and (4.3) gives:

$$\Delta Ps - \Delta Ex \approx - \Delta E(p_o^* + \frac{\Delta p}{2}) > 0 \ . \qquad (4.5)$$

If export taxation leads to an increase in export revenues for the cartel ($\Delta Ex > 0$), then there will be an even greater increase in production profit. A negative $\Delta Ex$ value can be accompanied by a positive value for $\Delta Ps$.

For the empirical determination of changes in revenue and profit as a result of export taxation, expressions (4.3) and (4.4) are formulated in terms of price elasticities. A simple equilibrium model is used for this purpose. For the export supply of the cartel E and the import demand of countries outside the cartel $I^*$ the following holds:

$$E = E(p) \qquad (4.6)$$

$$I^* = I^*(p^*) \qquad (4.6)$$

with

$$\frac{\Delta E}{\Delta p} > 0$$

$$\frac{\Delta I^*}{\Delta p^*} < 0 \ .$$

The price relationship between the two groups of countries is:

$$p^* = p(1 + t) \quad , \tag{4.8}$$

where t is the ad valorem export tax. Taking into account the assumption of absence of any trade restrictions in the initial equilibrium situation (t = 0), for the differential form of equation (4.8) we have:

$$\Delta p^* = \Delta p + p^* \cdot \Delta t + \Delta p \cdot \Delta t \quad . \tag{4.8a}$$

The product market is in equilibrium if

$$E = I^* \quad , \tag{4.9}$$

or in differential form

$$\Delta E = \Delta I^* \quad . \tag{4.9a}$$

Inserting the differential forms (4.6) and (4.7) and equation (4.8a) into equilibrium condition (4.9a) gives:

$$\frac{\Delta E}{\Delta p} \cdot \frac{p}{E} \cdot \frac{E}{p} (\Delta p^* - p^* \Delta t) \cdot \frac{1}{1+\Delta t} = \frac{\Delta I^*}{\Delta p^*} \cdot \frac{p^*}{I^*} \cdot \frac{I^*}{p^*} \cdot \Delta p^* \tag{4.10}$$

In order to simplify equation (4.10) two price elasticities are defined: the price elaticity of export supply of the cartel

$$\mu = \frac{\Delta E}{\Delta p} \cdot \frac{p}{E} \tag{4.11}$$

and the price elasticity of import demand outside the cartel[20] $\mu^*$

$$\mu^* = \frac{\Delta I^*}{\Delta p^*} \cdot \frac{p^*}{I^*} \quad . \tag{4.12}$$

The relative change in the product price outside the cartel as a consequence of export taxation can now be calculated from equation (4.10):

$$\frac{\Delta p^*}{p^*} = \frac{1}{1 - \frac{\mu^*}{\mu}(1 + \Delta t)} \Delta t \tag{4.13}$$

Expression (4.13) can be used to calculate from equation (4.8a) the resulting relative change in the product price within the cartel:

$$\frac{\Delta p}{p} = ( \frac{\Delta p^*}{p^*} - \Delta t) \frac{1}{1+\Delta t} \qquad (4.14)$$

Through equation (4.14) we can then determine from equation (4.11) the relative quantitative fallback in exports:

$$\frac{\Delta E}{E} = \mu \cdot \frac{\Delta p}{p} \qquad (4.15)$$

In interpreting the results of equations (4.13), (4.14) and (4.15) it is assumed that the export supply of the cartel and the import demand of the countries outside the cartel react neither perfectly elastically nor perfectly inelastically to price changes:

$$0 < \mu < \infty ,$$

$$-\infty < \mu^* < 0 .$$

The direction and magnitude of price and quantity changes as a result of an export tax to the value of $\Delta t$ can thus be given as:

$$0 < \frac{\Delta p^*}{p^*} < \Delta t ,$$

$$\frac{\Delta p}{p} < 0 ,$$

$$\left| \frac{\Delta p}{p} \right| < \Delta t \quad \text{and}$$

$$\frac{\Delta E}{E} < 0 .$$

These ratios are equivalent to the changes illustrated in figure 4.1. For a given ad valorem export tax the relative increase in the commodity price p* outside the cartel will be the greater, the more price inelastic is the reaction of import demand outside the cartel and the more price elastic the reaction of the suppliers within the cartel. Correspondingly, the smaller the absolute value of * and the greater the value of , the less the commodity price p within the cartel sinks.

Leaving out the index 0 for the initial equilibrium situation in equation (4.3) and reformulating the right side so that the relative changes from equations (4.13), (4.14), and (4.15) can be inserted, we can empirically calculate an expression for the change in export revenues of the supply cartel:

$$\Delta Ex = [1 + \mu^*(1 + \frac{\Delta p^*}{p^*})] \frac{\Delta p^*}{p^*} \cdot Ex \quad . \tag{4.16}$$

In equation (4.16) $Ex = E\, p^*$ is equal to the export revenue of the cartel prior to export taxation.

The change in production profits as a result of export taxation can be similarly reformulated on the basis of equation (4.4) to give:[21]

$$\Delta Ps \approx [1 + \mu^* \cdot \frac{\Delta p^*}{p^*} (1 - \frac{1}{2} \cdot \frac{\mu^*}{\mu})] \frac{\Delta p^*}{p^*} Ex \quad . \tag{4.17}$$

From equation (4.16) one can derive the necessary conditions under which a supply cartel can actually achieve increased export revenues through export taxation:

$$\mu^* > - \frac{1}{1 + \frac{\Delta p^*}{p}} \quad . \tag{4.18}$$

For infinitesimal changes in the tax rate ($\Delta t \to dt$) the relative price change outside the cartel will also be infinitesimal ($\Delta p^* \to dp^*$), and equation (4.18) can be written as:

$$\mu^* > -1 \quad . \tag{4.19}$$

This is precisely the statement derived earlier on, that export cartels are only successful when the absolute value of "derived demand elasticity" is smaller than one.[22]

The algebraic as well as the preceding graphical exposition were based on the assumptions listed at the beginning of the second section. In order to determine the limits of such an export cartel analysis, this section on theoretical deductions concludes with a discussion of the proximity to reality of the assumptions made.

Firstly, it has been assumed that the demand pattern within the export cartel for the product under consideration will remain unchanged even after the introduction of an export tax. This assumption is normal in all tax analyses, and presupposes either a distributive machinery which evenly shares out all gains and losses from trade restrictions or a government spending policy in line with consumer preferences. Although these conditions are seldom fulfilled (especially not in those cases where income redistribution is an explicit goal of export restriction policy), it is difficult to do otherwise than assume a given demand pattern. The reason for this lies in the difficulties involved in measuring the exact amount of redistribution within a cartel and in the limited knowledge of the expenditure behavior of different social groups. At best one can hazard a guess at the direction of presumed change in the demand pattern within the cartel as a consequence of export restrictions; an exact evaluation of the shift in the demand curve is not feasible. Thus the results obtained above disregard to some extent the distribution effects in the supplying countries.

The second assumption concerns the identification of private with social costs in the production of the restricted commodity. Together with the supposition that private producers within the cartel behave as perfect competitors, one can use the observed private supply curve as the relevant social supply curve for the cartel group.[23] This procedure has to be modified if there are divergences in the production costs of the respective products. Turning again to figure 4.1, if, for example, private marginal costs are higher than social costs, then the export supply curve E shifts to the right. If the aim of export taxation is to maximize export revenues, the optimal export quantity remains unaltered since costs are not involved in their determination. If however profit maximization is the ultimate goal, then the optimal export quantity will be greater than in the case of equal private and social costs. Maximum revenue and profit can only be achieved by applying higher export taxes.[24] In principle, divergencies in production costs -- insofar as they are measurable -- do not constitute a valid argument against the use of the above model.

A third simplification introduced into the analysis was the assumption that suppliers within the cartel behave as perfect competitors. If the cartel's export supply is already monopolized, then it serves no purpose to levy an export tax since equilibrium in trade in this instance would in any case be at the point of maximum producers' profit. Only in cases where national objectives differ from the objectives of private monopolies do corrective governmental trade policies make sense.

Fourthly, absence of any retaliation on the net importers' side has been assumed. But as Corden puts it, it seems highly improbable "that foreign governments will happily stand by and allow income to be redistributed against them".[25] It is logical to assume that if they are in a position to do so, the countries affected by export restrictions will attempt to curb imports of the goods in question.[26] If these goods are essential in the short run, or if the importing countries see the danger of a further reduction in the world market supply of the commodity as a result of a process of mutual retaliation, they may try to turn to other product markets and exert their own monopoly power there.[27] Behavior of this type oversteps the limit of the simple equilibrium model used here; for one thing the possibilities of retaliation depend on the specific market characteristics of the originally restricted good, and for another the conditions on the markets would have to be integrated into a multiproduct model.

The fifth restriction on the general applicability of the above model stems from the fact that only export tariffs have been considered, whereas in reality quantitative restrictions are just as often used to control exports. This omission is justifiable as long as perfect competition prevails before export restrictions are introduced, since provided the hypothetical quota is set at the same level as would be reached by exports under a system of tariff restrictions, and quotas are allocated by government auction, then an export quota would lead to exactly the same change within the cartel and outside it as would an export tax. On the basis of figure 4.1 one can say that it is irrelevant to the results of the analysis whether the restriction on export quantities from $E_o$ to $E_1$ is brought about by the imposition of a tax t per unit of exports or by simply restricting the export quantity to $E_1$. A difference in export quantities in the case of quotas as opposed to taxes will[28] only occur if domestic monopolies exist in trade or production. As has already been pointed out, in neither of these instances is the above model applicable.

The foregoing discussion indicates that the empirical statements made here only provide a clue to the analysis of cartels, and that for more complete information one must turn to detailed product and country studies.

ASSESSMENT OF THE POSSIBILITIES OF SUCCESS OF EXPORT CARTELS ON THE BASIS OF EMPIRICAL RESULTS

For several years developing countries have been making greater efforts in international negotiations to achieve a reordering or world raw material trade. Talks to this end under the auspices of UNCTAD also deal with the question of stabilizing raw material prices and raising them above the long-term trend. The motivating force behind these potential market interventions is the desire of the developing countries to stabilize and increase their export revenues. The industrial countries have been resisting such moves, particularly as far as price increases are concerned, and for some time now have employed delaying tactics in raw material negotiations.

The negotiating power of both sides is to a considerable extent dependent on the ability of the developing countries to achieve the desired revenue increases by unilateral action. The algebraic model developed in the second section is used here to assess quantitatively the extent to which countries exporting the ten core commodities of the UNCTAD Integrated Programme (cocoa, coffee, tea, sugar, cotton, jute, sisal, rubber, copper, tin) are able to achieve their objectives by acting jointly to enforce export restrictions.

In accordance with the structure of the model presented earlier, the analysis of interventions in raw material markets is of a comparative static nature. Calculations are based on average annual production and export **quantities** for the years 1976 to 1978, and the results are thus not disturbed by the effects of erratic price changes on raw material markets. Only in the final step does the calculation of absolute changes in export revenues and profits require the inclusion of average export **values** for the years 1976 to 1978.[29]

Price elasticities estimated by other authors on the basis of time series analysis are used to determine the reactions of production and consumption to export restrictions. For a number of products supply in particular reacts to price changes with a delay of several years. The elasticities used here are long-run elasticities which measure the total effect of market interventions after all adjustment processes have taken place. Appendix 4.II describes how the required elasticities are calculated from the basic data.

Calculations have been made for two hypothetical cartel constellations:

Case (a): all raw material exporting developing countries join together to form an export cartel;

Case (b): only large-scale exporters among the developing countries join to form an export cartel. "Large-scale" exporters are defined here as all suppliers who on average from 1976/78 commanded at least a 5 percent share in total world exports of the raw material in question.

One can take it that in reality the structure of export cartels lies somewhere between the two extreme cases (a) and (b); it would be impossible for a cartel to include all developing country exporters, neither would it be feasible to include exclusively large-scale suppliers.

The following section takes a look at the structure of world market production and world exports for the ten UNCTAD core commodities. The quantitative effects of unilateral export restrictions are analyzed in the following section, and then compared with the results of two other studies. Finally, conclusions from the empirical results are drawn in the last section.

Production and Export Structures on Individual Raw Material Markets

Table 4.4 gives the average 1976-78 figures for production and export of individual raw materials. Column (3) shows that for seven of the ten core commodities (cocoa, coffee, tea, jute, sisal,

Table 4.4 Survey of Annual Production and Export of the Ten Core Commodities of the UNCTAD Integrated Programme (averages for 1976-78)

| Commodity | Group(s) of SITC Rev. 2 | World production (in 1000 metric tons) | Developing countries' share in world production (%) | World exports (as a percentage of world production) | Developing country suppliers as a whole (%) | Developing country suppliers with at least a 5% share in world exports (%) |
|---|---|---|---|---|---|---|
| (1) | | (2) | (3) | (4) | (5) | (6) |
| Cocoa beans | 072.1 | 1422 | 100.0 | 74.8 | 100.0 | 79.7 |
| Coffee, green and roasted | 071.1 | 4177 | 100.0 | 79.3 | 100.0 | 45.0 |
| Tea | 074.1 | 1781 | 88.3 | 48.2 | 97.0 | 71.9 |
| Sugar, raw cent. & raw (raw eq.) | 061.11 061.2 | 103158 | 61.6 | 25.3 | 69.3 | 43.2 |
| Cotton lint | 263.1 | 12937 | 57.0 | 31.7 | 50.6 | |
| Jute & similar fibres | 264 Ex 265.8 | 4395 | 98.9 | 13.1 | 100.0 | 6.6 (Turkey) 90.6 |
| Sisal | 265.4 | 445 | 98.2 | 60.9 | 98.5 | 90.4 |
| Natural rubber | 232 | 3686 | 100.0 | 89.5 | 100.0 | 86.9 |
| Copper | 287.1 682.1 | 7757 | 42.3 | 63 | 57 | 42 |
| Tin[1] | 287.6 687.1 | 182 | 89.7 | 100 | 83 | 77 |

1) Period 1975-77

Sources:
FAO, Production Yearbook, 1978; FAO, Trade Yearbook, 1978; UN, Statistical Yearbook, 1978; UN, Yearbook of International Trade Statistics, 1978; World Bank, Commodity Trade and Price Trends, 1979.

rubber and tin), almost 90 percent or more of total world production comes from developing countries. Well over half of world sugar and cotton production is from developing countries, and just short of half of copper production.

The impact of trade restrictions on raw material prices, production, and consumption, is affected by the share of the traded quantity in world production. Column (4) in table 4.4 shows that for cocoa, coffee, rubber and tin, world exports make up three quarters or more of world production. Almost half of total production of tea, sisal, and copper is traded, and for sugar, cotton, and jute the share is less than one third.

According to column (5), developing countries are responsible for almost all world exports of cocoa, coffee, tea, jute, sisal, and rubber. Eighty percent of the tin traded on the world market comes from developing countries, and between fifty and seventy percent of sugar, cotton and copper. If one takes into account only those developing countries having a share of at least 5 percent in world exports, then a comparison between columns (6) and (5) shows that the total exports are relatively heavily concentrated on individual countries: between them, large-scale suppliers make up at least three quarters of total developing country exports for seven products. The three exceptions are coffee, sugar, and cotton.

The data contained in table 4.4 indicate that regardless of price elasticities of supply and demand, developing countries have a decisive position in the international markets for cocoa, coffee, tea, sisal, rubber, and tin. On the sugar, cotton, and copper markets, developing countries are in a weaker position.

Effect of a Unilaterally Enforced Raw Material Price Increase of 10 Percent

There are two possible ways of interpreting the formulae derived in the second section. Either one can assume that members of the relevant supply cartel levy an export tax of a particular value on the products under consideration, giving rise in this case to different effects on the price outside the cartel,[30] and on other variables,[31] depending on the elasticities of supply and demand for the individual products. Or one can treat it as a question, and ask how high the export taxes of a supply cartel must be in order to be able to achieve a 10 percent increase in the price of all goods considered on the world markets. The price increase is associated with changes in the export revenues of the cartel members. In order to be able to make a comparison of the results for individual products, the second procedure is to be adopted here.

Using equations (4.13) to (4.15) and the basic data given in Appendix 4.II one is able to calculate the rate of export taxation that a developing country supply cartel must introduce, as well as the resulting percentage decrease in export quantities of the cartel, if the price of the raw materials studied here is to be raised 10 percent above the level which would otherwise have been attained. The results are given in table 4.5. A comparison between the two cartel structures (a) and (b) shows that on the whole the greater market share of developing countries in case (a) means that it is not necessary to put such tight controls on exports in case (a) as it is in case (b). Comparatively low export taxes or export cut-backs are evident in the cases of cocoa, tea, sisal, and tin. For coffee and jute a cartel of the type (b) requires considerably tighter restrictions than a cartel of the type (a). In order to increase the world market prices of sugar, cotton, and copper by 10 percent it is on the whole necessary for developing countries to resort to very tight restriction measures. A cartel consisting exclusively of the large-scale producers would not be able to push through price increases for these three products. In the case of rubber relatively high export taxes and relatively low export cut-backs would be necessary, due to the particular elasticity constellation of this product.

Table 4.5  Export Tax Rates and Export Cut-Backs Necessary to Induce a 10 percent Increase in World Market Prices (in percent)

| Commodity | Case (a): The export tax is adopted by all developing country suppliers | | Case (b): The export tax is adopted by developing country suppliers having at least 5 percent share in world exports | |
|---|---|---|---|---|
| | export tax $t$ | export reduction $E/E$ | export tax $t$ | export reduction $E/E$ |
| Cocoa  | 19 | − 4  | 27 | − 6 |
| Coffee | 17 | − 3  | 48 | −13 |
| Tea    | 14 | − 3  | 16 | − 6 |
| Sugar  | 26 | −14  | 936 | −35 |
| Cotton | 59 | −41  | market share insufficient | |
| Jute   | 10 | − 1  | $46/49^1$ | $-39/-15^1$ |
| Sisal  | 13 | − 1  | 15 | − 1 |
| Rubber | $55/22^1$ | − 5 | $148/33^1$ | − 7 |
| Copper | 247 | −42 | $^2$ | −63 |
| Tin    | 24  | − 2 | 31 | − 3 |

Remarks:
1) Two values are given if there is a marked divergence between the price elasticities of supply and demand from different sources. See Appendix B.
2) A 10 percent price increase is only enforceable by means of quantitative export restrictions.

The change in export revenues as a result of the unilateral enforcement of a 10 percent increase by a hypothetical export cartel can be calculated using equation (4.16). Columns (2) and (6) of table 4.6 give the relative changes in export revenues for the alternative cartel constellations. As can be seen, in case (a) developing countries can succeed in raising their revenues from 7 of the 10 core commodities by between 5 and 9 percent. In the case of the other three commodities, sugar, cotton, and copper, sharp decreases in import demand will cause the export revenues of the cartel members to decrease. In case (b) suppliers are jointly able to achieve the goal of increased export revenues only for 5 of the 10 core commodities (cocoa, tea, sisal, rubber and tin). In the case of all other commodities, including coffee and jute as well, diminished revenues are to be expected.

In order to assess the magnitude of the effects of export restrictions discussed here in monetary terms, we must convert the relative changes in export revenues at 1977 prices into absolute changes.

Column (3) of table 4.6 shows that in case (a) developing countries would have yearly $ 650 million more in foreign exchange receipts as a result of restrictions on coffee exports. For cocoa, tea, rubber and tin, they would be able to take in $ 100 million more for their exports, and for jute and sisal each about $ 10 million more. Unilateral restriction measures would cause foreign exchange losses of over $ 1,000 million for cotton and copper, and of around $ 250 million for sugar. The extent to which the situation changes from case (a) to case (b) can be seen in the fact that a coffee cartel comprising the most important suppliers would suffer yearly losses in export revenue of around $ 200 million. For jute as well restrictive measures would cost the country $ 10 million a year in export revenues. For the other products increased export revenues would be just about halved, and actual losses would increase as compared with case (a).

Table 4.7 gives a global summary of the results for each individual product. Column (2) shows that altogether, developing countries would suffer losses in their foreign exchange incomes to the amount of $ 1.5 billion, if they were to raise unilaterally the prices of the ten core commodities of the UNCTAD Integrated Programme by 10 percent. The same measure would lead to an increase in foreign exchange receipts of $ 1.1 billion if one were to exclude sugar, cotton, and copper.

The changes in export profits calculated according to equation (4.17) and appearing in tables 4.6 and 4.7 gives a more favourable impression of the chances of developing countries to make economic gains out of unilateral export commodity restrictions than was the case with changes in export revenues: reduced export quantities as a result of price increases mean that raw material production and production costs will also fall in the long run. Thus, ceteris paribus, the greater the fall back in the cartel's export quantities, the more widely will changes in profits diverge from changes in revenues. In interpreting the figures one should take into consideration firstly that equation (4.17) is only an approximation, and secondly, that the entire calculations rest on the assumption that in the initial equilibrium situation private and social marginal costs are equal

Table 4.6: Changes in Export Revenues and Profits of Developing Countries as a Consequence of a Unilateral Price Increase of 10 Percent. (yearly averages for 1976-1978, values in US-$ at constant prices of 1977)[1]

| Commodity | Case (a): All developing country suppliers are members of the cartel | | | | Case (b) Only those developing country suppliers with at least 5% share in world exports are members of the cartel | | | |
|---|---|---|---|---|---|---|---|---|
| | Change in cartel's | | | cartel's initial export revenue $ million | Change in cartel's | | | cartel's initial export revenue $ million |
| | export revenue percent | export revenue $ million | export profit $ million | | export revenue percent | export revenue $ million | export profit $ million | |
| (1) | (2) | (3)=(2)x(5) | (4) | (5) | (6) | (7)=(6)x(9) | (8) | (9) |
| Cocoa | 6 | 143 | 237 | 2502 | 3 | 63 | 185 | 2065 |
| Coffee | 7 | 650 | 932 | 9699 | -4 | -184 | 330 | 4639 |
| Tea | 7 | 96 | 142 | 1475 | 4 | 43 | 104 | 1123 |
| Sugar | -5 | -239 | 350 | 4532 | -28 | -912 | -290 | 3254 |
| Cotton | -35 | -1024 | -12 | 2901 | market share insufficient | | | 328 |
| Jute | 9 | 14 | 15 | 154 | -33/-72 | -46/-92 | 2/92 | 139 |
| Sisal | 9 | 9 | 9 | 94 | 9 | 8 | 8 | 84 |
| Rubber | 5 | 117 | 229/2412 | 2607 | 3/22 | 63/432 | 169/1952 | 2253 |
| Copper | -37 | -1333 | -317 | 3639 | -59 | -1772 | -1062 | 3000 |
| Tin | 7 | 96 | 127 | 1319 | 6 | 79 | 115 | 1225 |

Remarks:
1) For copper and tin averages of 1975-1977. "Constant prices of 1977" means all values deflated 1977 by the c.i.f. index of prices of developed country manufactured exports to all destinations.
2) See remark (1) of Table 4.5.

Sources: See table 4.4.

Table 4.7: Summary Changes in Export Revenues and Profits of Developing Countries as a Consequence of a 10 percent Increase in Commodity Prices. (in $ million at constant prices of 1977).

| Commodity group (1) | Case (a): All developing country suppliers are members of the cartels | | Case (b): Only those developing country suppliers with at least 5% share in world exports are members of the cartels | |
|---|---|---|---|---|
| | Change in cartel's export revenues (2) | Change in cartel's export profits (3) | cartel's initial export revenues (4) | Change in cartel's export revenues (5) | Change in cartel's export profits (6) | cartel's initial export revenues (7) |
| 10 core commodities | -1471 | 1724 | 28922 | -2621[1] | -406[1] | 17782[1] |
| 9 core commodities (excluding copper) | -138 | 2041 | 25283 | -849[1] | 656[1] | 14782[1] |
| 7 core commodities (excl. sugar, cotton and copper) | 1125 | 1703 | 17850 | 63 | 946 | 11528 |
| Cocoa, tea, sisal, rubber, tin | 461 | 756 | 7997 | 256 | 607 | 6750 |

Remark: (1) Without cotton

Source: Table 4.6.

to the world market price for each commodity. According to table 4.7 developing countries as a whole can achieve a favourable combination of revenues and profit increases by imposing export taxes on seven core commodities (cocoa, coffee, tea, jute, sisal, rubber, tin), in which case their export profits would increase by about $ 1.7 billion a year.

## Comparison of the Results with Those from Two Other Studies

The values calculated in this study are incomparably lower than those appearing in two other studies on the problem of unilateral raw material price increases through cartel formation.$_{32}$ The reason for this lies partly in the different assumptions underlying the calculations and partly in serious errors committed by Baron et al. and McNicol in the course of their calculations.$_{33}$ In both cases it is assumed that all producing countries of a particular raw material increase the market price by 10 percent (Baron et al.) or 20 percent (McNicol). Thus, neither before nor after the price increase are there any producers remaining outside the supply cartel. Under this assumption the calculated increases in foreign exchange receipts for developing countries must necessarily work out higher than those in the present study, since according to Baron et al. and McNicol the developing countries retain their market share whereas in the cases (a) and (b) investigated here they lose part of their share and thus also part of their revenues. The approach used in the present study is a more adequate tool for providing an answer to the question of the extent to which developing countries are in a position to increase their export revenues through unilateral restrictions on individual commodity markets. One can not merely assume that raw material exporting industrialized countries will join with the developing countries in forming a supply cartel.

Despite the different assumptions made, one would expect the results of the three studies to be in approximate agreement in the case of those commodities where developing countries between them provide (almost) total world production. Table 4.4 shows that cocoa, coffee, jute, sisal, and rubber come under this category. However, comparing the figures of Baron et al. and McNicol with those of table 4.6, very marked differences come to light. Appendix 4.III demonstrates that the calculations in the other two studies must be erroneous. On average the figures of Baron et al. and McNicol are 200 to 300 percent too high for all ten UNCTAD commodities.

## Conclusions to be Drawn from the Empirical Results

Tables 4.6 and 4.7 show that in the case of seven of the ten UNCTAD core commodities (cocoa, coffee, tea, jute, sisal, rubber, tin) developing countries are in a strong enough market position to be able to increase their long run foreign exchange receipts and export profits by unilaterally restricting exports. For five of these commodities (cocoa, tea, sisal, rubber, tin) it is not necessary for the cartel to comprise all developing country suppliers, it is sufficient if it includes only those with at least a 5 percent share in world exports.

One should not be tempted to draw the hasty conclusion that in the foreseeable future raw material trade will be largely cartelized. The values calculated in the present study rest on assumptions which create a very favourable situation for the raw material exporting developing countries. In reality, however, many arguments support the belief that in the long run considerable difficulties will arise in the attempt to impose export restrictions. Thus the revenues and profit increases calculated here are to be taken as maximum values, in some cases to be corrected downwards. The following are among the difficulties to be taken into consideration:[34]

(a) Competitive relationships may evolve between developing countries, naturally making it difficult for them to consent to common trade policies within a cartel formation.

(b) For many developing countries raw material exports are a decisive source of foreign exchange revenue. In the case of retaliation measures by consumer countries, foreign exchange gaps occur for the supplying countries.

(c) The number of potential cartel members is probably so large, that reaching agreement and organizing a watchdog system for controlling conduct will be almost impossible. If control lapses, clandestine sales and purchases at reduced prices are almost certain to occur.

(d) The market may be invaded by an alternative supply source, hitherto unprofitable because of excessive fixed costs.

(e) Cutbacks in the supply of raw materials lead to internal problems in the cartel countries, particularly in the employment sphere.

(f) Long-term price increases are likely given incentive to substitution processes on the demand side, which go beyond the adjustment processes observed up to now.

(g) The strategic behaviour of international trade oligopolies hinders the implementation of price increases.

Recognising on the one hand the relatively small amount of income redistributed in favour of raw material exporting developing countries in the case of a ten per cent price increase (see tables 4.6 and 4.7) and on the other hand the many problems involved in the formation of a lasting cartel, one eventually comes to the conclusion that there is no real danger of long-run cartel formation for the ten UNCTAD core commodities.

## Appendix A

## Disaggregation of the Applied Model

The necessary price elasticities of import demand outside the cartel $\mu^*$ and export supply within the cartel $\mu$ for completing the empirical data in equations (4.13), (4.14) and (4.15) are seldom directly available. These equations must therefore be disaggregated to demand and supply both outside and within the cartel.

For import demand $I^*$:

$$I^*(p^*) = D^*(p^*) - X^*(p^*) > 0 \qquad (4A.1)$$

and equivalently for export supply E:

$$E(p) = X(p) - D(p) > 0 \qquad (4A.2)$$

where D is demand and X is supply. Equations (4A.1) and (4A.2) are differentiated according to prices and expanded so that both sides are expressed in terms of elasticities. With:

$$\varepsilon^* = \frac{\Delta X^*}{\Delta p^*} \cdot \frac{p^*}{X^*} > 0$$

$$\eta^* = \frac{\Delta D^*}{\Delta p^*} \cdot \frac{p^*}{D^*} < 0$$

$$\varepsilon = \frac{\Delta X}{\Delta p} \cdot \frac{p}{X} > 0$$

$$\eta = \frac{\Delta D}{\Delta p} \cdot \frac{p}{X} < 0$$

and equilibrium condition (4.9) from the text one has for the export supply elasticity:

$$\mu = \varepsilon \cdot \frac{X}{E} - \eta \left( \frac{X}{E} - 1 \right) \qquad (4A.3)$$

and for the import demand elasticity:

$$\mu^* = -\varepsilon^* \frac{X^*}{E} + \eta^*(\frac{X^*}{E} + 1) \tag{4A.4}$$

Inserting equations (4A.3) and (4A.4) into equations (4.13) and (4.15) from the text gives:

$$\frac{\Delta p^*}{p^*} = \frac{1}{1 + \dfrac{\varepsilon^* \cdot \dfrac{X^*}{E} - \eta^*(\dfrac{X^*}{E} + 1)}{\varepsilon \dfrac{X}{E} - \eta(\dfrac{X}{E} - 1)} + (1+\Delta t)} \Delta t \quad, \tag{4A.5}$$

$$\frac{\Delta E}{E} = -[\varepsilon^* \frac{X^*}{E} - \eta^*(\frac{X^*}{E} + 1)] \frac{\Delta p^*}{p^*} . \tag{4A.6}$$

The relative change in price within the cartel countries $\Delta p/p$ is given by equation (4.14). Thus all necessary variables appear as a function of the price elasticities of demand and supply both within and outside the cartel. Furthermore, a role is played by the division of production shares between the cartel countries and the rest of the world.[1]

NOTES
1. For a more detailed interpretation see van Duyne (1975).

## Appendix B

### Data Base

The price elasticities of export supply $\mu$ of the cartel countries and of import demand $\mu^*$ of the rest of the world, for calculating the effects of export taxes, were derived from basic data on export and production quantities and on price elasticities of supply and demand. The data on quantities are the average values for the years 1976 to 1978. The estimated values for supply and demand elasticities come from the time series analyses calculated by various authors using simple regression theory.[1] Since the present work investigates comparative static effects, the short-term elasticities taken from the mentioned studies were converted into long-term values.

In some cases the estimated values for price elasticities differ substantially from author to author and statistical criteria do not enable one to give preference to one over another. In such cases calculations were made on the basis of two alternative elasticities.

The basic data are summarized in table 4A.1 and 4A.2.

NOTES

1. The exception is the estimation of price elasticities for copper, which was carried out using a larger, interdependent model.

Table 4.A.1. Basic Market Share and Elasticity Values, 1976-78.
Case (a): All developing country suppliers are members of the cartel

| Commodity | Data for cartel group countries | | | Data for non-cartel countries | | | |
|---|---|---|---|---|---|---|---|
| | Production/export quantity share X/E | Longrun price elasticities of supply of demand | | Export supply elasticity | Production/export quantity share X*/E | Longrun price elasticities of supply of demand | | Import demand elasticity |
| Cocoa  | 1.34 | 0.34     | -0.13 | 0.50      | 0      | 0        | -0.39 | -0.39 |
| Coffee | 1.26 | 0.33     | -0.31 | 0.50      | 0      | 0        | -0.30 | -0.30 |
| Tea    | 1.89 | 0.34     | -0.22 | 0.84      | 0.25   | 0.41     | -0.17 | -0.32 |
| Sugar  | 3.52 | 0.24     | -0.10 | 1.10      | 2.20   | 0.34     | -0.20 | -1.39 |
| Cotton | 3.56 | 0.27     | -0.15 | 1.35      | 2.68   | 1.07     | -0.34 | -4.12 |
| Jute   | 7.56 | 0.6/0.2  | -0.05 | 4.86/1.84 | 0.09   | 0.6/0.2  | -0.05 | -0.11/-0.07 |
| Sisal  | 1.64 | 0.1/0.2  | -0.05 | 0.20/0.36 | 0.03   | 0.1/0.2  | -0.05 | -0.05/-0.06 |
| Rubber | 1.12 | 0.1/0.4  | -0.5  | 0.17/0.51 | 0      |          | -0.5  | -0.50 |
| Copper | 1.17 | 0.4      | -0.9  | 0.62      | 1.60   | 2        | -0.4  | -4.24 |
| Tin    | 1.05 | 0.2      | -0.2  | 0.22      | 0.12   | 0.2      | -0.2  | -0.25 |

Remark: 1) Production of non-cartel countries in relation to exports of cartel countries.

Table 4.A.2  Basic Market Share and Elasticity Values, 1976-78.
Case (b): only those developing countries that are members of the export cartel have at least a 5 percent share in world exports of the respective commodity.

| Commodity | Data for cartel group countries | | | Data for non-cartel countries | | | Import demand elasticity |
|---|---|---|---|---|---|---|---|
| | Production/ export quantity share X/E | Longrun price elasticities of supply of demand | | Export supply elasticity | Production/ export quantity share X*/E | Longrun price elasticities of supply of demand | |
| Cocoa   | 1.29 | 0.34     | -0.13     | 0.48      | 0.39 | 0.34     | -0.36      | -0.63       |
| Coffee  | 1.26 | 0.33     | -0.31     | 0.50      | 1.54 | 0.33     | -0.30      | -1.27       |
| Tea     | 2.05 | 0.36     | -0.27     | 1.02      | 0.83 | 0.32     | -0.16      | -0.56       |
| Sugar   | 1.82 | 0.19     | -0.05     | 0.39      | 7.35 | 0.30     | -0.15      | -3.46       |
| Cotton  | 1.93 | 0.07     | -0.18     | 0.30      | 5.98 | 0.64     | -0.15      | -36.47      |
| Jute    | 2.53 | 0.6/0.2  | -0.05     | 1.59/0.58 | 5.91 | 0.6/0.2  | -0.05      | -3.89/-1.53 |
| Sisal   | 1.53 | 0.1/0.2  | -0.05     | 0.19/0.34 | 0.25 | 0.1/0.2  | -0.05      | -0.09/-0.11 |
| Rubber  | 1.03 | 0.1/0.4  | -0.5      | 0.12/0.43 | 0.26 | 0.1/0.4  | -0.5       | -0.66/-0.73 |
| Copper  | 1.08 | 0.4      | -0.9      | 0.50      | 2.65 | 1.75     | -0.45      | -6.28       |
| Tin     | 1.0  | 0.2      | -0.2      | 0.20      | 0.31 | 0.2      | -0.2       | -0.32       |

Remark: 1) Production of non-cartel countries in relation to exports of cartel countries.

Appendix C

Analysis of Miscalculation of Export Revenue
Increases in Two Studies[1]

One of the aims of the two studies considered here is to calculate the level of increased foreign exchange receipts for developing countries if all producers of the ten core commodities of the UNCTAD Integrated Programme were to join together to form a supply cartel and raise the price of the ten commodities by 10 percent (Baron et al. 1977, 37) or 20 percent (McNicol 1978, 69).

Baron et al. calculate foreign exchange receipt increases for each product on the basis of 1974 quantities and 1975 prices and then add these values to give a total value.[2] Their results show that "Assuming a price increase of 10 percent and considering only the core commodities, when raw material cartels exist the export receipts of developing countries will increase by around 8 billion US $."[3]

McNicol makes his calculations in two stages. First he ascertains the "effects of price increases on revenue" on all producers. It is not made clear here whether he is talking of the export revenues of the producing countries or the revenues of the private producers. The calculation of the export receipt increases are made on the basis of the consumed quantities in 1971 and from mean commodity prices for the period 1968-1974. After this McNicol examines the "increase in revenue to less developed countries" resulting from the price increase. The changes in revenue for each product are then multiplied by the export shares of the less developed countries, from which it may be assumed that export revenues are being referred to. In the case of a general price increase of 20 percent McNicol's results show yearly increases in gross revenues of $ 4.8 billion for less developed countries as a whole.

It can be shown that in both the cited studies the given changes in foreign exchange receipts from raw material exports are highly exaggerated. In the study of Baron et al. the reason seems to lie in only one serious error; in McNicol's study, however, a series of errors have been made which render it impossible to stipulate exactly what has been calculated. Without going into details here it is to be assumed that other estimates in the studies of Baron et al. and McNicol are also erroneous since they likewise are based on the data criticized here. The two studies are analyzed individually below.

a) The Study of Baron et al.

Column (2) in table 4A.3 gives the 1974 export quantities of the developing countries for the ten core commodities. Column (3) shows the prices of these products for the year 1975. In order to conserve as far as possible the premises of the study of Baron et al. instead of taking the prices from official statistics they have been calculated on the basis of the data in Baron et al.'s book. The resulting values diverge only slightly from those published elsewhere.[4] The export revenues of the developing countries for the period 1974-75 (column 4) were calculated from the quantity and price data. These values were then compared with the increases in export revenues resulting from a 10 percent price increase for all commodities, as derived by Baron et al. Column (6) gives the ratios of the claimed revenue increases to original revenue. In seven of the ten cases the rate of increase is higher than ten percent. These results can not be correct: given total price inelasticity of demand, a price increase of ten percent can not give rise to a revenue increase of more than ten percent.

The reason for the incorrect results probably lies in the wrong choice of data pertaining to quantities; instead of the export quantities of the developing countries Baron et al. have obviously used total world consumption quantities in their calculations. Thus, rather than calculating the increase in foreign exchange receipts of the developing countries what in fact has been calculated (leaving aside the possibility of changes in stocks) is the increase in revenues of private producers in all countries, including industrialized nations.

This would also explain why the results in table 4A.3 in this Appendix are excessively high for sugar and cotton: only about 25 percent of world sugar production and about 32 percent of world cotton production is exported, 69 and 51 percent respectively pertaining to exports from developing countries.[5]

The error for coffee is relatively small according to table 4A.3 since about 79 percent of world production is exported, 100 percent of this coming from developing countries.[6]

b) <u>McNicol's Study</u>

It is a somewhat more laborious task to demonstrate the error in McNicol's study since his calculations, as shown above, are based on an unnecessarily complicated formula for ascertaining average prices. Furthermore, there is more than one error in the study. In order to reduce the intricacy of the calculations, the proof of errors is undertaken in two stages. Firstly, the complicated price calculations are left aside and an analysis of the McNicol results is done on the basis of the simplified assumption that he used not only the quantities, but also the prices of 1971 for his calculations. This gives an approximate idea of the quality of his figures. Secondly, the calculations for the first four commodities in McNicol's table (cocoa, coffee, tea, sugar) have been repeated according to his own method, showing the incomprehensibility of the procedure he uses.

Column (2) in table 4A.4 gives the commodity export values of developing countries (including Cuba) for the year 1971. The source of this data is the statistics given by McNicol himself. Column (4) of the table shows that for 8 of the 10 commodities the increase in export revenues of the developing

Table 4.A. 3   Percentage Increase in the Export Revenues of Developing Countries as a Result of a 10 Percent Increase in Commodity Prices (According to the Study of Baron et al.)

| Commodity (1) | Group(s) of SITC, Rev. 2 | Export quantity of developing countries 1974 (1000 metr.tons) (2) | Commodity prices 1952 ($/kg) (3) | Export revenues 1974-1975 (4)=(2)x(3) | Claimed increase in export revenues after a 10 percent increase (millions of $) (5) | As percent of export revenues (6)(5)/(4) |
|---|---|---|---|---|---|---|
| Cocoa beans, | 072.1 | 1169 | 1.50 | 1754 | 295.87 | 17 |
| Coffee, green and roasted | 071.1 | 3231 | 1.60 | 5170 | 439.56 | 9 |
| Tea | 074.1 | 719 | 1.37 | 985 | 230.70 | 23 |
| Sugar, raw. centr. and raw (raw eq.) | 061.11 061.2 | 17089 | 0.50 | 8554 | 4958.08 | 58 |
| Cotton lint | 263.1 | 1788 | 0.99 | 1770 | 1446.62 | 82 |
| Jute and similar fibres | 264 Ex 265.8 | 868 | 0.38 | 330 | 111.42 | 34 |
| Sisal | 265.4 | 429 | 0.62 | 266 | 68.88 | 26 |
| Natural rubber | 232 | 3180 | 0.66 | 2099 | 310.36 | 15 |
| Copper | 287.1 682.1 | | 1.23 | 58304 | 90.05 | 0 |
| Tin | 287.6 687.1 | | 6.90 | 9844 | 90.52 | 10 |
| Total | | | | 27735 | 8050.06 | 29 |

Sources:
1) FAO, Trade Yearbook, 1976
2) The values are derived by dividing column (8) by (4) in table 1 of Baron et al. 1977, 9.
3) Baron et al. 1977, 38.
4) UN, Yearbook of International Statistics, 1978.

countries ought to be higher than the effected price increase of 20 percent. In at least 5 cases they exceed the 20 percent mark so clearly that even a valuation of the quantities with average 1968 to 1974 prices should not alter the basic results.

Table 4A.4  Percentage Increase in Export Revenues of the Developing Countries as a Result of a 20 Percent Increase in Commodity Prices (According to McNicol's Study, but with Simplified Assumptions).

| Commodity (1) | Export revenue of developing countries (inc. Cuba), 1971* (in millions of $) (2) | Claimed increase in export revenues after a 20 percent price increase** (in millions of $) (3) | (as percentage of export revenues) (4) = (3)/(2) |
|---|---|---|---|
| Cocoa  | 741.2  | 387  | 52 |
| Coffee | 2361.7 | 501  | 21 |
| Tea    | 562.8  | 119  | 21 |
| Sugar  | 1901.3 | 2123 | 112 |
| Cotton | 1535.8 | 504  | 33 |
| Jute   | 197.5  | 23   | 12 |
| Sisal  | 64.0   | 25   | 39 |
| Rubber | 944.9  | 170  | 18 |
| Copper | 2162.0 | 831  | 38 |
| Tin    | 617.7  | 161  | 26 |

Sources:
\* World Bank, Commodity Trade and Price Trends, 1975.
\*\* McNicol 1978, 71.

It is not as easy as it was in the case of Baron et al. to localize the origin of the erroneous calculations in McNicol's work since the high percentages in column (4) of table 4A.4 do not apply to all commodities of which a small proportion of world production is exported or for which developing countries have only a small export share. An example for this is cotton.
Examining McNicol's calculations on an individual basis, it emerges that:
a) All his calculations are based on the formulae beginning on page 122 of his book. This is where the first mistake lies. McNicol designates revenue as R, production as q, and price as P. The following thus holds:

$R = q \cdot P$ .

For the absolute change in R one has:

$$\Delta R = ( \frac{\Delta q}{q} + \frac{\Delta P}{P} + \frac{\Delta q}{q} \cdot \frac{\Delta P}{P} ) \cdot R .$$

McNicol also gives finite magnitudes for the change in revenue, but makes his calculations in infinitesimal magnitudes. For formula (A.35) on page 122 he thus gets:

$$\Delta R = ( \frac{\Delta q}{q} + \frac{\Delta P}{P} ) \cdot R .$$

All estimates of revenue increases made on the basis of the last formula above are exaggeratedly high.⁷ The exaggeration is the greater, the higher the assumed price increases for the individual commodities.

b) In Table A-1 on page 119 McNicol presents the basic data used in his book. According to him, prices and quantities are calculated from the statistical volume <u>Commodity Trade and Price Trends</u>, 1975 of the World Bank. The prices he takes are "seven-year moving averages ending in the last year reported". However, he does not mention the weighting he used to arrive at the averages. It remains unclear why "moving averages" have to be calculated. It is assumed here that McNicol has calculated the arithmetical mean from the commodity prices for the years 1968 to 1974 (1974 is the last year recorded in the World Bank statistics). Table 4A.5 shows the corresponding quantitative values emerging from these calculations.

Table 4A.5   Average Commodity Prices for the Period 1968-1974

| Commodity | Arithmetical price averages | | Prices given by McNicol |
|---|---|---|---|
| | Current $ per kg | 1967-69 constant $ per kg* | $ per kg |
| (1) | (2) | (3) | (4) |
| Cocoa | 1.059 | 0.808 | 0.808 |
| Coffee | 1.098** | 0.873** | 0.892 |
| Tea | 1.097 | 0.889 | 0.690 |
| Sugar | 0.188*** 0.288**** | 0.128*** 0.168**** | 0.254 |

Remarks:
\* Deflated by the c.i.f. index of prices of developed countries' manufactured exports to all destinations.
\*\* Prices for the four internationally traded qualities weighted with their world export share at the beginning of the 70s.

*** US Preferential Rate.
****International Sugar Council, "World" daily price.

Sources:
World Bank, Commodity Trade and Price Trends (1975); Federacion Nacional de Cafeteros de Colombia, Boletin de Informacion Estadistica sobre el Cafe, Numero 48, Bogota (1978); McNicol 1978, 119.


The prices of cocoa and coffee in columns (3) and (4) of table 4A.5 are so similar, that one can assume that in his own calculations McNicol used the deflated average prices of 1968 to 1974. The values for tea and sugar, however, are a different matter. The average tea price used by McNicol is lower than all individual tea prices for the period 1968 to 1974, regardless of whether they are stated at constant dollar values or whether deflated prices were taken.[8] For sugar the average price given by McNicol is significantly higher than the average values in columns (2) and (3) of table 4A.5 . McNicol's values could only stem from the time series of the deflated prices for sugar if a weighting of at least 0.5 was put on the 1974 prices in the process of calculating the average. The outcome is that the prices given by McNicol are arrived at in an uncomprehensible manner and are in part erroneous.

c) The quantities used by McNicol are "estimated for 1971 computed from data provided by the same source". He calls these quantities "base production". Since no data on quantities is given in the cited source, one may assume that McNicol converted the values given in the World Bank statistics into quantities.[9] However, these World Bank statistics provide only export values and to call the calculated quantities "base production" is therefore incorrect. Moreover, official statistics on production and export data are available, so the complicated method of calculation used by McNicol is unnecessary.

Even leaving aside the last argument, and accepting the manner in which McNicol has made his calculations, one is still obliged to reject the data he gives for the simple reason that they are wrong. In order to show this, column (2) in table 4A.6 gives the average yearly export values of all countries for the four selected products. The averages are from the years 1970-72. Dividing these export values by the corresponding average prices gives estimates for yearly export quantities over the period 1970-72. These are shown in column (3). Comparing these figures with the ones in column (4), it can be seen that in making the calculations one has made fairly good estimates for 1971 export quantities. The figures calculated by McNicol (supposedly from the same source) are given in column (5). They diverge completely from the correct values.

Table 4A.6  Comparison Between Quantities Used by McNicol and Actual World Export Quantities for 1971

| Commodity (1) | Total world export values (average 1970-72)[4] (in millions of dollars) (2) | Calculated export quantities[1] (average (in 1000 metric tons) (3) | Actual export quantities 1971[5] (in 1000 metric tons) (4) | McNicol's "base production 1971"[6] (in 1000 metric tons) (5) |
|---|---|---|---|---|
| Cocoa | 776.3 | 1132 | 1190 | 3544 |
| Coffee | 2989.5 | 2810 | 3315 | 3579 |
| Tea | 702.3 | 658 | 767 | 1244 |
| Sugar | 2861.8 | 25189[2] 17455[3] | 21365 | 71400 |

Remarks:
1) Calculated by dividing column (2) by the average price for each respective product for the years 1970-72 (in $ per kilogram).
2) Calculated with the help of the US Preferential Rate.
3) Calculated using the "world" daily price of the International Sugar Council.

Sources:
4) Export values and commodity prices from World Bank, Commodity Trade and Price Trends, 1975
5) FAO, Trade Yearbook, 1975.
6) McNicol 1977, 119.

NOTES

1. Baron et al. 1977; McNicol 1978.
2. In the cited table Baron et al. do not disclose the year to which the calculations refer. From data earlier on in their book one can assume that the years cited in the above text are used (Baron et al. 1977, 9). The choice of different years would not substantially alter the statements in the present Appendix.
3. Baron et al. 1977, 39.
4. See for example World Bank, Commodity Trade and Price Trends (1979).
5. See table 4.4, columns (4) and (5) in the main text.
6. See table 4.4, Columns (4) and (5) in the main text.
7. McNicol uses this erroneous concept in his other calculations as well.
8. It is even lower than all tea prices between 1951 and 1974. This is important in answer to the possible criticism that the wrong time span has been taken into account in the current Appendix.
9. World Bank, Commodity Trade and Price Trends, 1975.

NOTES

1. Most of the objectives discussed here appear elsewhere in this report and have been analyzed by Bergsten, 1975. See also Schenkel, 1980, 5-24. An interesting survey of the aims of export controls at the beginning of the 20th century is given in the League of Nations, 1937.
2. Armament exports have of course been subject to almost constant regulation because of their security implications. This aspect is not considered here.
3. It is not intended here to give a comprehensive review of existing export controls. Only typical examples are chosen. A more detailed list, based on various OECD, IMF and GATT inventories, of export restrictions appears in chapter 2.
4. See Bergsten 1975, p. 6.
5. See, for example, Frankfurter Allgemeine Zeitung, 17 March 1979, where European leather processing industries complained about export restrictions in Latin America and the US.
6. Meadows 1972.
7. As Bergsten notes, export restrictions in this case will probably be pursued through production cutbacks because of the great stockpiling costs involved in controlling exports only. See Bergsten 1975, p. 8.
8. See IMF 1980.
9. See an earlier analysis by Rothwell 1963.
10. UN 1974.
11. Maizels 1977, 141-59.
12. It should be noted that the Havana Charter was never ratified.
13. UN 1974.
14. See, in this connection, the papers referred to in Chapter 2 where Nathanson and Weinblatt give an overview of the frequency of export control measures according to the type of measures and the countries enforcing them. Schenkel attempts to quantify the percentage of world trade in individual goods affected by export restrictions (Schenkel 1980, 25-33).
15. An exception is the registering at GATT of export controls of other countries by the US. See US Dept. of Treasury (1976).
16. See Schenkel 1980, 25-33.
17. See the earlier discussion in the previous section.
18. Where $E < 0$ is valid.
19. Where $E < 0$ and $p < 0$ are valid.
20. Since $E/p > 0$ and $I^*/p^*$, $0$, the signs of the elasticities are: $0 <$ and $* < 0$.
21. Equation (4.17) differs from that used by Baron, Glismann and Stecher, which gives a too positive value for the change in producers' surplus as a result of export restrictions. See Baron et al. 1977, 137.
22. See, for instance, van Duyne 1975.
23. If private suppliers behave non-competitively, the private cost curve must be used instead.

24. This statement depends on the specific form of the foreign demand curves. See the corresponding analysis of isoelastic demand curves in Corden 1974, 162 f.
25. Corden 1974, 162.
26. The classical exposition of retaliations results within the optimum tariff discussions is given by Johnson (1953).
27. Whether subsequent retaliation does indeed lead to further decreases in trade quantities depends on the shape of the national supply curves.
28. See the basic discussion on the problem of equivalence given by Bhagwati (1966, 53-67); (1968, 142/46) and Shibata (1968, 53-67).
29. The principle of quantity-based calculations was not fully possible in the cases of copper and tin due to the lack of relevant data. Furthermore, calculations for these two products refer to the period 1975-1977.
30. See equation (4.13).
31. See equations (4.14) to (4.17).
32. See Baron et al. 1977, 37 s.; McNicol 1978, 68 s.
33. The errors are explicitly dealt with in Appendix III.
34. Only some of the related problems are dealt with briefly here. For a more detailed analysis see Keppler 1981, 64 .

REFERENCES

Adams, Gerard F. and Jere, R. Behrman 1976. Econometric World Agricultural Commodity Markets: Cocoa, Coffee, Tea, Wool, Cotton, Sugar, Wheat, Rice. Cambridge, Mass..:
Baron, Stefan, Glismann, Hans H. and Stecher, Bernd 1977. Internationale Rohstoffpolitik - Ziele, Mittel, Kosten. Tubingen:
Behrman, Jere R. 1978. Development, The International Economic Order, and Commodity Agreements, Reading, Mass.
Bergsten, C. Fred 1974. Completing the GATT: Towards New International Rules to Govern Export Controls. Washington, D.C.: British-North American Committee.
Bhagwati, Jagdish 1966. On the Equivalence of Tariffs and Quotas. In: Trade, Growth and the Balance of Payments, Essays in Honor of Gottfried Harberler, edited by Robert E. Baldwin et al.
Corden, M.W. 1974. Trade Policy and Economic Welfare. Oxford:
FAO 1978. Production Yearbook. Rome: FAO.
___ 1975, 1976, 1978. Trade Yearbook. Rome: FAO.
Federacion Nacional de Cafeteros de Colombia 1978. Boletin de Informacion estadistica sobre el cafe 48. Bogota.
Fisher, Franklin M., Cootner, Paul H. and Bailey, Martin Neil 1972. An Econometric Model of the World Copper Industry, Bell Journal of Economics 3:
Frankfurter Allegemeine Zeitung. 17 March 1979.
IMF 1976. Export Restrictions: A Historical Sketch. In Export Restrictions and International Rules Governing Their Use. Washington, D.C.: IMF.
___ 1979. Annual Report on Exchange Arrangements and Exchange Restrictions. Washington, D.C.: IMF.
___ 1980. Government Finance Statistics Yearbook. Washington, D.C.: IMF.
Johnson, Harry G. 1953. Optimum Tariffs and Retaliation, Review of Economic Studies 21:
Keppler, Horst. 1981. The Effects of Commodity Export Taxes on World Market Prices and LDCs Export Receipts. In International Commodity Trade: Latin America, edited by CEDLA Amsterdam: EEC.
Lam, Ngo Van. 1978. Incidence of Tin Export Taxation in West Malaysia. Developing Economies 16:
League of Nations. 1937. Report of the Committee for the Study of the Problem of Raw Materials. Geneva: League of Nations.
Maizels, Alfred. 1977. Primary Commodity Markets and their Regulation. In Reshaping the World Economic Order, edited by Herbert Giersch. Tubingen:
McNicol, David L. 1978. Commodity Agreements and Price Stabilization. Lexington, Mass.:
Meadows, Dennis L. 1972. The Limits to Growth. New York:
OECD. 1974. Export Restrictions - Inventory of Measures Currently in Force. Paris: OECD.

Rothwell, K. L. 1963. Taxes on Exports in Underdeveloped Countries. Public Finance 18.
Schenkel, Hubertus. 1980. Wirschaftstheoretische und wirtschaftspolitische Probleme von Ausfuhrbeschrankungen. Gottingen:
Shibata, Hirofumi. 1968. A Note on the Equivalence of Tariffs and Quotas. American Economic Review 58:
United Nations. 1974. Resolutions Adopted by the General Assembly on the Report of the Ad-Hoc Committee of the Sixth Special Session: Declaration and Plan of Action on the Establishment of a New International Economic Order. New York: UN.
───── Statistical Yearbook. New York: UN.
───── Yearbook of International Trade Statistics. New York: UN.
United States Government. Export Taxes - An Interagency Report on Export Restrictions. Prepared for submission to the GATT as a Background Paper for the ongoing Tokyo Round Multilateral Trade Negotiations. Washington, D.C.: IS GPO.
Van Duyne, Carl 1975. Commodity Cartels and the Theory of Derived Demand, Kiklos, 28:
World Bank. 1979. Commodity Trade and Price Trends. Washington, D.C.: The World Bank.

# 5
# Export Restrictions as a Means of Redistributing World Income: An Appraisal

J. Weinblatt
R. Nathanson

This chapter analyzes the effect of export restrictions of raw materials in a macro-economic framework. It seeks to identify the conditions required to justify the implementation of export restrictions by a commodity exporting industry; the changes in national incomes of the countries involved; the impact on world welfare; and the extent to which foreign aid can serve as a substitute for export restrictions.

The focus is on the two central motives for imposing export restrictions, namely the desire to increase national income and the desire to stimulate processing in the exporting country. These restrictions are assumed to serve both as a mechanism through which both transfer income from developed to developing countries and to provide an incentive to increase domestic industrial production.[1]

NECESSARY CONDITIONS FOR SUCCESSFUL EXPORT RESTRICTIONS

In the case of the developed or the developing country where the goal of export restrictions is limited to the protection of a specific sector and to the increase of its income, the necessary condition required for success is that appropriate demand elasticities exist on world markets. These elasticities should be relatively low. A naive model would state that they should have absolute values of less than one. The theoretical meaning of facing low world price elasticities for a producer is that he could potentially exercise monopolistic or quasi-monopolistic power.

The result of an analysis based on such an approach falls into the domain of micro-economic partial equilibrium analysis; it thus conceptually belongs to the general framework of the Marshall-Lerner elasticities approach to balance of payments. Of course, the elasticities approach is no more than an attempt to derive stability conditions for the foreign exchange market; and therefore its purpose is to show when a devaluation (that leads to a deterioration of the terms of trade) could create a balance of payments surplus (or decrease a deficit). Here we deal with an attempt to improve the terms of trade by raising the relative prices of exported goods. Thus, the famous Marshall-Lerner stability condition is the inverse of that required to justify export restrictions.

The analysis of export restrictions may be confined to the elasticities approach when the scope of the policy is limited to one or a few specific sectors, as is probably the case with many of the export restrictions applied in the developed world. However, some of the restrictions exercised in developed countries and the great majority of those in developing countries have been adopted in order to achieve goals reaching far beyond the narrow interests of one or a few producers. Several national macroeconomic goals have been pursued via export restriction. Thus, the condition derived within the elasticities approach turns out to be a necessary but not a sufficient condition. Some macroeconomic factors that are ignored in this approach should be added to the analysis.[2] From a pure Keynesian point of view, the latter approach ignores the net multiplier effects of changes in exports, and in spending on locally produced goods for the home market, and on exportable and imported goods. To complete the analysis one must incorporate cross relations among relative prices and demand and supply (note that there must be a non-traded good present for exports and imports to have independent prices). We shall concentrate on the macroeconomic aspects of a comprehensive framework.

## TOWARD THE FORMULATION OF SUFFICIENT CONDITIONS

In this sub-section we develop the conditions for successful export restrictions. Both the elasticity issue and macroeconomic considerations are combined and international interactions are taken into account. The model is a simplified version of the Hicks-Mosak general equilibrium analysis of demand relations with Keynesian income multipliers. Exchange rates are assumed to be fixed and normalized to unity.

The analysis is based on a three-equation, two-country system:

$$Y_h = E_h(Y_h) + P_{xf} x_{hf}(P_{xf}, Y_f) - P_z[z_h(Y_h, P_z) - z_{hh}(P_{xh}, P_z)] \quad (5.1\text{-a})$$

$$Y_f = E_f(Y_f) + P_z[z_h(Y_h, P_z) - z_{hh}(P_{xh}, P_z)] - P_{xf} x_{hf}(P_{xh}, Y_f) \quad (5.1\text{-b})$$

$$B_h = P_{xf} x_{hf}(Y_f, P_{xf}) - P_z[z_h(Y_h, P_z) - z_{hh}(P_{xh}, P_z)] \quad (5.1\text{-c})$$

where
Y = national product;
E = total national expenditure;
z = quantity of the final good (exported from country f to country h);
$z_h$ = quantity of z consumed in country h;
$z_{hh}$ = quantity of z produced and consumed in country h;

$x_{hf}$ = quantity of commodity x (the primary good) exported from country h to country f;

$P_z$ = the world price of the final good z (assumed to be equal in the two countries, i.e., the law of one price holds);

$P_{xh}$ and $P_{xf}$ = the price of commodity x in countries h and f, respectively. After restrictions are imposed it is assumed to differ from one country to another;

$B_h$ = the balance of trade in country h (the two country assumption implies $B_h = -B_f$).

The subscripts h and f denote the home and foreign countries, respectively. The exchange rate is omitted from the equations since it is assumed to be fixed and equal to one. We assume country h to be the exporter of the primary good, x and both a producer and an importer of the manufactured good, z. Thus h represents a group of developing economies while f represents a group of developed countries.

In order to determine the impact of export restrictions in country h, of, say, $P_x$, we need to differentiate the system in (1) as follows:

$$\frac{d Y_h}{dP_{xf}} = \frac{\partial E_h}{\partial Y_h} \frac{d Y_n}{dP_{xf}} + x_{hf} + P_{xf} \left( \frac{\partial x_{hf}}{\partial P_{xf}} + \frac{\partial x_{hf}}{\partial Y_f} \frac{d Y_f}{dP_{xf}} \right) - \quad (5.2\text{-a})$$

$$- (z_h - z_{hh}) \frac{dP_z}{dP_{xf}} - P_z \left( \frac{\partial z_h}{\partial Y_h} \frac{d Y_h}{dP_{xf}} + \frac{\partial z_h}{\partial P_z} \frac{dP_z}{dP_{xf}} - \right.$$

$$\left. - \frac{\partial z_{hh}}{\partial P_{xh}} \frac{dP_{xh}}{dP_{xf}} - \frac{\partial z_{hh}}{\partial P_z} \frac{dP_z}{dP_{xf}} \right)$$

$$\frac{dY_f}{dP_{xf}} = \frac{\partial E_f}{\partial Y_f} \frac{dY_f}{dP_{xf}} + (z_h - z_{hh}) \frac{dP_z}{dP_{xf}} + P_z \left( \frac{\partial z_h}{\partial Y_h} \frac{dY_h}{dP_{xf}} + \right. \quad (5.2\text{-b})$$

$$\left. + \frac{\partial z_h}{\partial P_z} \frac{dP_z}{dP_{xf}} - \frac{\partial z_{hh}}{\partial P_{xh}} \frac{dP_{xh}}{dP_{xf}} - \frac{\partial z_{hh}}{\partial P_z} \frac{dP_z}{dP_{xf}} \right) - x_{hf} -$$

$$P_{xf} \left( \frac{\partial x_{hf}}{\partial P_{xf}} + \frac{\partial x_{hf}}{Y_f} \frac{dY_f}{dP_{xf}} \right)$$

$$\frac{dB_h}{dP_{xf}} = x_{hf} + P_{xf} \left( \frac{\partial x_{hf}}{\partial Y_f} \frac{dY_f}{dP_{xf}} + \frac{\partial x_{hf}}{\partial P_{xf}} \right) - (z_h - z_{hh}) \frac{dP_z}{dP_{xf}} \qquad (5.2\text{-c})$$

$$- P_z \left( \frac{\partial z_h}{\partial Y_h} \frac{dY_h}{dP_{xf}} + \frac{\partial z_h}{\partial P_z} \frac{dP_z}{dP_{xf}} - \frac{\partial z_{hh}}{\partial P_z} \frac{dP_z}{dP_{xf}} - \frac{\partial z_{hh}}{\partial P_{xh}} \frac{dP_{xh}}{dP_{xf}} \right),$$

The solution to system (5.2) provides the following expression:

$$\frac{d_{Yh}}{dP_{xf}} = T \left( \frac{S_f}{S_h S_f + S_h m_f + S_f m_h} \right) \qquad (5.3\text{-a})$$

$$\frac{d_{Yf}}{dP_{xf}} = T \left( \frac{-S_h}{S_h S_f + S_h m_f + S_f m_h} \right) \qquad (5.3\text{-b})$$

$$\frac{dB_h}{dP_{xf}} = T \left( 1 - \frac{m_h S_f + m_f S_h}{S_h S_f + S_h m_f + S_f m_h} \right), \qquad (5.3\text{-c})$$

where

$\partial E/\partial y \equiv e$, the marginal propensity to expend;
$(1-e) \equiv s$, the marginal propensity to hoard;

$P_{xf} \dfrac{\partial x_{hf}}{\partial Y_f} \equiv mf$, the marginal propensity to import in country f;

$P_z \dfrac{\partial z_h}{\partial Y_h} \equiv mh$, the marginal propensity to import in country h;

$\varepsilon_{xf}$, the price elasticity of demand for x in f;
$\varepsilon_{zh}$, the price elasticity of demand for z in h;
$\mu_{zh}$, the price elasticity of supply for z in h.

$$T = X_{hf}(1 + \varepsilon x_f) - [z_h(1 + \varepsilon z_h) - z_{hh}(1 + \mu z_h)] \frac{dP_z}{dP_{xf}}$$

$$+ P_z \frac{\partial z_{hh}}{\partial P_{xh}} \frac{dP_{xh}}{dP_{xf}}$$

If the necessary condition for export restrictions is met, then $[\varepsilon_{xf}]<1$ and if $[\varepsilon_{zh}]>1$ and $\mu z_h>0$ then $T>0$. When all marginal propensities are between the values of zero and one then

$$\frac{dY_h}{dP_{xf}} > 0, \quad \frac{dY_f}{dP_{xf}} < 0, \quad \text{and} \quad \frac{dB_h}{dP_{xf}} < 0.$$

The analysis of the effect of export restrictions can be broken down into two effects: the direct transfer effect (T), which is a first round effect, and the total effect, which takes into account feedback effects and macroeconomic factors.

## THE DIRECT TRANSFER EFFECT

Clearly, the greater the value of T the larger the income transfer from country f (representing the group of developed economies) to country h (representing the group of developing economies). The breakdown of T into its components shows that T consists of several factors, each important for the successful application of export restrictions when success is measured in terms of the income transfer generated. The expression $x_{hf}(1+\varepsilon_{xf})$ represents the power of economy h to directly increase its income from exports through export restrictions. The expression

$$-[z_h(1 + \varepsilon_{zh}) - z_{hh}(1 + \mu_{zh})] \frac{dP_z}{dP_{xf}}$$

is the direct change of national income in both countries that is due to the change of country h's import structure. It includes the decrease in total consumption of product z resulting from its rising price

$$[-z_h(1 + \varepsilon_{zh}) \frac{dP_z}{dP_{xf}}] ,$$

and the implication of an increase in Z's domestic production:

$$[z_{hh}(1 + \mu_{zh}) \frac{dP_z}{dP_{xf}}].$$

In other words, the latter expression represents the impact on further processing that stems from export restrictions on the national incomes of the two countries. The size of this impact depends, of course, on the capacity of the exporting country to perform further processing. This capacity is conditional on the existence of complementary factors in country h, such as adequate manpower, capital, skills, and know-how, inter-alia. All of these are represented above by $\mu_{zh}$, the price elasticity of supply. As can be seen above, the effect of the import structure changes on the level of incomes depends also on $dP_z/dP_{xf}$. This factor is assumed to be positive. It is easily seen that the greater this factor the more significant is the effect. $dP_z/dP_{xf}$ is negatively related to the value added in producing z and to the price elasticity of demand in country f (in which $P_z$ is assumed to be determined) and positively related to the price elasticity of supply in country f. Hence, an important issue in considering export restrictions for the sake of further processing is the value added in producing the processed good. Chances of success are better the lower the relative value added. The last component of T is

$$P_z \frac{\partial z_{hh}}{\partial P_{xh}} \frac{dP_{xh}}{dP_{xf}} ,$$

which represents the effect of the decreasing price of x in country h (resulting from export restrictions) on the capacity of further processing. $\partial z_{hh}/\partial P_{xh}$ is assumed to be negative and is larger in absolute value the smaller value added in producing z. $dP_{xh}/dP_{xf}$ is also assumed to be negative and is greater in absolute terms the lower the world demand and the domestic supply price elasticities.

THE TOTAL EFFECT OF EXPORT RESTRICTIONS

As can be seen from the equation system (5.3), the income transfer that is generated by export restrictions depends not only on the direct income shift T but also on the three different multipliers, $M_h$, $M_f$ and $MB_h$, where

$$M_h = \frac{S_h}{S_h S_f + S_h m_f + S_f m_h}$$

$$M_f = \frac{-S_h}{S_h S_f + S_h m_f + S_f m_h}, \text{ and}$$

$$MB_h = 1 - \frac{m_h S_f + m_f S_h}{S_h S_f + S_h m_f + S_f m_h}.$$

These multipliers are sensitive to the levels of the marginal propensities. The signs of their derivatives with respect to the different marginal propensities are as follows (assuming $0 < S_h$, $S_f$, $m_h$, $m_f < 1$):

(a) $\dfrac{dM_h}{dS_f} > 0$; (b) $\dfrac{dM_h}{dS_h} < 0$; (c) $\dfrac{dM_h}{dm_f} < 0$; (d) $\dfrac{dM_h}{dm_h} < 0$ (5.4)

(a) $\dfrac{dM_f}{dS_f} > 0$; (b) $\dfrac{dM_f}{dS_h} < 0$; (c) $\dfrac{dM_f}{dm_f} > 0$; (d) $\dfrac{dM_f}{dm_h} > 0$ (5.5)

(a) $\dfrac{dMB_h}{dS_f} > 0$; (b) $\dfrac{dMB_h}{dS_h} > 0$; (c) $\dfrac{dMB_h}{dm_f} < 0$; (d) $\dfrac{dMB_h}{dm_h} < 0$ (5.6)

We shall focus on some of the above signs. Derivatives (5.4a) and (5.5a) imply that the income transfer from f to h is more efficient the greater is Sf. Thus, for a given level of export restrictions the decrease (increase) in national income of the importing (exporting) country is smaller (larger) the higher is the marginal propensity to hoard (MPH) in the foreign importing country, f. The higher is the MPH of the exporting country, the lower is the efficiency of export restrictions in redistributing income between the two countries.

Improvement of the balance of payments in country h also depends on the marginal propensities. The above signs point out that the balance of payments improvement in country h is positively related to the marginal propensities to hoard, $S_h$ and $S_f$, and negatively related to the marginal propensities to import, $m_h$ and $m_f$.

An important question is whether export restrictions could result in a fall of national income and a deterioration of the balance of payments in the developing country even if the direct effect T is positive. Theoretically, this could happen when the developing countries' marginal propensity to hoard ($S_h$) is negative. There is no theoretical contradiction between the stability of the system and a prevailing negative $S_h$. The practical meaning of such a phenomenon is that even if the microeconomic considerations (elasticities) support the implementation of export restrictions, macroeconomic considerations may overrule them. This could be the case where export restrictions are harmful to both the exporting and the importing countries. While it is not unreasonable to hypothesize a negative marginal propensity to hoard in developing countries, especially when the process of development involves rapidly increasing government expenditure and private consumption, empirical estimates do not suggest that such is the case.

Export restrictions affect world income as shown in equation (5.7).

$$\Delta Y_h + \Delta Y_f = T \frac{S_f - S_h}{S_h S_f + S_h m_f + S_f m_h} \qquad (5.7)$$

where $\Delta Y_h = \dfrac{dY_h}{dP_{xf}}$ and $\Delta Y_f = \dfrac{dY_f}{dP_{xf}}$

Clearly, the direction of change in world income depends on the sign of the numerator. If $S_f > S_f$ world income grows; world income declines of $S_f < S_h$. This result is somewhat surprising: Export restrictions are generally believed to **redistribute** income between or among countries only at the cost of a decline in world income. The latter view is consistent with a microeconomic approach that implies that export restrictions introduce a distortion in the allocation of world resources. The above finding shows that this need not be the case. Nevertheless, it should be clearly stated that the possibility of achieving a higher world income requires both that $S_f > S_h$ and that idle resources exist in the developing country at the initial point. Existing unemployment in one country (h) is a suboptimal situation, thus the restriction of exports may shift the world from one suboptimal situation to another. This type of change does not rule out a possible improvement within the process, however.

For the above analysis to be practically relevant the likelihood that the two above mentioned conditions actually must be examined. Unemployment is known as a chronic problem of developing countries. Moreover, empirical studies show that there is a tendency for marginal propensities to save to rise in tandem with income per capita.[3] This finding is compatible with the Keynesian analysis implying that marginal propensities to save are greater than average propensities to save, which was explained by the Lewis Hypothesis and supported empirically by Kuznets (1960), Houthakker (1961), and others. It seems, therefore, realistic to expect the marginal propensity to hoard to be higher in developed economies than in developing ones.

Some reservations should be expressed about the above discussion. The analysis does not imply that export restrictions, even when they lead to an increase in world income, are the best way to redistribute world income. Export restrictions may be accompanied by undesirable by-products, such as cost-push inflation and unemployment in the importing country and possibly demand-pull inflation in the exporting country. Moreover, there may be other more efficient income transferring mechanisms, such as foreign aid (which will be discussed later).

A second reservation concerns the question of whether the change in world income as presented above is a change in real income or only in its nominal value. The way the income changes are computed implies that they are measured in terms of the non-tradable goods, that do not appear explicitly in the analysis but serve as a kind of numeraire and are implicitly embodied in E, the domestic expenditure. If, however, the aim is to measure changes in real income measured in terms of a tradable good, one could manipulate the expression in (5.4) by measuring the changes in world income in terms of the final good, z:

$$\Delta(\frac{Y_h}{P_z}) + \Delta(\frac{Y_f}{P_z}) = \frac{\Delta Y_h}{P_z} + \frac{\Delta Y_f}{P_z} - \frac{\Delta P_z}{P_z}(\frac{Y_h}{P_z} + \frac{Y_f}{P_z}) \qquad (5.8)$$

where Pz denotes the price of the final good, z.

Expression (5.8) could be positive or negative. That is, export restrictions could increase or decrease real world income depending on the relative change of "nominal" income, $Y_h + Y_f$, and on the reaction of prices of final goods, $P_z$, to changes in prices of raw materials. We could conclude that chances for an increase in world real income are better the greater is $S_f - S_h$ and T and the lesser the sensitivity of world prices of manufactured goods to price changes of primary commodities. In other words, when the macroeconomic conditions are favorable to export restrictions ($S_f - S_h > 0$), then the restrictions are less harmful and could be of benefit to world income the smaller the importance of the restricted commodity to world production. A possible interpretation of the expression in (5.8) is that it consists of two components:

$$\frac{\Delta Y_h + \Delta Y_f}{P_z},$$

which is the net macroeconomic effect of a transfer in real income from the developed to the developing country, and

$$-\frac{\Delta P_z}{P_z}\left(\frac{Y_h + Y_f}{P_z}\right),$$

which is a kind of measure of the excess burden generated by the technique chosen to redistribute world income.

## FOREIGN AID

Even when export restrictions increase world income they may not represent the best mechanism with which to transfer income from one group of countries to another. Such restrictions create distortions in the allocation of world resources and generate the "excess burden" caused by higher prices of final goods. In a world in which free trade and free access to markets is a goal, measures must be taken to avoid such measures. Countries which benefit from the prevention of export restrictions should compensate those countries which may suffer as a result. One way to facilitate such compensation is to establish an organized system of foreign aid. In this section we examine the implications of such transfers and analyze whether or not aid is superior to export restrictions in terms of world welfare.

The analysis of the impact of foreign trade can be pursued with the same instruments used to analyze export restrictions. The total effect of the income transfer generated by foreign aid is:

$$\Delta Y_h = A \frac{S_f}{S_h S_f + S_h m_f + S_f m_h} \quad \text{and} \quad \Delta Y_f = A \frac{-S_h}{S_h S_f + S_h m_f + S_f m_h}$$

where A denotes the amount of foreign aid.

It is easy to see that if the volume of foreign aid is the same as the nominal income transfer generated by export restrictions, T, then the nominal changes in the countries' incomes are exactly the same in both cases. Furthermore, world income obtained in both cases is identical. However, this finding is somewhat misleading. When changes in world income are measured in terms of the traded final good, z, foreign aid is a better solution for world economy than export restrictions. When $A = T$ the total change in world real income is:

$$\Delta\left(\frac{Y_h}{P_z}\right) + \Delta\left(\frac{Y_f}{P_z}\right) = \frac{A}{P_z}\left(\frac{S_f - S_h}{S_h S_f + S_h m_f + S_f m_f}\right).$$

This change is larger than the change obtained through export restrictions since world prices of final goods, $P_z$, remain unchanged and the "excess burden" appearing in expression (5.8) is spared.

There are other differences between foreign aid and export restrictions. National income of country h increases more in real terms through foreign trade, but the composition of output may be less desirable than that achieved through other means. Foreign aid may not stimulate further processing. Recall that further processing was motivated by two factors: a lower domestic price in country h for the input x and a higher world price for the final good z. These two effects disappear with foreign aid and domestic production is stimulated in the developing country across the board by increased demand. Thus, all sectors, including the non-traded goods sector, enjoy growth. This is not necessarily a drawback for country h since there is no particular reason to believe that the processed good is the good in which country h maintains a comparative advantage. If, however, such an advantage prevails, foreign aid does not curb it in any way.

SUMMARY AND CONCLUSIONS

The effects of export restrictions on primary commodities as analyzed in this chapter reveal the complexity and ambiguity of the problem. The combination of a microeconomic and macroeconomic approach to the issue shows that even when microeconomic characteristics show that export restrictions are favorable to exporting LDCs, there may exist macroeconomic factors that could make this policy undesirable to the exporting country. We have shown that when export restrictions are favorable to the developing exporting countries they need not reduce world income. Such restrictions create an income transfer from the developed to the developing countries but under quite realistic conditions such a transfer actually induces growth in world income.

Finally, we found that foreign aid is always a more efficient device with which to transfer income from the importing to the exporting countries. This conclusion is limited to the transfer of income and not to other objectives that may be incorporated as goals of export restrictions, e.g. further processing and industrialization of the exporting countries. A major reservation to the above conclusion is that while imposition of export restrictions is a fully sovereign decision by the exporting country or countries, foreign aid is subject to intensive international bargaining and to the approval of the other donor countries.

NOTES

1. For a more comprehensive survey of the motives for export restrictions, see chapter 2.
2. Various critics of the elasticities approach have raised this point. See Meade 1951, Negishi 1968, and Dornbush 1975.
3. See Chenery and Syrquin 1975.

REFERENCES

Chenery, H. and Syrquin, M. 1975. Patterns of Development, 1950-1970. Oxford: Oxford University Press.
Dornbusch, R. 1975. Exchange Rates and Fiscal Policy in A Popular Model of International Trade. American Economic Review 65: 859-71.
Houthakker, H.S. 1961. An International Comparison of Personal Saving. Bulletin de L'Institut International de Statistique 38: 56-69.
Kuznets, S. 1960. Quantitative Aspects of the Economic Growth of Nations, V: Capital Formation Proportions: International Comparisons for Recent Years. Economic Development and Cultural Change 8: 1-96.
Meade, J.E. 1951. The Theory of International Economic Policy. In The Balance of Payments. Vol. I. London: MacMillan.
Negishi, T. 1968. Approaches of Devaluation. International Economic Review, 9: 218-28.

# 6
# Restrictions of Exports from LDCs and Their Impact on World Economy

*J. Weinblatt*
*R. Nathanson*

INTRODUCTION

The antagonism created in developed countries by the potential and actual implementation of export restrictions on primary commodities is due, above all, to the fear that cost-push effects and stagflation could result. The total impact of export controls by commodity exporting countries includes both a redistribution effect and an apparent unemployment-inflation effect. Studies on inflation and foreign price shocks deal with several possible implications.[1] They all point out that a probable result of external price shocks of primary commodities is a combination of rising inflation rates and growing unemployment. The Economic Report of the President of the U.S. (1977) shows that while for the years 1963 to 1969 there was a clear trade-off between the rate of inflation and the level of unemployment (Phillips curve) in the years 1971-1972 and 1973-1974 the relationship between these two variables was positive. The 1973-1974 period was, of course, one in which commodity prices in general and petroleum prices in particular skyrocketed. It appears, then, that the Phillips curve has been shifting upwards as a direct or indirect result of rising commodity prices. To grasp the problem fully, we must analyze not only the direct cost-push effect of inputs prices but also the probable response of monetary and fiscal authorities to price and employment changes.

A MODEL OF MONETARY ACCOMMODATION TO AN EXOGENEOUS SUPPLY SHOCK

Assume an aggregated production function[2]

$$Y \quad Y(\overset{+}{L}, \overset{+}{K}, \overset{+}{\pi}), \tag{6.1}$$

where  L ≡ labor input;
K ≡ capital input;
π ≡ imported input;
Y ≡ income (final output).

The supply price of the final output, Y, is formulated with the following homogeneous function of degree one for the average money wage, W:

$$P^S = P^S(\overset{+}{Y}, \overset{-}{K}, \overset{-}{\pi}, \overset{+}{W}) \qquad (6.2)$$

$P^S$ is a supply function that can be treated as an industrial marginal cost function:

$$P^S = W[\overset{-\ +\ +}{Y_L(L, K, \pi)}]^{-1}, \qquad (6.3)$$

where $Y_L \equiv$ labor marginal product at the full employment level $\overline{L}$,

$$Y_L = \left.\frac{\partial Y}{\partial L}\right|_{\overline{L}}.$$

The labor market is formulated as follows:

$$W^D = P\, e(L); \qquad (6.4)$$

$$W^S = S(L, P), \qquad (6.5)$$

where $W^D \equiv$ wages determined by employers' labor demand function;
$W^S \equiv$ wages determined by employees' labor supply function;
$e \equiv$ marginal productivity factor;
$P \equiv$ price level.

$W^S = W^D$ is the equilibrium condition on the labor market and it implies:

$$P\, e(L) = S(L, P). \qquad (6.6)$$

The equilibrium condition on the goods and services market, (the IS equation), is:

$$i = Y_K(\overset{+}{L}, \overset{-}{K}, \overset{+}{\Pi}), \qquad (6.7)$$

where $i \equiv$ the expected short-term real interest rate;
$Y_K \equiv$ the marginal productivity of capital, $\partial Y/\partial K$.

The equilibrium condition on the money market is given by:

$$Q(Y, i+r) = \frac{M}{P^D} \quad 3 \tag{6.8}$$

and the LM equation is:

$$Mo = P^D \, Q[Y, (i+r)], \tag{6.9}$$

where  r ≡ the expected short-term rate of inflation;
       Q ≡ money demand (for liquidity);
       $M_0$ ≡ money supply at full-employment level;
       $P^D$ ≡ the demand price level.

By substituting equation (6.1) into equation (6.9) we obtain:

$$Mo = P^D \, Q[Y(L, K, \pi), (i+r)]. \tag{6.10}$$

Equations (6.10) and (6.7) generate a demand price, $P^D$, which is a function of employment.

Substituting equation (6.7) into equation (6.10) we obtain:

$$P^D = Mo[Q(Y(\overset{+}{L}, \overset{+}{K}, \overset{+}{\pi}), Y_K(\overline{L}, \overline{K}, \overset{+}{\pi}) + r)]^{-1}. \tag{6.11}$$

In this equation the higher the level of $\pi$, the greater are Y and $Y_K$ and the lower is $P^D$. Thus, an external price shock on imported inputs implies a decrease in $\pi$ that in turn raises $P^D$.

In order to achieve full employment equilibrium, the following condition must be met at the level of full employment:

$$P^D = P^S \tag{6.12}$$

Substituting equation (6.3) and equation (6.11) into equation (6.12) we obtain:

$$Mo[Q(Y(L, K, \pi), Y_K(\overline{L}, K, \pi)+r)]^{-1} = Wo[\underset{L}{Y}(L, K, \pi)]^{-1}. \tag{6.13}$$

This equilibrium is presented geometrically in figure 6.1. Every point on the $P^D$ curve represents an equilibrium at which IS=LM. Considering only the "normal" case, in which IS intersects LM from above, the $P^D$ curve is downward sloping. The full employment price Po has to satisfy condition (6.13) for given levels of the parameters in the equation. An external price shock on primary commodity markets that reduces $\pi$ causes an upward shift of both $P^D$

and $P^S$. Is full employment damaged as a result of the external price shock? The answer depends on the relative change of $P^D$ and $P^S$ induced by the external price shock. Diagramatically it is easy to see that if $P^D$ and $P^S$ shift to $P^{D'}$ and $P^{S'}$ (figure 6.1), respectively, the level of employment will decrease and an expansionary policy (probably monetary) will be needed to restore full employment. If, however, the external shock generates a change in $P^D$ and $P^S$ such as $P^{D''}$ and $P^{S'}$ respectively, the level of employment remains unaltered and no special policy is needed.

Figure 6.2

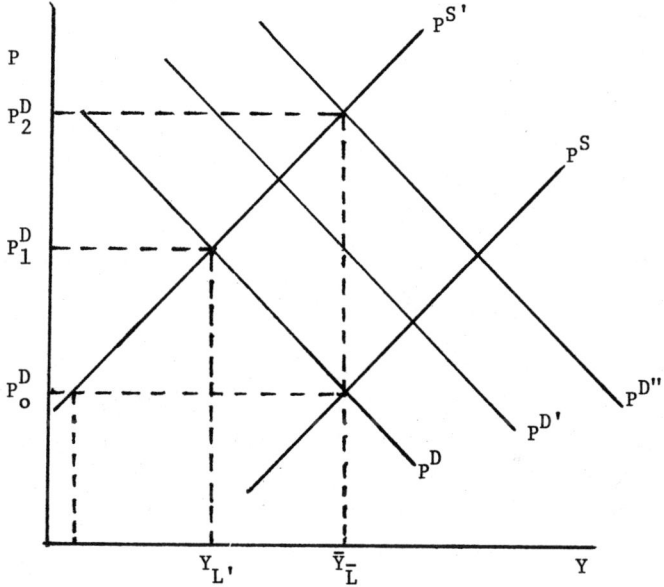

The proportional changes of full employment demand and supply prices per unit change of $\pi$ is computed as follows:

$$-\frac{\partial \bar{P}^D}{\partial \pi} \cdot \frac{1}{\bar{P}^D} = \frac{Q_{Y} \cdot Y}{Q} \frac{Y_\pi}{Y} + \frac{Q_r \, Y_K}{Q} \frac{Y_{K\pi}}{Y_K} = A \qquad (6.14)$$

$$-\frac{\partial \bar{P}^D}{\partial \pi} \cdot \frac{1}{PD}$$

has to be compared with the proportional change of the full employment supply price $\bar{P}^S$.

$$-\frac{\partial \bar{P}^S}{\partial \pi} \frac{1}{\bar{P}^S} = \frac{Y_{L_\pi}}{Y_L} \equiv B \quad . \tag{6.15}$$

Full employment is not maintainable without changing the money supply when A<B. In this case the difference between B and A is the proportional change in the money supply to restore full employment.

## EMPIRICAL ANALYSIS

### The Methodology

In order to test the impact of price changes of imported primary commodities on the level of economic activity in importing developed countries we have developed a simultaneous equation system presented below.

The system was estimated with a two-stage least-squares technique for pooled data combining a cross section over developed countries for two years, 1974 and 1975.[4] Ten primary commodities were chosen and aggregated for this purpose.[5] The major criterion for selecting these commodities was the fact that for all of them complaints regarding their restriction by the exporting country were filed and reported to the IMF and other organizations.[6] Moreover, each of the commodities represents an important share in the exporting countries' exports (more than 50 percent).[7]

Apart from the complaints, there are other signs indicating the possible use of restrictive measures on the export of these commodities. The most outstanding one is the change in their price during the period of the study, 1973 to 1975. During this period all of the selected commodities had at least one annual price increase of 45 percent or more. The average price rise for each of these commodities was higher than the average commodity price change as computed by the IMF.

By testing the effect of these price changes that are partly attributable to export restrictions we shall be able to estimate the impact of such measures on world economic activity, especially in major importing developed countries. The estimates of the equation system serve to assess the effect of price changes on variables related to economic activity and the rate of inflation in the developed importing countries. They thus allow us to assess the possible damage caused by export restrictions.

### The Equations

The simultaneous model is comprised of the five following equations:

Inflation equation

$$n\dot{P}j = \alpha_1 + \beta_{10}\ln\dot{P}cj + \beta_{11}\ln Uj + \beta_{12}\ln Mj/Poj$$

$$+ \beta_{13}\ln(\frac{IMcj}{IMj}\dot{P}cj) + \beta_{14}D75 + \varepsilon_1 \qquad (6.15)$$

Unemployment equation

$$nUj = \alpha_2 + \beta_{20}\ln Uj\text{-}1 + \beta_{21}(\ln Pj - \beta_{10}\ln\dot{P}cj)$$

$$+ \beta_{22}\ln Mj/Popj + \varepsilon_2 \qquad (6.16)$$

GNP equation

$$GNPj = \alpha_3 + \beta_{30}GNPj\text{-}1 + \beta_{31}IMcj + \beta_{32}\dot{U} + \varepsilon_3 \qquad (6.17)$$

Commodity imports equation

$$nIMcj = \alpha_4 + \beta_{40}\ln IMcj\text{-}1 + \beta_{41}\ln GNPj + \beta_{42}\ln\dot{P}c + \varepsilon_4 \qquad (6.18)$$

Money supply equation

$$nMj = \alpha_5 + \beta_{50}\ln Mj\text{-}1 + \beta_{51}\ln\dot{P}cj + \beta_{52}\ln GE + \beta_{53}\ln TB + \varepsilon_5 \qquad (6.19)$$

where:
$\dot{P}j$   the annual rate of change of the GNP deflator in country j;
$\dot{P}cj$   the annual rate of change of the commodity imports price index in country j;[8]
Uj   percent of unemployed in total labor force;
Mj   real money supply, measured in US dollars;
Pop   population;
IMcj   total value of imported selected commodities to country j measured at constant 1975 prices;[9]
IMj   total imports to country j measured at constant prices;
D75   dummy variable for the year 1975;
GNPj and GNPj-1   Real Gross National Product of country j in the current year and with one year lag, respectively, both measured at constant 1975 prices;
GE   government expenditure at constant prices;
TB   balance of payments surplus.

The inflation equation (6.15) shows the vulnerability of domestic inflation to exogenous price shocks. This relationship depends on both the magnitude of the commodity price change Pcj and the degree of openess of the economy to imports of the selected primary commodities IMcj/IMj. Clearly, the rate of inflation is also (and perhaps initially) affected by the money supply in the economy. Since the equations are estimated on a set of (pooled) cross-sectional data over countries, the money supply variable Mj has been normalized by the size of population, Popj. The unemployment equation (6.16), when combined with the inflation equation (6.15), gives the unemployment-price relationship, reflected geometrically by the Phillips curve. The rate of inflation variable has been introduced in this equation not with its total (logarithmic) value but as a residual above 10 nPcj, which is the direct effect of an external price shock on the rate of inflation. Theoretically, the component of domestic inflation that has a trade-off relationship with unemployment is the demand-pull inflation generated either by money supply and government expenditure changes or by any structural change of private demand patterns. Thus, it would be wrong to relate the entire rate of inflation to the level of unemployment when it is clear that at least some of the inflation is due to cost-push effects generated by external price shocks.

The dummy variable D75 appears here to capture specific unidentified factors causing the stagflation of 1975. The money supply per capita Mj/Pop appearing in both equations represents the policy variable with which governments accommodate unemployment generated by exogenous cost-push effects. When equations (6.15) and (6.16) are combined to formulate a Phillips-type equation, external price shocks (changes of Pcj) potentially affecting both the inflation rate and unemployment could be presented geometrically as a shift of the curve. Accommodating changes in the money supply would be represented by a movement along the Phillips curve, incorporating changes of both inflation rates and unemployment in opposite directions.

Equation (6.17) is the type of aggregative production function in which we are interested largely in the relationship between GNP and the volume of imported primary commodities IMcj. Equation (6.18) is a demand function relating imported commodity price changes to the volume of commodity imports. Equation (6.19) serves to reveal the monetary policy in times of changing commodity prices. It enables us to estimate government responses to an external price shock. When incorporated into the simultaneous system, this equation also provides insight into the effect of this policy on the various variables related to the economic activity.

This model shows that during periods of accommodation to external supply shocks a combination of rising inflation with growing unemployment is expected. It is true that in the above model we analyze the monetary expansion that is required to maintain full employment in times of rising prices of imported commodities. However, this is a long process and in practice there is no guarantee that full employment will indeed be fully restored. It seems more realistic to assume a partial government response to the exogenous price shock. Thus, both unemployment and inflation will rise, at least for a limited period of time. If the exogenous price change is not a one time shock but rather a process carried out over time, then a continuous sequence of rising inflation and unemployment could prevail.

To sum up, an accommodation of resources following a supply shock can occur either by adjusting the money supply to the level of full employment (causing rising prices) or by letting the level of employment decrease, with smaller concomitant price changes. This is not a dichotomic situation since the latter solution has a large number of different degrees of unemployment and inflation.

Empirical Findings

An econometric estimate of the model presented above yielded the following results:

Inflation equation

$$\ln \dot{P}j = -2.14 + 0.06 \ln \dot{P}cj - 1.73 \ln Uj + 0.31 \ln Mj/Popj \quad (6.15)$$

$$(-5.96) \quad (2.48) \quad (-2.67) \quad (1.91)$$

$$+ 0.11 \ln[(IMcj/IMj)\dot{P}cj] + 0.35 Dj$$

$$(1.86) \quad (2.15)$$

$$R^2 = .757$$

Unemployment equation

$$\ln Uj = -.056 + 0.97 \ln Uj{-}1 - 0.44 \ln \dot{P}j \quad (6.16)$$

$$(-3.50) \quad (22.78) \quad (-2.57)$$

$$+ 0.05 \ln Pcj - 0.16 \ln Mj/Popj$$

$$(2.13) \quad (-1.82)$$

$$R^2 = .947$$

GNP equation

$$GNPj = 20535.4 + 0.71\ GNPj{-}1 + 23.92\ IMcj \quad (6.17)$$

$$(5.13) \quad (13.65) \quad (10.74)$$

$$-42379.9\ Uj$$

$$(-4.82)$$

$$R2 = .971$$

Commodity imports equation

$$\ln IMc_j = -1.12 + 0.91 \ln IMc_{j-1} + 0.64 \ln GNP_j \qquad (6.18)$$

$$(-2.24) \quad (39.12) \qquad (2.74)$$

$$- 0.41 \ln Pc_j$$

$$(-2.28)$$

$$R^2 = .932$$

Money supply equation

$$\ln M_j = 0.15 + 0.99 \ln M_{j-1} + 0.08 \ln \dot{P}c_j \qquad (6.19)$$

$$(7.10) \quad (48.16) \qquad (7.79)$$

$$+ 0.09 \ln GE_j + 0.16 \ln TB_j$$

$$(2.66) \qquad (1.88)$$

$$R^2 = 0.972$$

(Figures appearing in parentheses are T values).

This equation system reveals some of the relationships relevant to the analysis in this Chapter. Price changes of imported commodities as measured in this study positively and significantly affect both the rate of inflation and the rate of unemployment (equations (6.15) and (6.16)). Clearly, countries are more vulnerable to external price shock the greater is the proportion of imported commodities in their total imports (equation (6.15)). The commodity imports demand equation shows a relatively low quantity response to changes of the price rate, $\dot{P}c_j$ (-0.41), for the commodity group chosen.

Total real GNP in the importing countries is positively affected by changes of commodity imports. According to equation (6.17), a change of $1 million in commodity imports would change GNP by an average of $23.93 million, an average for all the countries and all commodities included in the sample. It is important to keep in mind that the importing countries are mostly developed economies with large manufacturing sectors, that are relatively vulnerable to changing supplies of raw materials.

The price changes elasticity as measured in equation (6.18) is not the neoclassical elasticity relating price changes to quantity changes but rather a measure relating quantity changes to changes in the rate of price change. The 0.41 measured thus represents a more complicated concept than that normally implied by price elasticity. When actual commodity price changes that occurred during the period of the study are used to derive an average price elasticity that stems from the above measure (0.41) the outcome is a price elasticity between 0.75 and 0.9. Thus, the implied price elasticity is relatively low. This is, of course, compatible with the fact that the selected commodities in this study have all been subject to export restrictions. Thus, the export restricting countries have chosen the appropriate commodities for this purpose and have in most cases achieved their goal of increasing export earnings.

In equation (6.19), the money supply equation, we estimate the average reaction of monetary authorities (or of economic policymakers) to a foreign price shock. We can easily see that money supply is positively and significantly related to changes in the price of imported commodities. This reaction is not too strong in its measured arithmetical value, but it is statistically significant and has a clear repercussion on the economy, as will be shown later. Moreover, it shows that, on average, there is a tendency among policymakers in developed countries to counterbalance for external price shocks by increasing the money supply.

As can be observed in equations (6.15) and (6.16), this monetary policy indirectly accelerates the rate of inflation generated by the direct effect of the external price shock. On the other hand, it reduces the rate of unemployment created indirectly by imported commodity price changes. Thus, it partly offsets the recessionist impact of the external price shock at the cost of increasing the rate of inflation. In other words, a demand-pull inflation is generated through changes in the money supply in order to cure (at least temporarily) the deflationary effect of cost-push inflation.

We shall illustrate the impact of an external price shock originating in the group of selected commodities. Assume a change of 100 percent in the rate of imported commodity price changes. Such an assumption is perfectly realistic and such changes (and much larger ones) have occurred in recent years. Changes in the annual rate of commodity price increase from 10 to 20 percent or from 30 to 60 percent do not seem unusual or extraordinary in the world of primary commodities. Such an initial change would imply average consequences computed from the above equation system and summarized in table 6.1. Some of the results of table 6.1 are exhibited in a Phillips-type diagram in figure 6.2. The initial situation for the average economy in the sample is represented by point A on the Phillips curve R. The external commodity price shock shifts the curve upwards to R'. This price shock can lead to either of two extreme situations, represented by points B and C and any combination in between on the curve R'. The extreme points are represented by only one change of the parameters $\dot{P}j$ or U. Either the rate of domestic inflation rises 9 percent (e.g., from 10.0 percent to 10.9 percent) and unemployment is unchanged, or unemployment rises 5 percent (e.g., from 5.00 percent to 5.25 percent) and the inflation rate remains unchanged. From equation (6.19) we see that an external price shock results in an increase of the money supply, which generates a move on the curve R' to D, where the final result (ignoring feedback effects) consists of a rate of inflation 2.5 percent higher and an unemployment rate 3.8 percent higher than in the initial situation at A.

Table 6.1   The Effect of a 100 Percent Increase in the Rate of Commodity Price Changes* (in Percent)

| | |
|---|---|
| Direct effect on the rate of inflation | +8.8 (assuming U unchanged) |
| Direct effect on unemployment u | +5 (assuming Pj=0) |
| Direct effect on money supply | +8 |
| Direct effect on commodity imports IMcj | -41 |
| Indirect effect on GNP (through changes of IMcj and unemployment) | -3.3 |
| Effects on Pj accounting for embodied changes of Mj** | 2.5 |
| Effect on Uj accounting for embodied changes of Mj | 3.8 |

*A change of this magnitude implies an average annual change of Pcj from 30 percent to 60 percent for the years of the study.
**That is the first round effect, ignoring feedback effects within the simultaneous system (that are very small and practically negligible).

A few points should be raised in this context. The above results, in spite of being statistically significant, appear small in magnitude. It is true that if export restrictions or a price shock such as the one assumed in the example above were to occur for a large number of primary commodities the result could have been more harmful for the importing economies. However, it must be stated that the ten commodities in this study were not selected randomly. These are primary commodities whose exports have actually been restricted. Few other commodities have been subject to such restrictions, since most other commodities lack the characteristics suitable for the implementation of export restrictions. Elsewhere it has been shown that, except for certain exceptional commodities, LDCs cannot really improve their export earnings by restricting their primary commodity exports.[10]

An important qualification of the above findings is that they all refer to short-term trends. Thus, the impact of external price shocks as measured here is relevant for short-run analysis. It seems reasonable to assume that in the long-run, the effects are weaker, since in the long-run economies learn how to adjust to changes in general and to external price shocks in particular.

Figure 6.2

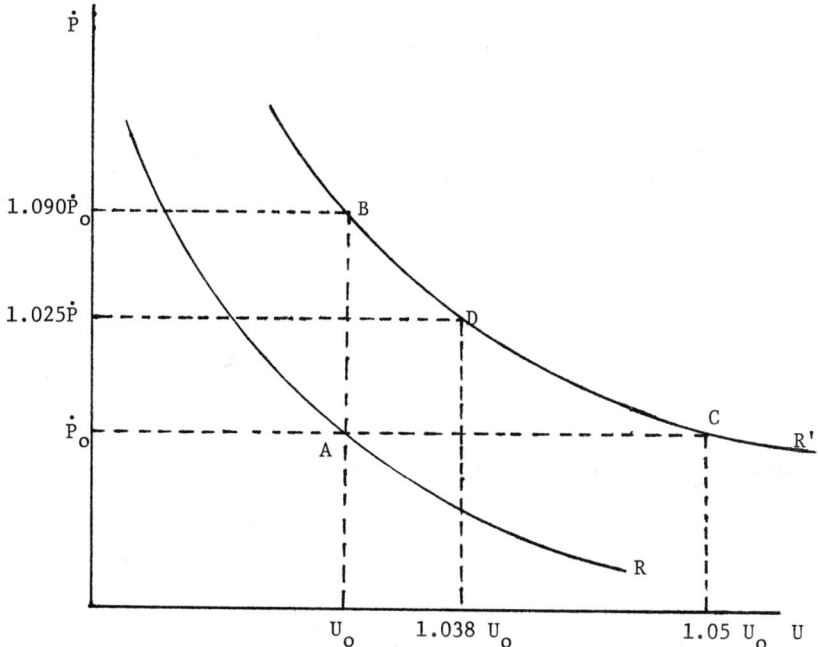

Appendix A

List of importing countries

| | |
|---|---|
| US | South Korea |
| Japan | New Zealand |
| Canada | Singapore |
| Italy | South Africa |
| UK | Norway |
| Spain | Netherlands |
| France | Israel |
| West Germany | Sweden |
| Switzerland | Greece |
| Australia | Ireland |
| Belgium | Austria |
| Finland | Denmark |

Appendix B

Average World Share of Developing Countries'
Exports of Ten Core Commodities
(in percent)

| Commodities | 1970-72 | 1974-76 | 1975-77 |
|---|---|---|---|
| Bananas | 93.3 | 98.4 | 92.7 |
| Cocoa | 99.2 | 97.7 | 96.5 |
| Coffee | 96.8 | 92.8 | 92.1 |
| Rubber | 97.7 | 95.8 | 96.1 |
| Timber | 24.6 | 25.4 | 25.0 |
| Bauxite | 69.7 | 77.4 | 78.4 |
| Copper | 54.4 | 52.8 | 56.8 |
| Manganese | 56.1 | 50.2 | 49.7 |
| Phosphates | 53.6 | 68.7 | 63.2 |
| Tin | 85.5 | 88.9 | 82.6 |

Source: Commodity Trade and Price Trends (Washington, DC: The World Bank, 1979, 1978, 1979).

NOTES

1. See Gordon 1976, Turnovsky and Kaspura 1974, Bruno and Sachs 1979, and others.
2. This model is based on Phelps 1978 and Gordon 1975. For a critical discussion, see Gramlich 1979.
3. $Q/r = Q_r(Y_r, i) = MD/P$.
4. The list of selected countries appears in appendix A.
5. Their list appears in appendix B.

6. See chapter 3.
7. See appendix B.

8. $P_{cj}^{74} = \dfrac{\Sigma_i P_{cij}^{74} IM_{cij}^{75}}{\Sigma_i P_{cij}^{75} IM_{cij}^{75}}$ 100 is the price index of the ten imported commodities, where $IM_{cij}^{75}$ = imported quantity of commodity i in 1975.

9. $IM_{cj}^{74} = \dfrac{\Sigma_i P_{cij}^{74} IM_{cij}^{74}}{P_{cj}^{74}}$.

10. See chapter 8.

REFERENCES

Bruno, M. and Sachs, J. 1979. Macro-Economic Adjustment With Import Price Shocks: Real and Monetary Aspects. <u>Discussion Paper No. 793</u>. Jerusalem: The Maurice Falk Institute.

Gordon, R.J. 1975. Alternative Responses of Policy to External Supply Shocks. <u>Brookings Papers on Economic Activity</u> 6: 183-206.

----- 1976. Recent Development in the Theory of Inflation and Unemployment. <u>Journal of Monetary Economics</u> 2: 185-219.

Gramlich, E.M. 1979. Macro-Policy Responses to Price Shocks. <u>Brookings Papers on Economic Activity</u> 1: 125-66.

Phelps, E.S. 1978. Commodity Supply Shock and Full Employment Monetary Policy. <u>Journal of Money, Credit and Banking</u> 10: 206-22.

Turnovsky, S. and Kaspura, A. 1974. Analysis of Imported Inflation in A Short Run Macro-Economic Model. <u>Canadian Journal of Economics</u> 7: 355-80.

# 7
# Monetary Effects of Export Restrictions on World Commodity Markets

*J. Weinblatt*
*Miriam Rodrik-Farhi*

INTRODUCTION

During the first half of the 1970s world commodity prices rose above the general trend, as a result of the exercise of monopoly power by some LDCs. The LDCs' aim was to obtain a higher share of world income. Export restrictions were adopted as the means to achieve this goal.[1] The ensuing sudden reversal of the terms of trade in favor of commodity exporting LDCs caused surprise and dismay among the importing countries. World markets, which until then had been accustomed to inexpensive raw materials and compliant LDC suppliers, went into disarray.[2] Economists around the world tried to cope with the shock and predict its outcome for the commodity importing countries. Accommodating fiscal and monetary policies were adopted simultaneously.
  The imposition of export restrictions effected a new distribution of resources. The level of reserve holdings by the commodity exporting countries increased, as did the world money supply. The general tendency was, of course, higher world prices.
  It is generally agreed that a supply shock of international character has a cost-push effect for commodity importing countries. As a result, prices rise, causing a reduction in output and employment unless policies to accommodate the shock are adopted. The level of economic activity of a particular economy at the time of the shock is, of course, of great importance, but it is argued that there are several other preconditions for the smooth adjustment of the individual economies and of the world economy to the shock. These include predictable expectations about the new economic reality, especially concerning price and money supply changes and domestic production sufficiently flexible and stable to react rapidly to relative price changes, enabling a better utilization of the more expensive commodities without requiring massive technological changes. In fact, domestic economies seem to be strongly characterized by sticky prices and wages everywhere. Thus, in the short-run the effective choice among alternative policies is reduced to one, namely, an accommodating monetary policy.[3] While a supply shock curbs economic growth, this accommodating policy favors inflation and the economy ends up in a stagflationary process of reduced growth and

higher inflation. In other words, the Phillips curve shifts upwards as a direct or indirect result of rising commodity prices. In addition, commodity exporting countries recycle their freshly acquired foreign reserves into the monetary systems of the developed countries, adding further dynamism and a new element of imported inflation to world economic relations.

ANALYTICAL BACKGROUND

Movements in the prices of traded goods form an integral part of Hume's price-specie flow method of adjustment and are treated as part of the mechanism that transmits world inflation.[4] Since Hume, the influence of import prices on domestic prices in an open economy has been widely investigated. Import prices are regarded as a cost-push factor. Brunner (1974) treats import prices along with the trade volume as a major element responsible for transmiting inflation among economies.

Some economists, e.g., Johnson (1977b), advocate a policy of non-activating domestic credit after an initial exogenous shock that reduces the level of reserves under fixed exchange rates, so that the shock will be absorbed by real variables and the economic agents be forced to live with the fact of the shock without chasing after their previous levels of profits or real wages. Following the same line of reasoning Poole (1975), pointing out the historical tendency for overreaction to external economic events, favors neutral policy settings in the face of the 1973 shocks from farm and fuel products.

At the other extreme we find Okun (1975), who maintains that disregarding the macroeconomic effects of abrupt commodity shortages causes total real output to fall by more than a decline in the primary product, through an extra induced loss of processed output.

Adams (1979) favors considering the impact of primary commodity prices in a full accommodation system, thus recognizing not only the direct costs, but also the resulting demand feedback.

In theoretical studies the analytical treatment of macroeconomic problems has also accounted for exogenous supply shocks. Findlay and Rodriguez (1977) emphasize the need for the explicit introduction of imported intermediate inputs into macroeconomic models of the open economy. They build a Keynesian model of an open economy with perfect international capital mobility under flexible exchange rates and introduce an intermediate imported input, analyze the effects monetary and intermediate imported input and analyze the effects of monetary and fiscal policy.

Phelps (1978) and Gordon (1975) both inquire into the possible responses to commodity supply shocks, each using a different macroeconomic model and tracing the extreme cases of full and no accommodation to the shock.

Van Duyne (1979) assumes flexible exchange rates and analyzes the macroeconomic effects of the 1973-74 commodity price boom. He shows that the commodity market disruptions of that period had significant effects on prices, exchange rates, trade, and capital flows and that these effects persisted long after the initial shock had passed.

In this section we build the theoretical background that integrates the effects of sudden price changes of primary commodities on various economic variables, namely changes in reserves, R; changes in the supply of money, M; changes in the growth of output, G; and changes in the domestic price level, P.

The sudden changes in the cost of the commodity input - the supply shocks - resemble business cycles in that they affect all or many sectors of the economy simultaneously and thus involve aggregated output fluctuations. Yet these shocks are distinctly different from business cycles. Business cycles are assumed to take care of themselves, that is, peaks and troughs follow an invisible hand. However, supply shocks are absorbed into the economy at the cost of sharp reductions from trend output and thus of the existing level of employment. Some kind of policy action is therefore necessary to smooth out the process.

In order to analyze the effects of supply shocks, we distinguish between the group of shock-generating and the group of shock-absorbing countries. Countries that apply price and quantity restrictions on commodity exports generate a shock if they have monopoly power on those commodities, while countries importing these "restricted" commodities absorb the shock.

The effects of this shock in both groups of countries are first felt in their respective balance of payments accounts. In a world of quasi-fixed exchange rates the balance of payments of the exporting group improves[5] while the balance of payments of the importing one deteriorates. The reflection of this change in the balance of payments will be seen in R and will affect the domestic variables of each group.

In the literature, the supply of money is generally assumed to be an exogenous variable because it is subject solely to the decisions of the monetary authorities. Yet such decisions are not a function of stochastic disturbances but rather are a function of changes in the demand for money, in the world price level, in the balance of payments, inter alia. The supply of money is thus considered to be endogenous.[6]

A change in the rate of reserve accumulation of both importing and exporting countries reflects the differences between the aggregate receipts and payments of residents and of the monetary authorities for a given period of time, e.g., between the beginning of the shock and the time of evaluation. A current deficit is implied if the rate is negative; a current surplus if the rate is positive. Two different and asymmetrical issues are involved in each of the implications.

A deficit, which is usually accompanied by an initial deterioration of reserves, contracts the supply of money. In theory this should cause a downward price adjustment. However, since prices tend to be rigid downwards either an excess demand for money is created and unemployment results or such an outcome is offset by accommodating the supply of money to fight unemployment at the cost of accelerating inflation.[7]

A surplus initiates a domestic disequilibrium process in which the supply of money increases. At this point there are three possible outcomes or any combination of them: The monetary authority can abstain from reacting further; the increased reserves can be recycled into foreign countries through increased imports; or the monetary authority can sterilize the excess reserves. In the first case, domestic prices will simply adjust to the increased money supply. In the second case, characteristic of developing countries, economic activity will expand and inflation will accelerate. In the last case, reserves will simply accumulate, with no side effects.

In the cases of both a surplus and a deficit, a commodity price shock that causes a shift of reserves from importing to exporting countries is also likely to result in a higher level of international liquidity. This can be explained by the fact that both deficit and surplus countries have a tendency to expand their supply of money as an accommodating domestic policy; eventually one country's currency becomes the other countries' reserves.[8] The extent of world inflation is then determined by changes in the supply of international liquidity and by the magnitude of the commodity price shock. The degree of inflationary pressure for each economy will vary indirectly with the openness of the economy relative to the world. That is, this pressure will be weaker for economies enjoying high levels of trade, currency convertibility, and freedom of labor and capital movements.

One way of insulating the individual economy - and eventually the world - from the inflationary pressures of the trading countries whose supply of money has increased is to adopt the system of floating exchange rates. The emphasis in the adjustment process then shifts from the level of reserve accumulation to the exchange rate, and the domestic economy remains free from the influences of changes in international liquidity.

From 1973 onwards the developed world moved to floating exchange rates but the system has not been characterized by true free floating, because not all countries adopted the system and even those that did prevented their currencies from floating freely by intervening in the exchange market to prevent currency depreciation or appreciation as a result of balance of payments changes created by international currency speculation. The European snake is a perfect example of protection against a free float. Other countries have continued to hold assets in the form of foreign reserves and have added significantly to their stock of reserves.[9] Thus, there is room to believe, as Williamson (1974) argued, that demand and supply for foreign reserves are invariant with respect to the foreign exchange system used. A change in reserves, then, is still a good indicator of balance of payment disequilibria even under "floating" exchange rates. ("Managed" or "dirty" float would be more accurate terms describing the existing situation).

To sum up, the following issues provide the theoretical basis of the model that follows:

(1) A surplus or a deficit is a flow equilibrium process, i.e., it must be absorbed into the economy by the decisions of

monetary authorities. The implication is that unless and/or until it is absorbed by the national economy, a surplus or deficit represents a transient shock adjustment process.

(2) Although it is not assumed that the monetary authorities follow a rigidly fixed exchange rate system, it is assumed that under conditions of surplus (increase in foreign reserves) caused by an increase in export prices, for example, the demand for money in the economy increases and initiates a disequilibrium process in which the demand for money is greater than its supply. For this disequilibrium to disappear, monetary authorities must eventually either increase the supply of money or appreciate the currency. The length of the lag in the adjustment process will vary.

We assume, then, that: the supply of money is endogenous, and reacts to a set of macro-economic variables; that velocity is stable; and that the money markets clear faster than the goods market (neoclassical assumption).

THE EMPIRICAL MODEL

In order to estimate and predict the behavior of reserves, prices, supply of money, and growth, we have attempted an aggregation of countries into two groups: developing countries (LDCs) and developed countries (DCs). For simplicity we assume that only the developing world exports primary commodities (excluding oil) and imposes export restrictions while the developed world imports those commodities whose prices have risen. It is further assumed that the price elasticity of the commodity imports is low. Thus, in a system of quasi-fixed exchange rates a higher rate of reserve transactions is expected to take care of the increased trade volume.

Our model is a four-equation simultaneous system that empirically tests the effects of a real commodity supply shock ($\dot{P}c$) on monetary variables, namely the rate of change in money supply ($\dot{M}s$); the rate of reserve accumulation ($\dot{R}$), the level of domestic inflation ($\dot{P}d$); and the rate of growth of the economy ($\dot{g}$) for LDCs and DCs, respectively. The period of analysis is from 1959 to 1978.

The effect of a supply shock upon investment, unemployment, productivity, and growth depends upon the absorption of this shock through the variables of the economy. Thus, ($\dot{M}s$) is expected to reflect the policy measure used to absorb the supply shock; ($\dot{P}d$) and ($\dot{R}$) are expected to be directly affected by this exogenous factor; while ($\dot{g}$) will be affected only ex post. We adopt the neoclassical assumption that the goods markets clear after the money markets of the world. The exogenous variables used in this model are change in the volume of trade ($\dot{T}V$); change in the commodity price index ($\dot{P}c$); and yearly lags for the change in supply of money and price of commodities ($\dot{M}s_{-1}$, $\dot{M}s_{-2}$, $\dot{P}c_{-1}$).

(1) The World Inflation Equation: $\dot{P}d(\dot{P}c, \dot{M}s, \dot{M}s_{-1}, \dot{M}s_{-2}, \dot{g})$

During a period of world inflation the assumption of a close correlation between the level of world prices and that of traded commodities seems reasonable. Commodity prices are considered an exogenous factor (an outside shock) affecting the importing and exporting countries separately.

We expect that $(\partial \dot{P}d/\partial \dot{P}c) > 0$ for the importing countries, but it may be that the expression does not persist long enough to be of statistical importance, because although a single rise in commodity prices will affect the level of prices, it cannot permanently increase the rate of world inflation unless it is accompanied by faster monetary growth. Only if the degree of monopoly power due to the export restrictions rises can increases in the prices of traded commodities be a source of continuing inflation. For commodity exporting countries, if the commodity price rise results from export restrictions, domestic prices of these commodities fall and reduce their general rate of inflation.

The effects of changes in the supply of money and in the level of reserves on the change in the domestic price level depend on a simple extension of the quantity theory of money. An expansion in international reserves increases the monetary base and, given a stable money multiplier, causes an expansion of the money supply. The growth in the supply of money will, after some delay, cause prices to rise unless a positive change in the level of economic activity (growth) can absorb this new level of money supply. Accordingly, and in line with Friedman's predictions on the lagged effect of the quantity of money on prices, we expect $\partial \dot{P}d/\partial \dot{M}s$, $\partial \dot{P}d/\partial \dot{M}s_{-1}$ and $\partial \dot{P}d/\partial \dot{M}s_{-2}$ all to be positive.

Another way of defining the relationship between prices and the supply of money is through changes in aggregate demand (Laidler, 1976). When aggregate demand changes due to an exogenous or endogenous factor, this causes a change in the demand for money. When the supply of money varies to accomodate the demand for it, the change in prices is one of the results. In this case, change in the supply of money is considered a proxy for changes in aggregate demand.

The sign of $\partial \dot{P}d/\partial \dot{g}$ is more ambiguous. A positive sign is expected unless growth is a result of increased productivity or better capacity utilization.

(2) The Policy Rule Equation: $\dot{M}s(\dot{P}d, \dot{M}s_{-1}, \dot{R})$

We adopted a narrow definition of money (M1), largely because of data inconsistencies. Assuming a stable demand for money and given $\dot{P}d$, $\dot{R}$, and $\dot{M}s_{-1}$, the changes in M1 reflect inter alia the short-term targets of policy to prevent a serious decline in economic activity. The introduction of past changes in the money supply as an independent variable reflects the assumption that money supply is dynamically determined.

Generally, $d\dot{M}s/d\dot{M}s_{-1}$ is expected to be positive, unless past changes in the supply of money cause a countercyclical policy response of money supply. Thus, $d\dot{M}s/d\dot{M}s_{-1}$ can also be negative.

This is the case where authorities want to reverse their actual monetary policy. In both cases, this lagged variable picks up any element of serial dependence or lagged adjustment.

In the international economy the excess supply of reserves translates itself into an excess supply of money simultaneously or with some time lag. It is argued that increases in international reserves cause a worldwide monetary expansion that results in a higher level of world inflation.[11] On the other hand, $(\partial \dot{M}s/\partial \dot{R}) \leq 0$ can also occur where:

(a) The supply of money is increasing despite decreasing reserves (domestic credit is created by monetary authorities by deficit financing).

(b) The inflow of reserves is being sterilized by the monetary authorities. This is a stock adjustment process in the balance of payments and it is highly improbable that the authorities would be able to continue such a policy in the face of pressures that originate in the domestic economy.

(3) The International Reserves Equation: $\dot{R}_1(\dot{T}V, \dot{g}, \dot{M}s)$

To estimate changes in the level of reserves, we used two distinct equations for developed and developing countries, respectively. Changes in the level of reserves for developed countries are considered to be the function $\dot{R}_1(\dot{T}V, \dot{g}, \dot{M}s)$.

A change in the level of reserves in relation to the supply of money is separated from changes in the reserves in relation to changes in the volume of trade (total exports). A positive sign of the $(dR_1/DTV)$ is the result of changes in the trade volume affecting the level of reserves in the same direction.

The sign of $\partial \dot{R}_1 / \partial \dot{g}$ is ambiguous since growth may require either the running down of reserves, in which case $(\partial \dot{R}_1/\partial \dot{g}) < 0$, or the dominating of a greater share of the international market, in which case $(\partial \dot{R}_1/\partial \dot{g}) > 0$, or simply $(\partial \dot{R}_1/\partial \dot{g}) = 0$. Because the DCs tend to experience growth biased to non-tradables $(\partial \dot{R}_1/\partial \dot{g}) \leq 0$ is more probable.

The relationship whereby changes in the supply of money affect changes in the level of reserves is more complex. If a developed country inflates its supply of money at a rate higher than of its trading partners, the country will, ceteris paribus, suffer a deterioration in its balance of payments and a loss of international reserves. Thus, $(\partial \dot{R}_1/\partial \dot{M}s) < 0$. On the other hand, the DCs have the advantage of being able to pay for imports in their home currency and thus delay the reduction in their level of foreign reserves. Thus, when analyzing the group of DCs we can expect to find $(\partial \dot{R}_1/ \partial \dot{M}s) > 0$. Since there is no shortage of mechanisms available for recycling this expanding supply, and since no ceiling exists for the aggregate supply of reserves this increase is inflationary.

A different reserve equation has been used for the LDCs:

$$\dot{R}_2(\dot{T}V, \dot{M}s_{dc}, \dot{M}s_{dc-1}, \dot{P}c, \dot{g}).$$

Here, too, the change in the level of reserves of the LDCs is a function of their trade volume and growth rate. As in the case of developed countries and for similar reasons $\partial \dot{R}_2 / \partial \dot{T} V$ is positive.

The sign of $\partial \dot{R}_2 / \partial \dot{g}$ is more ambiguous. The LDCs are generally characterized by growth biased to tradable goods. $\partial \dot{R}_2 / \partial dg$ will be negative if the bias is toward imports and positive if the bias is toward exports.

An additional explanatory variable - namely changes in the price of commodities - has been used, since commodity exports make up LDCs' major source of reserve earnings. The sign, of course, is positive.

Furthermore, the LDCs' change in reserves is assumed to be a function of changes in the developed countries' supply of money ($\dot{Ms}_{dc}$) and in the developed countries' lagged supply of money ($\dot{Ms}_{dc-1}$). The logic underlying this relationship stems from the assumption regarding the lower degree of convertibility of the LDCs' currency. Positive relationships are expected.

(4) The Aggregate Supply Equation: $\dot{g}(\dot{Ms}, \dot{TV}, \dot{Pc}_{-1})$

The above function closes the model by adding the effects on growth of changes in trade volume, in the supply of money, and in the lagged prices of commodities. The changes in the supply of money incorporate the feedback effects of the other endogenous variables in the model, namely changes in the level of reserves and inflation. The effect is ambiguous: it may positively stimulate growth or it may cause a stagflation that only inflates the nominal value of growth without changing the real value ($\partial \dot{g} / \partial \dot{Ms}) \geq 0$.

The two other variables that affect growth, $\dot{TV}$ and $\dot{Pc}_{-1}$, capture the effect of international trade variations on growth. It is expected that growth varies directly with trade volume, ($\partial \dot{g} / \partial \dot{TV}) > 0$.

The change in the lagged prices of the traded commodities will affect the growth of DCs and LDCs differently. It will vary indirectly with DCs' growth and directly with LDCs' growth.

For developed countries this price variable also integrates the dependence of economic activity on the commodity imports. The lagged value is preferred to the unlagged one because (a) we assume that real effects of price changes on growth are felt with a lag only and that (b) stocks can exist in the importing countries, thus delaying the effects of changes in import prices.

The final simultaneous model:

$$\dot{Pd} = a_1 + b_{11}\dot{Pc} + b_{12}\dot{Ms} + b_{13}\dot{Ms}_{-1} + b_{14}\dot{Ms}_{-1} + b_{15}\dot{g} \qquad (7.1)$$

$$\dot{Ms} = a_2 + b_{21}\dot{Pd} + b_{22}\dot{Ms}_{-1} + b_{23}\dot{R} \qquad (7.2)$$

$$\dot{R1} = a_3 + b_{31}\dot{TV} + b_{32}\dot{Ms} + b_{33}\dot{g} \text{ (for DCs)} \qquad (7.3)$$

$$\dot{R1} = a_4 + b_{41}\dot{TV} + b_{32}\dot{Ms}_{dc} + b_{43}\dot{Pc} \text{ (for LDCs)} \qquad (7.3\text{-a})$$

$$\dot{g} = a_5 + b_{51}\dot{P}c_{-1} + b_{52}\dot{M}s + b_{53}\dot{T}V \qquad (7.4)$$

where $\dot{T}V$, $\dot{M}s_{-1}$, $\dot{M}s_{-2}$, $\dot{P}c$, $\dot{P}c_{-1}$ are exogenous variables; $\dot{M}s$, $\dot{R}$, $\dot{g}$, $\dot{P}d$ are endogenous variables; and dots denote annual rates of change.

## EMPIRICAL FINDINGS

The estimates of the model are presented and analyzed in this section. Since the effects of a commodity price shock are different in developed and in developing countries a distinction between the two has been made and the model estimated separately for each group of countries. The following simultaneous equation systems were estimated with a two-stage least-squares technique.

### Developed Countries

Table 7.1 shows the effect of changes in commodity prices on some of the economic variables for the aggregated group of developed economies. We distinguish between the direct effect of commodity prices (Pc) on domestic prices (Pd) and on economic growth (g) on the one hand and the indirect effects on money supply (Ms) and international reserves (R) and through them second-round effects on the other endogenous variables on the other.

From Table 7.1 it is apparent that commodity price changes generate higher rates of inflation and lower rates of economic growth for this group of countries. The effects are statistically significant. It is important to note that a negative effect on growth was found only when commodity price changes were introduced into the equation system with a one year lag. This finding is compatible with the commonly held belief that the effect of a commodity price shock on the level of economic activity is not immediate. Indeed, the deepest recession of the 1970s occurred in 1975, about one year after the oil commodity price boom.

The effect of commodity price changes on the rate of inflation in DCs reflects a part of the (short-run) upward shift of the Phillips curve. In theory such an external shock should result in a combination of faster inflation and higher unemployment, unless governments intervene with an expansionary monetary policy.[12] When this is the case the increase in unemployment could be spared or at least partly offset at the cost of still higher rates of inflation. The findings in Table 7.1 provide some insight into the process, that can be described as the following sequence of events.

A rise of commodity prices generates a higher rate of inflation, which increases the rate of change of money supply (equation (7.2)). After some time (one year approximately) unemployment rises as a result of the fall in the rate of economic growth (equation (7.4)). This change speeds up the rate of inflation (equation (7.1)), which again generates an increase in money supply changes. This last effect is followed by a partial

Table 7.1. The Effect of Commodity Price Shocks in the Developed Countries on the World Monetary System

| Independent variables | Dependent variables | | | | | | | |
|---|---|---|---|---|---|---|---|---|
| | $\dot{P}d$ | | $\dot{M}s$ | | $\dot{R}$ | | $\dot{g}$ | |
| | Coeff. | T | Coeff. | T | Coeff. | T | Coeff. | T |
| Endogenous variables | | | | | | | | |
| $\dot{P}d$ | – | – | 0.11 | 2.65 | – | – | – | – |
| $\dot{M}s$ | 0.84 | 0.72 | – | – | 0.52 | 2.59 | 0.84 | 1.59 |
| $\dot{R}$ | – | – | 0.21 | 2.13 | – | – | – | – |
| $\dot{g}$ | –0.051 | –1.97 | – | – | –0.25 | –1.74 | – | – |
| Exogenous variables | | | | | | | | |
| TV | – | – | – | – | 0.21 | 2.13 | 0.16 | 2.03 |
| $\dot{M}s-1$ | 1.17 | 2.49 | 0.87 | 1.98 | – | – | – | – |
| $\dot{M}s-2$ | 0.89 | 4.03 | – | – | – | – | – | – |
| $\dot{P}c$ | 0.053 | 2.72 | – | – | – | – | – | – |
| $\dot{P}c-1$ | – | – | – | – | – | – | –0.12 | –5.93 |
| Constant | 0.12 | 0.09 | 3.67 | 3.11 | 2.42 | 1.94 | –8.94 | –0.44 |
| $R^2$ | .812 | | .737 | | .846 | | .514 | |
| D.W. | 1.64 | | 2.34 | | 1.98 | | 1.87 | |

offset of the fall of economic growth (and the rise of unemployment). Since most DCs' currencies are fully convertible, the increase in their supply raises international liquidity. As suggested by Crockett, international liquidity is one of the main sources of international reserves.[13] Indeed, equation (7.3) shows that an increase in DCs' money supply creates additional international reserves in these countries. This, of course has a positive feedback effect on money supply (see equation (7.2)). In line with Heller's findings equation (7.2) shows a positive and significant effect of international reserves on money supply in DCs.[14] This effect has a repercussion on the level of inflation in the longer-run, implied by the fact that the lagged variable of money supply $Ms_{-1}$ has a stronger effect on inflation than the unlagged variable $Ms$. This finding is compatible with Heller's finding showing a positive relationship between international reserves and world inflation.

The model points out a complex interrelation between inflation and economic growth in the longer-run through the monetary system. A commodity supply price shock reduces the rate of growth of DCs (with a lagged effect), which creates an increase in the rate of accumulation of reserves. This in turn creates an increase in the rate of change of the money supply, which creates inflation on the one hand but reduces the slowdown of economic growth on the other.

Export restrictions on international commodity markets have two distinct effects on the DCs' monetary system and economic activity. The immediate response of the system is an accelerated rate of inflation and an expansion of money supply, which creates increased international liquidity and thus rising accumulation of reserves. At this stage the effect on real production is small and negligible. This phenomenon is explained by the existence of inventories of raw materials, which serve as buffers for the decline in production implied by quantitative disturbances of world commodity markets.

The description of this immediate response to commodity price shocks is backed up by data showing a rise of inflation rates, faster accumulation of international reserves, and practically no real change of the rate of growth and the levels of unemployment in 1974.

The real effect on economic activity generated by a supply shock appears in the longer-run as a prolonged effect. As time passes inventories cease to serve as a buffer from a slowdown in production. Signs of a recession appear and lead to a further acceleration of inflation, additional accumulation of reserves, and an additional rise in money supply, which somewhat offsets the deflationary effect on economic growth.

To sum up, commodity price shocks in general, and those initiated by export restrictions in particular, create an increased need for international and domestic liquidity. If this increment of liquidity is not provided (and there are usually antagonistic views regarding the expansion of money supply) then DCs fall into a state of stagflation accompanied with a decrease of their trade volume.

A major reservation to the above analysis should be stated at this point. The analysis is based on the signs of various coefficients in the equation model that are statistically significant. The magnitudes of the significant coefficients are such that they imply very mild effects (keep in mind that petroleum is excluded from the analysis). In other words, although export restrictions have a significant deteriorating effect on DCs' rates of inflation, money supply, economic growth, and so forth, this effect is not strong enough to impose a heavy burden in DCs' economies.

## Developing Countries

LDCs appear to be the major beneficiaries of export restrictions on commodity markets. An estimate of their impact on LDCs' economic growth, money supply and inflation will allow us to assess their efficiency as an instrument of economic growth.

In table 7.2 we present a model similar to the one presented in table 7.1. The main difference is that the equations in table 7.2 are estimates of the effect of commodity price changes on inflation, money supply, international reserves, and economic growth in LDCs. Commodity price changes have been introduced as an explanatory variable in the reserves equation and the DCs' money supply has been used as an independent variable in determining LDCs' changes in reserve accumulation.

Table 7.2. The Effect of Commodity Price Shocks in the Developing Countries on the World Monetary System

| Independent variables | Dependent variables | | | | | | | |
|---|---|---|---|---|---|---|---|---|
| | (1) $\dot{P}d$ | | (2) $\dot{M}s$ | | (3) $\dot{R}$ | | (4) $\dot{g}$ | |
| | Coeff. | T | Coeff. | T | Coeff. | T | Coeff. | T |
| Endogenous variables | | | | | | | | |
| $\dot{P}d$ | – | – | 0.71 | 2.12 | – | – | – | – |
| $\dot{M}s$ | 2.49 | 3.24 | – | – | – | – | -0.009 | -0.03 |
| $\dot{R}$ | – | – | 0.35 | 3.15 | – | – | – | – |
| $\dot{g}$ | 1.88 | 1.75 | – | – | 0.039 | 0.29 | – | – |
| Exogenous variables | | | | | | | | |
| $\dot{T}V$ | – | – | – | – | -0.042 | -0.11 | 1.08 | 2.32 |
| $\dot{M}s{-}1$ | – | – | 0.058 | 2.11 | – | – | – | – |
| $\dot{M}s{-}Dc$ | – | – | – | – | 2.81 | 2.67 | – | – |
| $\dot{P}c$ | -0.33 | -2.08 | – | – | 0.31 | 2.15 | – | – |
| $\dot{P}c{-}1$ | – | – | – | – | – | – | 0.017 | 2.18 |
| Constant | -14.17 | -2.28 | 3.69 | 1.58 | -10.57 | -1.39 | 4.775 | 3.41 |
| $R^2$ | .705 | | .823 | | .526 | | .621 | |
| D.W. | 1.84 | | 2.17 | | 2.46 | | 2.37 | |

The simultaneous equations system in table 7.2 shows an ambiguous effect of commodity price changes on the rate of inflation and the money supply in LDCs. We see in equation (7.1) that the direct effect of changes in the rate of change of prices on the domestic rate of inflation in LDCs is negative and significant. This finding appears surprising, although it should not be. In a theoretical analysis of export restrictions it is easy to show that when commodity prices rise on international markets due to export taxes or quotas in the exporting countries, the domestic commodity prices in the countries of origin are expected to fall. This is a result of excess supply of the commodities on their domestic markets. The counter-intuition stems from the fact that not all commodity price increases are generated by export restrictions. Nevertheless, most sharp commodity price changes are accompanied (at least in the longer-run) with export quantitative changes that create domestic supply surpluses. Thus, they affect the domestic prices in the opposite direction. This finding matches the hypothesis formulated by Nankani, implying that an increase in LDCs' export earnings is usually anti-inflationary.[15]

This is not the only effect of commodity international price changes on domestic inflation. An opposite effect is that which operates through reserves and money markets. A faster rate of commodity price changes increases the rate of reserves accumulation (equation 7.3), which results in a growth of the money supply (equation 7.2) which in turn creates additional inflationary pressure (equation 7.1).

The reserves equation (7.3) indicates a phenomenon of major importance. The only two variables significantly determining the level of reserves in LDCs are commodity international prices and the supply of money in the developed economies. This means that LDC reserve accumulation is in a sense an exogenous factor, depending on commodity prices, which are only partly determined by their policies, and by the DCs' money supply. We have previously seen that the DCs' supply of money reacts (indirectly) positively to changes of commodity prices. Now we see that some of the additional money supply in the developed world leaks not only to their own foreign reserves, but also to those of LDCs.

This, of course, creates additional domestic inflationary pressure in LDCs through the increased money supply initiated by an increase of reserves. In other words, the inflationary pressures in LDCs emerging from price shocks of their exported commodities depends on the following characteristics in DCs:

(a) The additional amount of inflation created in DCs as a result of a commodity price shock. Keep in mind that we assume that money supply is an endogenous variable that reacts to the rate of inflation. The magnitude of the inflationary effect of a commodity price shock depends on the proportion of total GNP or total resources these commodities constitute among the importing countries.

(b) The extent to which governments in DCs are eager to fight a potential recession caused by a commodity price boom by using monetary means. The expansion of money supply in DCs for this purpose creates additional inflation both in the developed and the developing exporting countries.

In the equation system relevant to DCs (table 7.1) no indication was found that commodity price changes cause a direct erosion of their foreign reseves. On the contrary, due to DCs increase of their money supply, a rise of reserves accumulation has been observed. On the other hand, we found in table 7.2 that LDCs' foreign reserves accumulation increases in periods of commodity price booms. These two findings when combined imply that the accumulation of reserves in LDCs is not a result of a transfer of reserves from DCs to LDCs but rather stems from the creation of new quantities of currency reserves in the DCs. Thus the increase of additional foreign reserves through export restrictions in LDCs did not occur at the expense of reserves in DCs, or at the cost of reducing international liquidity. The opposite is true and the cost was higher worldwide inflation and a mild slow down of economic activity in the DCs.

Finally, equation (4) in table 7.2 indicates that changes of commodity prices have a mild effect in the longer-run on the economic growth of LDCs. As can be seen, growth is more vigorously stimulated by an increase of trade volume. This finding hints to the well-known hypothesis that the cause of economic growth is served better when incentives are given to increase exports of manufacturers rather than artificially try to expand commodity export earnings. The last statement rests on the fact that for the last several decades the major contribution to export earnings growth in LDCs has been from manufactured goods.

## SUMMARY AND CONCLUSIONS

In this chapter an attempt has been made to estimate the monetary effects of a commodity price boom (excluding petroleum) and its implications for world inflation and economic growth. A distinction has been made between developed and developing economies. The direct and indirect commodity price effects were estimated with a simultaneous equation model for each of the country groups.

The econometric estimates show that a general commodity price has a direct and immediate effect on the rate of inflation in both developed and developing economies, but in opposite directions. While in DCs the general rise in commodity prices accelerates inflation, in LDCs it slows it down. Higher inflation in DCs generates an increase in the money supply, which results in an increase in international reserves in both DCs and LDCs. The result is a rise in the inflation rates. In DCs the rise is in addition to the initial price hike, while in LDCs it is a reversal of the initial decline in inflation rates.

In the longer-run the commodity price boom affects the rate of growth in both country groups: growth in LDCs accelerates while growth in DCs slows. These changes create a prolonged inflationary effect in both country groups. Thus, the income transfer effect possibly generated by export restrictions and commodity price shocks occurs in the longer-run as a phenomenon lagging after the implementation of the restrictive policy. This income redistribution is accompanied with inflation both in LDCs and DCs, and possibly with unemployment in DCs.

An important qualification of these findings is that, although they are statistically significant, they show a low magnitude of the effects. The real changes of income and economic growth created through the mechanism of commodity prices (excluding petroleum) are rather small, both for the importing DCs and the exporting LDCs. Thus, doubts are raised regarding the efficiency of this instrument to redistribute world income, especially in view of its undesirable inflationary effects, both in the short and in the longer-run.

APPENDIX: THE DATA

The empirical estimates are based on time series for the period 1960-1978. Data on world and domestic rates of inflation; primary commodity price index excluding petroleum; domestic money supply; and foreign reserves come from the IMF <u>International Financial Statistics</u>, various issues. Data on GDP and trade volume (total exports) were taken from UN: <u>Statistical Yearbook</u>, various issues.

NOTES

1. For a detailed analysis on the general performance of export restrictions in commodity markets, see chapter 2.
2. Similar cases can be found in recent times. For example, following the outbreak of the Korean war, raw material and farm prices increased sharply and income was transferred to developing countries that exported such commodities.
3. For a theoretical discussion on this subject, see chapter 6.
4. See Hume 1898.
5. This assumption is supported in another section of the article.
6. This argument is supported by Johnson 1977b and Frenkel and Johnson 1976.
7. On ratchet effects see Goldstein 1977 and Goldstein and Khan 1976.
8. See Crocket 1978 on liquidity and reserves.
9. Countries may accumulate reserves to finance payment imbalances when depreciation of currency is not desired; to serve as collateral for foreign borrowing; or to cover emergency situations such as war, uncertainty of economic and political development, etc.
10. See Frenkel and Johnson 1976.
11. For empirical evidence, see Heller 1976 and Khan 1979.
12. Phelps 1978, Bruno and Sachs 1979, Bruno 1982.
13. See Crockett 1978.
14. See Heller 1976.
15. See Nankani 1979.

REFERENCES

Adams, J.F. 1979. Must High Commodity Prices Depress the World Economy? An Appraisal of a World Monetary System. Journal of Policy Modeling 1: 201-15.
Brunner, K., and Meltzer, A., eds. 1976, Institutional Policies, Economic Performance. Amsterdam: North Holland.
Bruno, M. 1982. Adjustment and Structural Change under Supply Shocks. Institute for International Economic Studies S-106 91 Stockholm.
Bruno, M. and Sachs, J. 1979. Macro-Economic Adjustment with Import Price Shocks: Real and Monetary Aspects. Discussion paper No. 793. Jerusalem: The Maurice Falk Institute.
Crockett, A.D. 1978. Control over International Reserves. IMF Staff Papers 25: 1-24.
Findlay, R., and Rodriguez, C.A. 1977. Intermediate Imports and Macroeconomic Policy under Flexible Exchange Rates. Canadian Journal of Economics 2: 208-17.
Frenkel, J.A. and Johnson, H.G., eds. 1976. The Monetary Approach to the Balance of Payments. London: George Allen and Unwin.
Friedman, M. 1956. The Quantity Theory of Money Restatement. In Studies in the Quantity Theory of Money, edited by Milton Friedman, 3-21. Chicago. University of Chicago Press.
Goldstein, M. 1977. Downward Price Inflexibility, Ratchet Effects and the Inflationary Impact on Import Price Changes: Some Empirical Tests. IMF Staff Papers 24: 569-612.
Goldstein, M. and Khan, M.S. 1976. Large Versus Small Price Changes and the Demand for Imports. IMF Staff Papers 23: 200-25.
Gordon, R.J. 1975. Alternative Responses of Policy to External Supply Shocks. Brookings Papers on Economic Activity 6: 183-206.
Heller, R.H. 1976. International Reserves and World Wide Inflation. IMF Staff papers 23: 61-87.
Heller, R.H. and Khan, M.S. 1978. The Demand for International Reserves Under Fixed and Floating Exchange Rates. IMF Staff Papers 25: 623-49.
Hume, D. 1898. Of the Balance of Trade. In Essays, Moral, Political, and Literary. Vol. 1, 330-45. London: Longmans Green.
Johnson, H.G. 1977. Commodities, LDCs' Demands and DCs' Responses. In The New International Economic Order: The North-South Debate, edited by J. Bhagwati, 240-51. London: MIT Press.
Johnson, H.G. 1977. Money, Balance of Payments Theory, and the International Monetary Problem. Princeton University - International Finance Section.
Khan, M.S. 1979. Inflation and International Reserves: A Time-series Analysis. IMF Staff Papers 26: 699-724.
Nankani, G. 1979. Development Problems of Mineral Exporting Countries. World Bank Working Paper No. 354. Washington, D.C.: The World Bank.

Phelps, E.S. 1978. Commodity Supply Shock and Full Employment Monetary Policy. Journal of Money, Credit, and Banking 10: 206-22.
Poole, W. 1975. Monetary Policy during the Recession. Brookings Papers on Economic Activity 6: 123-39.
Van Duyne, C. 1979. The Macroeconomic Effects of Commodity Market Disruptions in Open Economies. Journal of International Economic 9: 559-82.
Williamson, J. 1973. Surveys in Applied Economies: International Liquidity. Economic Journal 83: 685-746.

# 8
# Exports from LDCs:
# Impacts on Economic Growth

*J. Weinblatt*
*Nora Schrager*

## 1. INTRODUCTION

The controversy over the issue of trade and development calls for an overview of the problem at its general aggregative level. The policy prescriptions are mostly general and apparently relevant to the comprehensive problems of developing countries. In the international forums the debates are on general issues and the decisions that are taken are of a broad nature. On the other hand, most economic studies of trade and development, and especially of exports from LDCs, are specific and deal with distinct commodity groups. It is true that most of the problems are of a microeconomic nature. However, in order to match research with the frequent policy recommendations it seems worthwhile to have a macroeconomic look at exports from developing countries. This is the approach adopted here.

We try to draw a general picture of the patterns of exports from LDCs by focusing on aggregate variables. We analyze the LDCs as one unit and observe both their total exports and their exports of large commodity groups.

In section 2 we analyze trends of exports from LDCs in the 1970s, distinguishing between exports to developed countries and to LDCs. In section 3 the analysis is refined by using a simultaneous econometric system to estimate world demand and supply elasticities for the large commodity groups. We estimate the contribution of the exports of these commodity groups on the growth and development of LDCs.

## 2. TRENDS IN LDCs' EXPORTS IN THE 1970s

### Shares in World Trade

The structure of LDCs' exports has always been characterized by a heavy concentration in primary commodities. As noted by Bhagwati, in spite of the substantial changes in the political structure of the world during the last thirty years, the nature of North-South economic relations has remained similar to that prevailing during the preceding centuries.[1] In other words, the process of decolonization had very little effect on the patterns of trade that existed during the colonial period. The developed economies remain for the most part the main producers and exporters of processed manufactured goods, while the ex-colonies continue to supply the DCs with primary commodities - basic food and minerals.

In Appendix 1 a list of LDCs is presented with the share of 33 main primary commodities in their individual exports. The figures in this list indicate that for the majority of LDCs most exports are concentrated in one of few primary goods. For most countries appearing in this list, the share of 33 primary commodities in their total exports is above 60 percent and reaches as high as 98 percent. The high commodity concentration is, of course, a source of major trade and development problems. Prices of primary commodities tend to be unstable, thus leading to serious instability of export earnings for the producing countries.

In addition to their chronic instability, exports of LDCs have been declining in relative terms since 1945. The LDCs' share of world trade fell from 35 percent in 1950 to approximately 18 percent in the early 1970s.[2] This trend is often attributed to the deterioration in LDCs' terms of trade. A fact that reinforces this claim is the apparent reversal in this secular trend during the 1970s. Table 8.1 shows that LDCs' share of total exports to developed market economies increased sharply in 1974 to 29.5 percent and was followed by years during which the share fluctuated between 26 and 31 percent. This new trend was accompanied by a sharp rise of primary commodity prices in 1974, which provides at least a partial explanation of the change in LDCs' weight in world exports.

Table 8.1 Share of Developing Countries' Exports in Total Exports Market Economies to Developed Market Economies (in percent)

|  | Food | Raw Materials | Manufactures | Total |
| --- | --- | --- | --- | --- |
| 1970 | 35.7 | 30.4 | 6.6 | 18.7 |
| 1971 | 32.2 | 29.6 | 6.2 | 18.5 |
| 1972 | 29.2 | 30.2 | 6.5 | 18.6 |
| 1973 | 28.8 | 29.2 | 7.6 | 20.2 |
| 1974 | 31.7 | 30.7 | 7.9 | 29.5 |
| 1975 | 28.1 | 29.5 | 7.3 | 26.7 |
| 1976 | 30.5 | 29.8 | 8.4 | 28.3 |
| 1977 | 34.9 | 30.4 | 9.4 | 28.3 |
| 1978 | 31.1 | 29.8 | 9.7 | 25.7 |
| 1979 | 30.1 | 31.0 | 10.3 | 27.9 |
| 1980 | 28.6 | 30.9 | 10.7 | 30.9 |

Source: UN Statistical Yearbook, 1982.

Although LDCs' share of total exports rose between 1970 and 1976, their share in food exports showed a slight decline and their share in raw materials exports remained more or less constant. Only manufactured goods experienced a relative rise in exports.

It must be kept in mind that the shares presented in table 8.1 were computed from current values of exports, thus the changes incorporate both price and quantity changes. While changes in food and raw materials shares could be attributed mainly to price changes, changes in manufactures shares could be attributed both to price and quantity changes, but mainly to the latter. This is the continuation of a trend that started earlier when LDC manufactures exports rose by 253 percent (from $4 billion to $14 billion) between 1960 and 1970, while their exports of food products rose by only 58 percent.[3] This trend was probably helped by tariff reductions in MDCs.

Table 8.1 reveals the fact that the share of food exports was falling throughout the 1970s while the share of raw materials remained constant. If we recall that this period was characterized by rising prices of primary commodities we cannot avoid the conclusion that price shocks in the food and agricultural sectors led to a quick shift in the importing countries to domestic substitutes. This did not occur in the raw materials sectors, where the search for substitutes is more complex and requires longer periods of adjustment. This points out one of the limitations of cartelization and price raising of agricultural commodities as a device for transferring income from MDCs to LDCs.

Appendix 1 shows that primary goods are a major and sometimes overwhelming source of export earnings for LDCs. This may suggest that they could use their "commodity power" to increase their real income through cartelization and the creation of international commodity agreements. This idea, though a possible solution for a few countries that are large exporters of some specific commodities, is not a general solution for the problem of poverty and unequal income distribution in the world.[4] As Low writes, "controls used in an attempt to boost price levels and redistribute income constitute an inferior form of aid...When longer periods are considered, most have also failed to transfer resources and improve the economic conditions of producing lands."[5] This situation stems from the fact that LDCs in total do not face demand price elasticities that are suitable for controls of this kind. One reason is that on average their share constitutes only about 30 percent of world exports of primary goods (see table 8.1). In other words, although primary commodities are the most important source of export earnings for LDCs, in general they do not produce enough of them to control world prices and trade. Thus, their ability to limit the access to commodity markets is relatively low.[6]

## Quantities Prices and Values

We now turn to observe trends of LDCs exports in a more detailed manner and to relate them to events in the world economy. The quantum index of exports presented in table 8.2 shows a general upward trend during the 1970s: total real exports rose by 62 pecent between 1970 and 1976. This trend was temporarily interrupted in 1975, due to the world recession, during which the GDP of developed countries did not grow (see table 8.4) and world trade suffered a substantial decrease of 3 percent. The breakdown of total LDCs' exports into three major component groups - food, raw materials, and manufactures - reveals that in the period analyzed food exports rose in quantity terms by 32 percent, raw materials by 32 percent and manufactures by 172 percent.

Table 8.2 Exports Quantum Indices of Flows from Developing to All Market Economies

|      | Food | Raw materials (exc. petroleum) | Manufactures | Total |
|------|------|--------------------------------|--------------|-------|
| 1970 | 100  | 100 | 100 | 100 |
| 1971 | 102  | 102 | 107 | 102 |
| 1972 | 109  | 112 | 128 | 114 |
| 1973 | 115  | 120 | 149 | 127 |
| 1974 | 105  | 118 | 167 | 130 |
| 1975 | 112  | 105 | 169 | 122 |
| 1976 | 122  | 106 | 205 | 140 |
| 1977 | 118  | 108 | 213 | 143 |
| 1978 | 122  | 111 | 238 | 150 |
| 1979 | 128  | 123 | 266 | 164 |
| 1980 | 132  | 132 | 272 | 162 |

Source: UN *Statistical Yearbook*, 1982.

Of the three export groups, food and raw materials suffered serious setbacks during the recession of the mid-1970s. In spite of the sharp price rises of both food and raw materials in 1974, the decline in raw material quantities exported occurred in 1975, a full year after the decline in food exports. This hints again to the different market structure of the two commodity groups. Food, being a consumer good, faces a fast reaction by buyers to large price changes. This is in addition to the possible longer-run effect of potential producers in developed economies to react to world price changes (the cobweb effect) by increasing the production of substitutes for the imports from LDCs. Raw materials exports face a slower reaction to price changes. It is not smaller in its order of magnitude, however.

During the period analyzed, the LDCs' quantities of manufactures exported grew more than that of primary goods.

Manufactures suffered less from world recession than food and raw materials and this can be considered a more stable and certain component of LDCs' exports. The comparison between the trends of the three commodity groups leaves no doubt about the ongoing process of industrialization in LDCs, which finds expression in the composition of their exports. We have too little information here to determine whether this industrialization is carried out through the further processing of available raw materials or in other fields. In any case, this trend of a growing share of manufactures in LDCs' exports prevailed despite the fact that prices of manufactures were rising at a slower pace than prices of primary goods (see table 8.3). Thus, one could conclude that manufactures exports have increased mainly due to positive shifts in supply and increasing competitiveness, rather than as a result of substantial changes in demand.[7]

Table 8.3  Exports Unit Value Indices of Flows from Developing Countries to All Market Economies

|  | Food | Raw Materials | Manufactures | Total |
|---|---|---|---|---|
| 1970 | 100 | 100 | 100 | 100 |
| 1971 | 100 | 97 | 99 | 108 |
| 1972 | 109 | 105 | 104 | 116 |
| 1973 | 138 | 140 | 141 | 156 |
| 1974 | 204 | 192 | 173 | 318 |
| 1975 | 195 | 181 | 167 | 311 |
| 1976 | 204 | 208 | 176 | 330 |
| 1977 | 267 | 221 | 202 | 371 |
| 1978 | 270 | 234 | 226 | 373 |
| 1979 | 289 | 283 | 264 | 474 |
| 1980 | 305 | 299 | 312 | 641 |

Source:  UN *Statistical Yearbook*, 1982.

We now turn to export price changes. As can be seen in table 8.3 sharp price increases occurred in 1973 and 1974. The drastic change in the value of the total export unit in 1974 is explained largely by the increase in petroleum prices. Nevertheless, prices of food and raw materials also rose substantially and they, together with petroleum, explain the world stagflation of 1974-1975.[8]

Prices of primary commodities rose during the 1970-1976 period faster than world prices, which were apparently pushed up by them. In the early 1970s, world inflation was moderated by a relatively low increase in primary commodity prices. This effect was reversed after 1973. Bearing in mind that prices of primary commodities and of final goods are mutually dependent, it is

Table 8.4 World GDP, GDP per Capita,* and Consumer Price Index (CPI) 1970 - 100

| Year | Developed Economies | | Developing economies | | C P I |
|------|------|------|------|------|------|
| | G D P (1) | GDP per capita (2) | G D P (3) | GDP per capita (4) | (5) |
| 1970 | 100 | 100 | 100 | 100 | 100 |
| 1971 | 104 | 103 | 104 | 102 | 106 |
| 1972 | 109 | 107 | 110 | 106 | 112 |
| 1973 | 116 | 113 | 118 | 111 | 124 |
| 1974 | 116 | 112 | 119 | 110 | 143 |
| 1975 | 116 | 111 | 118 | 107 | 161 |
| 1976 | 122 | 116 | 124 | 110 | 178 |
| 1977 | 126 | 119 | 132 | 112 | 201 |
| 1978 | 131 | 122 | 137 | 117 | 229 |
| 1979 | 136 | 126 | 145 | 120 | 257 |
| 1980 | 137 | 127 | 151 | 122 | 291 |

*Measured at fixed prices.
Sources: Columns (1), (2), (3), (4) - UN Statistical Yearbook (1982)
Column (5) - IMF: International Financial Statistics (1982).

impossible always to attribute a part of world inflation or all of it to changes in prices of raw materials. It could well be that rises in primary commodity prices are a lagging reaction to an earlier world inflation and hence are just an adjustment of relative prices that were temporarily disturbed by a world price fluctuation. Thus, when world inflation is attributed (at least partly) to changes in commodity prices this is arithmetically correct. However, a deep and serious search for genuine causality could in some cases reverse the sequence of effects.

The combination of rising export prices with growing quantities exported leads to a significant growth of exports values. The changes in the value of exports from LDCs during the period between 1970 and 1980 are shown in table 8.5. Total exports value increased during the period analyzed by 941 percent. This figure is somewhat misleading because it includes petroleum. The breakdown of exports excluding petroleum shows a growth in exports values of all components, but mainly in exported manufactures. Thus, in spite of a rate of price changes lower than that for primary commodities, the importance of manufactures as a source of exports earnings increased. This is due to the fast rate of growth of the quantities of manufactures exported.

Table 8.5 Total Value Indices of Export Flows from LDCs to all Market Economies

| | Food | Raw materials (exc. petroleum) | Manufactures | Total |
|---|---|---|---|---|
| 1970 | 100 | 100 | 100 | 100 |
| 1971 | 101 | 98 | 106 | 110 |
| 1972 | 119 | 117 | 132 | 132 |
| 1973 | 159 | 168 | 210 | 198 |
| 1974 | 210 | 224 | 288 | 414 |
| 1975 | 217 | 191 | 281 | 379 |
| 1976 | 248 | 220 | 361 | 460 |
| 1977 | 308 | 233 | 415 | 533 |
| 1978 | 316 | 255 | 523 | 559 |
| 1979 | 358 | 344 | 677 | 772 |
| 1980 | 392 | 388 | 815 | 1041 |

Source: UN Statistical Yearbook, 1982.

A major policy implication results from the above description. Primary commodities are still the major source of export earnings for LDCs, yet if the trends of recent years continue, the importance of manufactures will increase and eventually they will become the main source of foreign exchange. Therefore, a more logical way to increase LDCs' exports earnings is by accelerating exports of manufactures, which do not face elasticity problems and other drawbacks connected with the manipulation of primary commodities exports.

The analysis of trends in exports directions from LDCs indicates several interesting developments. Table 8.6 shows that the LDCs' share in developed countries' imports value increased during the 1970s. This fact represents mainly the increasing value of petroleum in international trade; the weight of LDCs in total export values of food and raw materials to developed market economies has been falling. The latter trend is partly explicable by the rapidly rising prices of primary goods and the shift in MDCs to substitutes, produced in their own developed economies. The only component of LDCs' exports to DCs growing more rapidly than world exports to MDCs is manufactures. There is a clear trend indicating the increasing weight of LDCs in developed countries' imports of manufactures. This weight is still very low but growing significantly from 6.4 percent in 1970 to 10.7 percent in 1980. Once again the statistics support the case for industrialization of exports as a device to increase export earnings.

Table 8.6    Exports Value Indices of Flows.

| | Food | Raw materials (exc. petroleum) | Manufactures | Total |
|---|---|---|---|---|
| A. From All Market Economies to Developed Market Economies | | | | |
| 1970 | 100 | 100 | 100 | 100 |
| 1971 | 108 | 99 | 112 | 111 |
| 1972 | 132 | 115 | 134 | 133 |
| 1973 | 183 | 171 | 180 | 183 |
| 1974 | 213 | 217 | 230 | 264 |
| 1975 | 227 | 186 | 229 | 257 |
| 1976 | 255 | 219 | 266 | 299 |
| 1977 | 289 | 237 | 305 | 338 |
| 1978 | 331 | 258 | 371 | 391 |
| 1979 | 383 | 341 | 467 | 503 |
| 1980 | 413 | 379 | 529 | 604 |
| B. From LDCs to Developed Market Economies | | | | |
| 1970 | 100 | 100 | 100 | 100 |
| 1971 | 98 | 97 | 103 | 109 |
| 1972 | 116 | 113 | 129 | 130 |
| 1973 | 153 | 163 | 208 | 194 |
| 1974 | 191 | 221 | 273 | 409 |
| 1975 | 184 | 117 | 249 | 360 |
| 1976 | 228 | 209 | 336 | 443 |
| 1977 | 290 | 228 | 388 | 507 |
| 1978 | 300 | 242 | 488 | 535 |
| 1979 | 330 | 328 | 644 | 732 |
| 1980 | 340 | 371 | 733 | 980 |

Source:   UN Statistical Yearbook, 1982.

To complete the review of trends in LDCs' exports, we must observe the development of trade among LDCs. Table 8.7 shows that trade among LDCs increased substantially in terms of values, quantities, and prices. A comparison of table 8.6 with table 8.2 shows that quantities exported by LDCs have grown faster than from the LDCs to all market economies. This is true not only for manufactures but also for food and raw materials.

Between 1970 and 1980 trade in manufactures among LDCs rose from 37 percent to 60 percent of total manufacture exports from LDCs. Moreover, the absolute money values of intra-LDC trade reached $15 billion in 1975, approximately equivalent to the total value of raw materials exported from LDCs to the rest of the world. These facts probably indicate a kind of Linder process that is developing in the trade of LDCs.[9]

Linder's hypothesis implies that bilateral trade is larger and more similar in its composition the more similar are the patterns of demand of the countries involved. Similarity of demand patterns is usually measured in terms of income per capita. Hufbauer, in a test of Linder's hypothesis, found that it explained trade among DCs, but found no evidence that trade among LDCs behaved along the lines Linder anticipated.[10] Hufbauer's test was carried out on 1965 trade data when only 26 percent of LDCs total manufactures exports were directed to LDCs. Since then there has been a great rise of this trade, indicating the development of a Linder process. This kind of evolution raises a major policy implication. If trade among LDCs is becoming more and more industrial and similar in its composition, then the chances for successful economic integration between them is increasing. Economic integration among exporters of primary commodities is almost meaningless. The only advantage it could provide to the countries involved is the possibility to produce on larger scales of production, thus stimulating economic growth. However, countries with similar patterns of industrial production and exports and with industrial sectors of substantial size could gain from integration by trade creation (among themselves) and hence in economic growth and increased industrial performance.

Intra-LDCs trade of food and raw materials grew significantly during the 1970s both in quantities and values (see table 8.7). It exceeded by a reasonable degree the growth rates of exports of these commodity groups from LDCs to the rest of the world. Thus, the share of LDCs in world imports of food and raw material is constantly increasing, having risen from 6.8 percent in 1970 to 12.0 percent in 1980. This fact inflicts an additional constraint on the possible manipulation by LDCs of primary commodity exports to promote their export earnings. The attempt to restrict exports of primary commodities by LDCs will (if the general trend continues) transfer less and less income from DCs to LDCs and more and more from one LDC to another. Thus, LDCs are becoming more and more vulnerable to possible interference in commodity markets by other LDCs. This is one expression of the possible conflict of interests between LDCs and its intensification cannot promote the well-being of the whole group of LDCs or a part of it. On the contrary, the figures suggest that cooperation and integration among LDCs seem to be a more promising policy to achieve economic growth.

Table 8.7  Exports from LDCs to LDCs

|  | Food | Raw materials (exc. petroleum) | Manufactures | Total |
|---|---|---|---|---|
| A. Unit Value Indices | | | | |
| 1970 | 100 | 100 | 100 | 100 |
| 1971 | 100 | 102 | 103 | 111 |
| 1972 | 108 | 107 | 108 | 116 |
| 1973 | 140 | 139 | 140 | 154 |
| 1974 | 200 | 180 | 177 | 295 |
| 1975 | 196 | 189 | 173 | 289 |
| 1976 | 205 | 206 | 182 | 311 |
| 1977 | 266 | 234 | 206 | 350 |
| 1978 | 270 | 238 | 232 | 349 |
| 1979 | 299 | 289 | 266 | 435 |
| 1980 | 326 | 306 | 328 | 577 |
| B. Total Value Indices | | | | |
| 1970 | 100 | 100 | 100 | 100 |
| 1971 | 114 | 106 | 114 | 109 |
| 1972 | 133 | 125 | 138 | 128 |
| 1973 | 185 | 193 | 209 | 210 |
| 1974 | 299 | 237 | 329 | 405 |
| 1975 | 319 | 231 | 353 | 411 |
| 1976 | 338 | 275 | 435 | 483 |
| 1977 | 400 | 312 | 513 | 627 |
| 1978 | 425 | 375 | 622 | 645 |
| 1979 | 525 | 525 | 838 | 918 |
| 1980 | 650 | 600 | 1054 | 1263 |
| C. Quantum Indices | | | | |
| 1970 | 100 | 100 | 100 | 100 |
| 1971 | 114 | 100 | 110 | 106 |
| 1972 | 125 | 117 | 137 | 120 |
| 1973 | 133 | 137 | 151 | 135 |
| 1974 | 150 | 131 | 187 | 148 |
| 1975 | 174 | 126 | 213 | 155 |
| 1976 | 168 | 132 | 236 | 169 |
| 1977 | 144 | 143 | 250 | 173 |
| 1978 | 150 | 164 | 273 | 182 |
| 1979 | 169 | 182 | 322 | 208 |
| 1980 | 193 | 187 | 338 | 215 |

Source:  UN Statistical Yearbook (1982).

## 3. REGRESSION ANALYSIS

In order to refine the analysis of exports from LDCs and their impact on economic growth we turn to regression analysis.

### The Method

In this section we attempt to characterize LDC exports in a general framework. We proceed with the analysis of all LDCs as one unit. When dealing with the destination of exports, we distinguish between LDCs and DCs. Exported commodities are broken down into five commodity groups as in the previous section and the one-digit code is adopted.

The selected commodity groups for the analysis are:

| One digit SITC code | Commodity group |
|---|---|
| 0,1 | Food |
| 2,4 | Raw materials, excluding fuel |
| 5 | Chemicals |
| 7 | Machinery |
| 6,8 | Other manufactures |

The statistical work for all variables is based on time series for the period between 1960 and 1976. The source for all the data is the UN *Statistical Yearbook*, 1982.

Simultaneous equation sets are computed for each of the above commodity groups. The demand equation is given by:

$$P_{ij} = \alpha_0 + \beta_0 X_{ij} + \beta_1 P_1^W + \beta_2 GNPM + \beta_3 D_{ij} + \beta_4 DX_{ij} + \quad (8.1)$$
$$+ \beta_5 DGNPM + \varepsilon_i$$

where

$P_{ij}$ = export unit value of commodity group i to country group j;

$X_{ij}$ = export value of commodity group i to country group j measured at constant prices of 1970;

$P_i^W$ = world export unit value of commodity i;

GNPM = GNP of importing countries;

$D_{ij}$ = dummy variable for the intercept = 0 for developed country of destination; = 1 for developing country of destination;

$DX_{ij}$ = dummy variable for the coefficient of $X_{ij} - \beta_0$.

DGNPM = dummy variable for the coefficient of GNPM $- \beta_1$.

This equation is estimated by using a pooling method combining time series with cross sectional data on the destination of

exports. Two possible destinations are accounted for--the group of developed market economies and the group of LDCs.
The supply equation is given by:

$$X_i = a_0 + b_0 P_i + b_1 X_i^w + b_2 GNPX + e_i \qquad (8.2)$$

where
$X_i$ = export value (at constant prices) from LDCs to the rest of the world;
$P_i$ = export unit value of $X_i$;
$X_i^w$ = world exports (at constant prices) of i;
GNPX = GNP of the exporting (developing) countries.

Economic growth equation is captured by equation (8.3):

$$GNPX = A + B_0 P_i + B_2 X_i + B_3 T + E_i, \qquad (8.3)$$

where T = time variable accounting for the changes of GNP independent from exports (prices and quantities) of commodity group i.

The three equations are estimated for each of the commodity groups with a two-stage least squares technique.
The three-equation system allows us to examine some of the issues related to export policies of developing countries. The demand and supply equations make it possible to estimate price and income elasticities of demand and price elasticities of supply at a general level. The economic growth equations reveal the relationship between export prices and quantities and the level of GNP for the exporting countries. We have not attempted to identify causation with respect to growth and exports. Both hypotheses--trade promotes growth versus growth promotes trade-- are consistent with a positive relationship between growth and exports. Here we examine the mechanism that relates the two, ignoring the question of causation. Is real GDP affected to a greater degree by export price changes or by export quantity changes? The answer depends on the nature of the exported commodities and on their world market structure. When both price and quantity are positively and significantly related to real GNP the exported commodity tends to lead to economic growth and the exporting country has little control over its world prices. Thus, an increase in quantity generated in the exporting economy and/or a world price rise initiated by forces on world markets both contribute to economic growth. When real GDP is positively related to price changes of the exported good and not to quantity changes price changes that are initiated outside the economy tend to stimulate a growth of real exports value and of GDP. However, quantum changes of exports in one sector could hold back economic growth or affect it negatively, especially if the induced structural changes are not in favor of comparative advantages.

Estimates of five distinct equation systems (one for each of the selected commodity groups) their analysis, and implications are presented in the next two subsections.

Results for Food and Raw Materials

As shown in the previous section, primary commodities constitute both the largest and the most problematic component of LDCs' exports. Markets for primary commodities are considered to be unstable due to inelasticities of demand and supply. They create the temptation for sellers to monopolize their sales and reduce quantities. In the dynamic context, they represent a declining sector due to their decreasing share in world exports.

Systems of equations representing demand, supply, and the contribution to growth of the two commodity groups are presented in table 8.8.

Table 8.8   Simultaneous Equations and $R^2$ Results for Demand, Supply, and Growth of Food and Raw Materials*

F O O D

Demand Equation

$$\ln P_{ij} = 0.004 \text{ GNPM} - 1.21 \ln X_{ij} + 0.79 P_i^w - 1.13 D_{ij} +$$

$$(2.24) \quad\quad (-2.94) \quad\quad (5.69) \quad (-2.61)$$

$$+ 0.02 \text{ DGNPM} - 0.27 \text{ DX}_{ij} + 2.38$$

$$(2.38) \quad\quad (-2.20) \quad\quad (1.8)$$

$R^2 = 0.983$

Supply Equation

$$\ln X_{ij} = 0.20 \ln P_{ij} + 0.08 \text{ GNPX} - 0.09 X_i^w + 6.95$$

$$(1.21) \quad\quad (0.21) \quad\quad (2.45) \quad (3.75)$$

$R^2 = 0.363$

Growth Equation

$$\text{GNPX} = 11.84 \ln P_{ij} + 0.08 \ln X_{ij} + 5.06 \text{ T} + 4.65$$

$$(13.35) \quad\quad (0.43) \quad\quad (70.39) \quad (1.26)$$

$R^2 = 0.991$

RAW MATERIALS

Demand Equation

$$\ln P_{ij} = 0.0003 \text{ GNPM} - 0.48 \ln X_{ij} + 1.12 P_i^w + -0.37 D_{ij} +$$
$$\phantom{\ln P_{ij} = } (1.98) \phantom{xxx} (-2.81) \phantom{xxxx} (22.34) \phantom{xx} (-0.99)$$

$$+ 0.001 \text{ DGNPM} - 0.29 DX_{ij} + 4.64$$
$$\phantom{+} (1.64) \phantom{xxxxx} (1.88) \phantom{xxx} (1.58)$$

$R^2 = 0.995$

Supply Equation

$$\ln X_{ij} = 0.14 \ln P_{ij} + 0.03 \text{ GNPX} + 1.32 X_i^w + 3.64$$
$$\phantom{\ln X_{ij} = } (0.936) \phantom{xxx} (0.09) \phantom{xxxx} (1.83) \phantom{xx} (2.94)$$

$R^2 = 0.283$

Growth Equation

$$\text{GNPX} = 11.74 \ln P_{ij} + 0.009 \ln X_{ij} + 5.21 T + 3.76$$
$$\phantom{\text{GNPX} = } (12.92) \phantom{xxx} (0.048) \phantom{xxx} (79.57) \phantom{x} (0.96)$$

$R^2 = 0.993$

*Figures in parentheses are t statistics

From the two demand equations it is easy to compute short (medium) run price and income elasticities of demand in developed and developing economies.

Table 8.9  Price and Income Elasticities for Food and Raw Materials

| Commodity | Price elasticity | | Income elasticity | |
|---|---|---|---|---|
| | DC | LDC | DC | LDC |
| Food | 0.81 | 0.67 | 0.69 | 0.64 |
| Raw Materials | 2.08 | 1.29 | 0.75 | 0.62 |

Of course, these are aggregate elasticities for very large commodity groups. Nevertheless, they can serve to assess the possible impacts of general exports policies. We see that price elasticities are slightly below one for food and significantly above one for the group of raw materials. In both cases the price elasticity of demand is higher in the developed economies. These estimates partially coincide with other more detailed findings.[11] The findings accentuate the general limitations of export restrictions policies as a device to increase exports earnings. The estimated price elasticities imply that earnings might be increased by cartelizing exports of food, but such a possibility is very limited and the major victims would be LDCs. The high price elasticities for raw materials rule out this kind of policy for this commodity group. It is true that there are specific commodities both in the food and in the raw materials group for which export restrictions could be profitable for the exporting countries. Nevertheless, the findings show that this could not be a general type of policy applied across the board on most or all primary commodities.

As expected the coefficients of the dummy variables for the intercepts ($D_{ij}$) show that LDCs are smaller demanders (importers) of food and raw materials from other LDCs than the DCs. Changes of world food and raw materials prices increase the demand for exports of these commodities from LDCs. The relationship is stronger for raw materials than for food. This phenomenon could be due to the fact that raw materials can be stockpiled to a greater extent than food.

The two supply equations indicate a rather rigid relationship between prices and supplied quantities. In both cases the price elasticity of supply is very low and statistically insignificant and can thus be assumed to be close to zero in the short-run.

The growth equations show an interesting relationship between the level of GNP and exports of the two commodity groups for LDCs. In both cases the time trend has strong and significant coefficients. Hence, exogenous factors, correlated with time and represented by T, substantially affect the level of GNP. Moreover, in both cases quantities obtain insignificant coefficients while export prices of the commodity groups are significantly and positively related to the level of national income. This finding indicates that in general it is almost impossible for LDCs to stimulate economic growth by manipulating the quantities of primary commodities exported. By observing also the two demand equations, we see that the demand price elasticity for food is probably not low enough to justify **restrictions** that have the **purpose** of stimulating economic growth. The relatively high price elasticity of demand for raw materials implies that an increase of exported quantities could raise export earnings. However, when combining this implication with the finding in the growth equations the logical deduction is that the incentives for growth are probably better when other sectors expand and increase their exports. In the cases of both food and raw materials, when export prices originate outside the economies, e.g., due to a price shock such as that of 1973, the terms of trade are externally improved and the level of real GNP rises.

Results for Manufactures

Equation sets of the type presented in the previous subsection are exhibited below for three main groups of manufactures.

Table 8.10 Simultaneous Equations and $R^2$ Results for Demand, Supply and Growth of Chemicals, Machinery, and Other Manufactures*

CHEMICALS

Demand Equation

$$\ln P_{ij} = 0.013 \text{ GNPM} - 0.42 \ln X_{ij} + 0.94 P_i^W - 2.64 D_{ij} - 3.24$$

$$(2.37) \qquad (-1.75) \qquad (4.81) \qquad (1.64) \qquad (1.89)$$

$R^2 = 0.968$

Supply Equation

$$\ln X_{ij} = 0.55 \ln P_{ij} + 0.014 \text{GNPX} + 0.61 X_i^W - 0.23$$

$$(3.06) \qquad (5.85) \qquad (4.86) \qquad (0.29)$$

$R^2 = 0.979$

Growth Equation

$$\text{GNP} = 2.32 \ln P_{ij} + 3.61 \ln X_{ij} + 4.37 T + 17.91$$

$$(6.20) \qquad (2.96) \qquad (17.19) \qquad (1.86)$$

$R^2 = 0.997$

MACHINERY

Demand Equation

$$\ln P_{ij} = 0.11 \text{ GNPM} - 0.22 \ln X_{ij} + 0.24 P_i^W + 0.10 D_{ij}$$

$$(1.86) \qquad (-2.02) \qquad (2.11) \qquad (1.82)$$

$R^2 = 0.887$

Supply Equation

$$\ln X_{ij} = 0.23 \ln P_{ij} + 0.23 \text{ GNPX} - 4.81$$
$$(2.12) \qquad (3.76) \qquad (-2.28)$$

$R^2 = 0.869$

Growth Equation

$$\text{GNP} = 1.48 \ln P_{ij} + 2.36 \ln X_{ij} + 4.69 \text{ T} + 16.31$$
$$(4.14) \qquad (2.95) \qquad (25.22) \quad (1.63)$$

$R^2 = 0.986$

OTHER MANUFACTURES

Demand Equation

$$\ln P_{ij} = 0.40 \text{ GNPM} - 0.15 \ln X_{ij} + 0.86 \; P_i^W + 0.13 \; D_{ij} - 0.88$$
$$(2.51) \qquad (0.87) \qquad (7.97) \qquad (2.12) \qquad (-0.61)$$

$R^2 = 0.958$

Supply Equation

$$\ln X_{ij} = 4.76 \ln P_{ij} + 0.17 \text{ GNPX} + 32.99$$
$$(1.92) \qquad (2.64) \qquad (1.47)$$

$R^2 = 0.556$

Growth Equation

$$\text{GNPX} = 3.76 \ln P_{ij} + 1.58 \ln X_{ij} + 4.96 \text{ T} - 3.73$$
$$(7.19) \qquad (1.84) \qquad (33.81) \quad (-0.45)$$

$R^2 = 0.997$

*Figures in parentheses are t statistics

The demand equations in table 8.10 exhibit high price and income elasticities. Price elasticities vary between 2.3 (chemicals) and 4.5 (machinery) and are higher in other manufactures. Income elasticity for chemicals is 2.2; it is higher for the two other commodity groups. Coefficients of the dummy variables $D_{ij}$ are positive and significant in all three cases, implying that intra-LDC imports of manufactures are larger than imports by LDCs from DCs when the size (GNPM) has been accounted for. The implication is clear: exports of manufactures from LDCs face favorable world conditions for substantial growth. High price elasticities show the profitability of increasing exports; high income elasticities mean that exports of manufactures from LDCs are a growing phenomenon. The higher demand by LDCs for other LDCs' exports supports the projection of increasing intra-LDC trade, which by taking advantage of similarities in consumption patterns could develop a kind of Linder process in their bilateral trade relations. These similarities and the advantages that they provide to the countries involved could offset the disadvantages that LDCs' industrial sectors have vis-a-vis DCs. They could also create alternative channels of trade to those ending in DCs, where effective protection is apparently unfavorable to LDCs' exports.

The supply equations in table 8.10 show positive and significant supply price elasticities. For machinery elasticity is, as expected, relatively low but for chemicals and especially for other manufactures it is high. This leads to the conclusion that manufactures in general and the group of SITC 6 and 8 in particular, are the appropriate base upon which to increase exports earnings. No effective constraints on the demand side seem to prevail and on the supply side there is the potential capacity to increase output and export earnings.

To complete the argument we observe the growth equations, which show that, as in the case of primary commodities, export price changes that originate outside of LDCs increase real GNP. However, unlike the case of primary commodities, quantum changes in manufactures exports do stimulate economic growth, implying that comparative advantages are embodied in manufactures rather than in primary commodities. It emerges from these equations that a growth of 1 percent in the quantum exports of manufactures increase real GNP by 1.5 to 3.6 percent. These figures represent, of course, a multiplier effect that manufactures exports have on GNP, probably through externalities or other multiplying effects.

## APPENDIX
Percentage of 33 Main Commodities in Total Exports, 1975-1977

### Agriculture

| South and Central America and the Caribbean | | Africa | |
|---|---|---|---|
| Argentina | 39.2 | Botswana | 98.8 |
| Barbados | 31.0 | Burundi | 98.8 |
| Bermuda | 22.7 | Cameroon | 68.1 |
| Brazil | 44.0 | Republic of Central Africa | 71.4 |
| Colombia | 69.1 | | |
| Costa Rica | 63.7 | Chad | 50.1 |
| Dominican Republic | 70.3 | Egypt | 50.9 |
| El Salvador | 69.7 | Ethiopia | 70.0 |
| Guadaloupe | 79.0 | Gambia | 90.8 |
| Guatemala | 62.8 | Ghana | 81.4 |
| Guayana (bauxite) | 78.9 | Ivory Coast | 74.3 |
| Haiti (bauxite) | 57.6 | Kenya | 54.2 |
| Honduras | 73.5 | Madagascar | 58.2 |
| Jamaica (bauxite) | 39.4 | Malawi | 89.0 |
| Martinique | 58.2 | Mali | 61.6 |
| Nicaragua | 67.7 | Mauritius | 74.6 |
| Panama | 45.0 | Mozambique | 43.7 |
| Paraguay | 44.2 | Rwanda | 84.1 |
| Peru (tin, zinc, copper) | 80.5 | Senegal (phosphate) | 57.6 |
| Uruguay | 41.4 | Sierra Leone | 34.1 |
| | | Sudan | 72.7 |
| | | Tanzania | 65.4 |
| | | Uganda | 96.8 |
| | | Upper Volta | 44.8 |

### Minerals

| Africa and South America | | Asia | |
|---|---|---|---|
| Bolivia | 87.9 | Bangladesh | 31.5 |
| Chile | 67.5 | Burma | 78.5 |
| Guinea | 81.3 | India | 24.7 |
| Liberia | 93.6 | Jordan | 30.6 |
| Mauritania | 90.9 | Malaysia | 70.5 |
| Morocco | 43.7 | Nepal | 68.2 |
| Namibia | 96.7 | Pakistan | 32.7 |
| Togo | 87.0 | Philippines | 60.0 |
| Zaire | 94.5 | Sri Lanka | 71.4 |
| Zambia | 56.8 | Thailand | 52.7 |
| | | Yemen Arab Republic | 63.0 |

NOTES

1. See Bhagwati 1977.
2. See Tinbergen 1976, 34.
3. See Morgan 1975, 314-15.
4. For example, petroleum and possibly bauxite.
5. Law 1975, 114.
6. Michaely (1962, Chapter 4) shows rigorously that world demand price elasticity of an economy is negatively related with the economy's weight in world exports.
7. Kravis (1970, 850-72) combining competitiveness with diversification into one export performance measure, concluded that LDC export performance is determined more by supply factors than by world demand.
8. See Bruno 1978.
9. See Linder 1961.
10. See Hufbauer 1970.
11. See Adams and Behrman 1976 and Behrman 1977.

REFERENCES

Adams, G.F. and Behrman J.R. 1976. Econometric Models on World Agricultural Commodity Markets. Cambridge, Mass.: Bellinger Publishing Co.
Behrman, J.R. 1977. International Commodity Agreements. Washington, D.C.: Overseas Development Council.
Bhagwati, J., editor, 1977. The New International Economic Order: The North-South Debate, Cambridge, Mass.: MIT Press.
Bruno, M. 1978. An Analysis of Stagflation in the Industrial Countries: Some Preliminary Results. The Maurice Falk Institute for Economic Research in Israel. Jerusalem: Discussion Paper 778.
Hufbauer, G.C. 1970. The Impact of National Characteristics and Technology on the Commodity Composition of Trade in Manufactured Goods. In The Technology Factor in International Trade, edited by R. Vernon. New York: NBER.
Kravis, I.B. 1970. Trade as a Handmaiden of Growth: Similarities Between the Nineteenth and Twentieth Centuries. Economic Journal.
Law, A.D. 1975. International Commodity Agreements. London: Lexington Books.
Linder, S.B. 1961. An Assay on Trade and Transformation. Uppsala, Almqvist and Wiksell.
Michaely, M. 1962. Concentration in International Trade. Amsterdam: North Holland.
Morgan, T. 1975. Economic Development. New York: Harper and Row.
Reshaping the International Order - A Report to the Club of Rome. 1976. New York: Dutton.

# 9
# The Effects of Export Restrictions on Economic Growth in LDCs

*J. Weinblatt*
*R. Nathanson*

1. INTRODUCTION

   This chapter deals with the macroeconomic effects of export restrictions in exporting countries. The economics of export restrictions and their relevance to international trade are analyzed with emphasis on the conditions under which export restrictions are successful. The study measures and analyzes the effectiveness of these restrictions in stimulating economic growth in the less developed countries.
   Recall that the microeconomic and macroeconomic factors that contribute to the success of these restrictions in stimulating economic development were identified in the theoretical analysis of chapter 5. At the microeconomic level we found that the income transfer from the importing countries (mainly DCs) to the exporting countries (mainly LDCs) is greater:
(1) The greater the monopoly power of the exporting country. The degree of monopoly power depends on the price elasticity of demand of the restricted commodity on world markets and the volume exported.
(2) The greater the capacity of the exporting country for further processing of the exported raw material. This capacity is conditional on the existence of complementary factors, such as adequate manpower and technology.
(3) The greater the importance of the exported commodity in the production of manufactured goods. When the value added in producing the processed good is lower, a commodity price shock generates a higher rise in the price of manufactures. Thus, the stimulus for domestic processing of the commodity in the exporting country is greater.

   At the macroeconomic level it was shown that taking into account multiplier effects, the total change in income of the exporting countries due to export restrictions depends, inter alia, on the marginal propensities to expend for domestic uses both in the importing and the exporting countries. The increase in the exporting country's national income is larger, the lesser the importing countries' marginal propensities to expend and the greater this propensity is for the exporting countries.

## SIDE EFFECTS OF EXPORT RESTRICTIONS

Because primary products generally constitute a major part of LDCs total exports, restrictions will substantially affect the volume and value of their total exports and the composition of their balance of payments. Such changes influence the internal monetary activity in LDCs and thus contribute to the determination of domestic price levels. In other words, under certain conditions export controls have a strong impact on domestic inflation.

Where they are subject to tax earnings deriving from the export of raw materials increase government revenues. When public expenditure is at least partially financed by export earnings and government policy is to expand development spending, a reduction of export earnings leads to an increase in the government's debt. Thus, government expenditure and/or its debt fluctuate according to fluctuations of export earnings, which are highly sensitive to changing demand and supply conditions in international commodity markets.[1] Hence cyclical changes of commodity prices affect total government revenue and may cause financial difficulties for the public sector. The degree of instability of governmental expenditure due to price fluctuations in commodity markets depends upon the weight of primary products in total exports. For countries included in this study we can assume that the dependency of public expenditure on export earnings creates inflationary pressures in periods of decreasing export revenue. A reinforcement to this view is expressed in Nankany (1979): "Since instability (of export earnings) is directly transmitted to fiscal revenues, ...governments tend to run fiscal deficits financed largely by central borrowing. The reduction of foreign exchange earnings also implies that imports do not increase aggregate supply. The result is demand-pull inflation."[2]

A possible effect operating in the opposite direction is described below. There exists a structural kind of inflation in raw material exporting countries often described as a result of absorptive capacity constraints. The balance of payments surplus caused by primary exports cannot be absorbed by the domestic economy. The additional foreign currency creates either an expansion of money supply (under a fixed exchange rate system) or a currency appreciation (under a floating exchange rate system). There may be rigidities in the economic systems of LDCs that are related to the lack of sufficient additional factors of production such as high-skilled labor and capital.

Finally, domestic inflation can be stimulated by world inflation of final goods. Thus, the greater the degree of openness of the LDC, the higher the impact of the rate of inflation in international markets.

To sum up, the evaluation of benefits resulting from export controls in a national context calls for the consideration of their side effects. The above discussion highlights the ambiguity concerning the effect of export controls on domestic inflation. There is no doubt that for different economies the implications could be different.

## 3. SOME CHARACTERISTICS OF THE COUNTRIES AND COMMODITIES SELECTED FOR THE STUDY

Twenty countries that are the main exporters of ten core mineral and agricultural commodities were selected for the study (see table 9.1 and 9.2). Note that for each commodity there may be several minor exporters which, individually, are unable to influence world markets. We have focused on countries and commodities for which evidence was found that restrictions (e.g., export taxes, quotas, embargoes, etc.) were imposed.[3] In the following section we look at some of their characteristics.

### The Countries

Revenue dependence on primary exports (see table 9.1). Because of the overwhelming share of commodities in export earnings, their protection in these countries is a matter not only of sectoral but of national concern. Although a slight general downward trend was experienced, the share of primary commodities in total exports did not change significantly during the last decade and continues to be of major significance. Brazil, Chile, Haiti, and Panama are exceptions. In Brazil, dependency on commodity exports was reduced from 63.5% in 1970-1972 to 40.0% in 1976-1978 as a result of a large expansion in its industrial sector.

Significant share in total world exports of the commodity. The total exports of each of ten core commodities from the selected LDCs constitute a large enough share in world exports to permit these LDCs to exert pressure on prices and quantities. This is true especially in cases where they have the potential power of capturing a substantial share of world exports of processed products based on their commodities (see table 9.2). Timber is an exception.

### The Commodities

The selected agricultural and mineral commodities originate almost exclusively from developing countries. The exceptions are timber, copper, and manganese, which are also exported by developed countries. They were included because they contribute a significant source of foreign currency in several of the selected countries (for example, timber in Malaysia, Jamaica, Cameroon; copper in Chile, Peru, Zambia; manganese in Gabon, Ghana). The share of all LDCs in world exports of the ten commodities did not change substantially between 1970 and 1978. This fact implies that in spite of the rapidly rising commodity prices and the strong incentive for substitutes, control of commodities remains in the hands of LDCs.

A distinction between agricultural products and minerals should be noted. Agricultural commodities can be relatively easily substituted in the short-run and consumers tend to cease purchasing the higher priced products and switch to substitutes. Moreover, stockpiling of agricultural goods is in many cases

Table 9.1  Share of Commodities in the Exports of Selected LDCs, 1970-1978 (in percent)

|  | 1970-1972 | 1974-1976 | 1975-1977 | 1976-1978 |
|---|---|---|---|---|
| South and Central America |  |  |  |  |
| Bolivia | 84.0 | 87.5 | 87.9 | 84.0 |
| Brazil | 63.5 | 46.4 | 44.0 | 40.4 |
| Chile | 81.4 | 69.7 | 67.5 | 64.6 |
| Colombia | 83.4 | 65.1 | 69.9 | 74.9 |
| Ecuador | 82.0 | 88.4 | 77.1 | 77.6 |
| Guyana | 63.3 | 80.7 | 78.9 | 77.0 |
| Haiti | 73.9 | 57.4 | 57.6 | 46.4 |
| Honduras | 88.1 | 74.6 | 73.5 | 80.4 |
| Jamaica | 43.8 | 34.9 | 33.4 | 33.9 |
| Panama | 83.3 | 41.6 | 45.0 | 37.3 |
| Peru | 89.6 | 72.2 | 80.5 | 75.9 |
| Africa |  |  |  |  |
| Cameroon | 70.1 | 69.5 | 68.1 | 69.9 |
| Gabon | 85.1 | 96.7 | 92.1 | 88.3 |
| Ghana | 74.2 | 79.0 | 81.4 | 73.4 |
| Ivory Coast | 80.1 | 73.6 | 74.3 | 73.2 |
| Morocco | 30.4 | 56.5 | 51.6 | 43.8 |
| Tanzania | 56.3 | 67.1 | 65.4 | 68.1 |
| Togo | 96.6 | 94.3 | 87.0 | 83.2 |
| Zambia | 97.4 | 98.1 | 97.0 | 97.3 |
| Asia |  |  |  |  |
| Malaysia | 80.7 | 70.7 | 70.5 | 69.4 |
| Total LDCs | 67.0 | 69.2 | 69.6 | 61.2 |

Source: Commodity Trade and Price Trends. Washington, D.C.: The World Bank, 1975, 1978, 1979, 1980).

relatively expensive and expectations regarding future prices cannot easily be translated into stocks. This explains why short-run price elasticities of demand are relatively higher for agricultural products than for minerals.[4]

Minerals are much easier to stockpile and therefore less sensitive to short-term effects of export restrictions. At the same time, switching to substitutes or to alternative sources of supply may prove difficult. Since the demand for minerals is determined primarily by the needs of the processing industries, the change in purchased quantities will occur at a later stage,

Table 9.2 The Average Share of Twenty LDCs' Exports in Total World Exports of Ten Core Commodities, 1974-1976 (in percent)

| | Cocoa | Coffee | Bananas | Timber | Rubber | Bauxite | Copper | Man-ganese | Phos-phates | Tin |
|---|---|---|---|---|---|---|---|---|---|---|
| South and Central America | | | | | | | | | | |
| Bolivia | – | 0.2 | – | 0.2 | 0.1 | – | 0.1 | – | – | 16.4 |
| Brazil | 13.0 | 23.1 | 3.0 | 0.9 | 0.1 | 0.1 | – | 17.3 | – | 1.5 |
| Chile | – | – | – | 0.2 | – | – | 16.7 | – | – | – |
| Colombia | – | 13.4 | 4.5 | 0.2 | – | – | – | – | – | – |
| Ecuador | 3.6 | 2.0 | 16.6 | 0.1 | – | – | – | – | – | – |
| Haiti | – | 0.6 | – | – | – | 2.2 | – | – | – | – |
| Honduras | – | 1.2 | 9.2 | 0.4 | – | – | – | – | – | – |
| Jamaica | 0.1 | 0.1 | 1.8 | – | – | 24.5 | – | – | – | – |
| Guyana | – | – | – | – | – | 14.4 | – | – | – | – |
| Panama | – | – | 7.2 | – | – | – | – | – | – | – |
| Peru | – | 1.1 | – | – | – | – | 3.3 | – | – | – |
| Africa | | | | | | | | | | |
| Cameroon | 6.9 | 2.3 | 2.3 | 0.5 | 0.5 | – | – | – | – | – |
| Gabon | 0.1 | – | – | – | – | 0.7 | – | 20.0 | – | – |
| Ghana | 27.9 | – | – | 0.8 | – | 0.6 | – | 3.4 | – | – |
| Ivory Coast | 15.6 | 6.6 | 1.8 | 2.5 | 0.5 | – | – | – | – | – |

Table continued

Table 9.2 Continued

| | Cocoa | Coffee | Bananas | Timber | Rubber | Bauxite | Copper | Man-ganese | Phos-phates | Tin |
|---|---|---|---|---|---|---|---|---|---|---|
| Africa (Continued) | | | | | | | | | | |
| Morocco | - | - | - | - | - | - | - | 2.3 | 37.9 | - |
| Tanzania | 0.1 | 1.6 | - | - | - | - | - | - | - | - |
| Togo | 1.7 | 0.2 | - | - | - | - | - | - | - | - |
| Zambia | - | - | - | - | - | - | 13.6 | - | - | - |
| Asia | | | | | | | | | | |
| Malaysia | 0.9 | - | 0.2 | 6.8 | 52.2 | 0.9 | - | - | - | - |
| Total | 69.9 | 52.4 | 46.6 | 12.6 | 53.4 | 43.4 | 33.7 | 43.0 | 42.6 | 62.1 |
| Total LDCs | 97.7 | 92.7 | 93.0 | 25.3 | 95.7 | 77.4 | 52.7 | 50.2 | 68.6 | 88.9 |

Source: Commodity Trade and Price Trends. 1978. Washington, D.C.: The World Bank.

when higher commodity prices or supply shortages begin to affect the output of the processed goods.

## 4. THE METHODOLOGY

The testing of the impact of export restrictions on export earnings and economic growth of LDCs lead to the formulation of a simultaneous equations system, presented below.
The system was estimated with a two-stage least-squares technique for pooled data, combining a cross section of developing countries and a time series for the period 1969-1974. The selected countries and commodities are listed in table 9.1 and table 9.2, respectively.
In assessing the outcome of quantitative restrictions in the context of economic development, we studied a possible sequence of events, starting with effective quantitative export controls, followed by higher international prices and larger export revenues for the restricting countries. This process accelerates economic growth, which might generate some undesirable side effects, such as inflation. Some exogenous variables are involved in the process and are accounted for in the system of simultaneous equations. The system is represented by equations (9.1) through (9.4).

Demand equation

$$\dot{P}_{xj} = \alpha_1 + \beta_{10}\dot{G}_w + \beta_{11}\dot{P}_{w-1} + \beta_{12}\dot{Q}_{xj} + \beta_{13}\dot{P}_{xj-1} + \varepsilon_1 \qquad (9.1)$$

Export earning equation

$$\dot{V}_{xj} = \alpha_2 + \beta_{20}\dot{P}_{xj} + \beta_{21}\dot{G}_w + \beta_{22}\dot{GP}_w + \beta_{23}DBAN + \beta_{24}DCOF + \qquad (9.2)$$

$$+ \beta_{25}DCOC + \beta_{26}DBAU + \beta_{27}DTIN + \beta_{28}DCOP + \beta_{29}DWOO +$$

$$+ \beta_{210}DMAN + \varepsilon_2$$

Economic growth equation

$$\dot{G}_j = \alpha_3 + \beta_{30}\dot{V}_{xj} + \beta_{31}\dot{VPIN}_j + \beta_{32}\dot{G}_{j-1} + \beta_{33}PV_{xj} + \beta_{34}DBAN + \qquad (9.3)$$

$$+ \beta_{35}DCOF + \beta_{36}DCOC + \beta_{37}DBAU + \beta_{38}DTIN + \beta_{39}DCOP +$$

$$+ \beta_{310}DWOO + \beta_{311}DMAN + \varepsilon_3$$

Inflation equation[5]

$$\dot{P}_j = \alpha_4 + \beta_{40}\dot{G}_j + \beta_{41}\dot{P}_{w-1} + \beta_{42}\dot{M}_j + \beta_{43}\dot{TB}_j + \varepsilon_4 \qquad (9.4)$$

where:

$P_{xj}$ = price index of commodity bundle exported to country j (100 = 1970);

$Q_{xj}$ = quantum index of commodity bundle exported by country j (100 = 1970);

$V_{xj}$ = value of commodity bundle exported by country j;

$G_w$ and $G_j$ = world income and country j's GNP, respectively, measured at constant prices of 1970;

$P_w$ and $P_j$ = world price index and j's GNP deflator, respectively;

$GP_w$ = world income per capita at constant prices of 1970;

$PIN_j$ = share of manufactures in j's GNP;

$\dot{VPIN}_j$ = the product of PIN $\dot{V}_{xj}$;

$PV_{xj}$ = the share of $V_{xj}$ in j's total exports;

$M_j$ = nominal money supply;

$TB_j$ = trade balance (exports value minus imports value);

D = dummy variables for various commodities:

    BAN = bananas;
    COF = coffee;
    COC = cocoa;
    BAU = bauxite;
    TIN = tin;
    COP = copper;
    WOO = wood;
    MAN = manganese;

When dummy variables are incorporated the intersect of the equation represents the control commodity, phosphates.[6]
All dots denote annual rates of change.
All subscripts $_{-1}$ denote a one year lag.
    The above simultaneous equations system enables us to trace the sequence described earlier.
    Equation (9.1) is a Marshallian type demand function. Its purpose is to release quantitative changes in exports to changes in the world price of the selected commodities. The measured relationship represents an average of the potential trend for .all nine commodities. The introduction of past world inflation $P_{w-1}$ into this equation has the purpose of capturing the effect of

world price changes on commodity world prices. Thus, this relationship is related on the one hand to the terms of trade argument, and expresses the effect of expectations regarding world inflation on commodity prices on the other. The underlying assumption is that the formation of expectations is adaptive rather than rational. The appearance of $P_{xj-1}$ as an explanatory variable in this equation implies that the process of commodity prices determination is dynamic and depends not only on present factors but also on past trends. In other words, the present could compensate or correct for past mistakes and defaults.

The effect of export restrictions on export earnings is expressed in equation (9.2). This equation completes equation (9.1) in revealing relevant relationships. Equation (9.1) shows the partial effect of various variables on commodity price changes. However, some of these variables affect the exported quantities, too. Since we are interested in final equilibrium positions concerning export revenues, equation (9.2) is added to the system. In this equation we have added to the economic variables a series of dummy variables for each of the selected commodities other than phosphates, which has been used as a control commodity. The dummy variables fulfill the purpose of differentiating among the different effects (due to different elasticities) of various commodities in generating changes of exported earnings resulting from export restrictions.

Equation (9.3) shows the contribution of a change in export earnings to the rate of economic growth of the exporting countries. We focus on the role of export restrictions in stimulating growth. Therefore, variables such as the share of primary goods in total exports ($PV_{xj}$) and the share of manufactures in GNP (PIN) have been incorporated into this equation. There is no doubt that these two variables are closely related to the capacity of an economy to benefit from restricting exports. In this equation as well, dummy variables representing the different commodities have been introduced in order to show their differential contribution to economic growth.

Equation (9.4) is an inflation equation designed to test an undesirable side effect resulting from export restrictions that cause accelerated economic growth.

## 5. EMPIRICAL FINDINGS

The estimates of the simultaneous equations model exhibited above are presented in table 9.3.

The demand equation (9.1) gives the average relationship between export prices of the ten primary commodities and a set of variables. As anticipated, the quantity variable $Q_{xj}$ and world GNP changes affect export prices in the expected direction. The two variables obtain a negative and a positive coefficient, respectively, both of which are statistically significant. Some of the implications of these results will be discussed later.

Two interesting findings in equation (9.1) are related to the coefficients of $P_{w-1}$ and $P_{x-1}$. First, we see that past world inflation has a positive effect on exported commodity prices. The

Table 9.3  Simultaneous Regression Equations System 2 SLS Estimates

| Independent Variables | Demand Equation $P_{xj}$ Coef. | $T^{xj}$ | Export earning Equation $V_{xj}$ Coef. | $T^{xj}$ | Economic Growth Equation $G_j$ Coef. | $T$ | Inflation Equation $P_j$ Coef. | $T^j$ |
|---|---|---|---|---|---|---|---|---|
| **Endogenous variables** | | | | | | | | |
| $V_{xj}$ | − | − | − | − | 0.216 | 7.59 | − | − |
| $G_{xj}$ | − | − | − | − | − | − | 0.581 | 1.64 |
| $P_j$ | − | − | − | − | − | − | − | − |
| $P_{xj}$ | − | − | 0.324 | 2.36 | − | − | − | − |
| **Exogenous variables** | | | | | | | | |
| $G_w$ | 4.69 | 6.90 | 0.717 | 1.53 | − | − | − | − |
| $GP_w$ | − | − | 0.703 | 0.04 | − | − | − | − |
| $V_x PIN_j$ | − | − | − | − | 0.00008 | 6.40 | − | − |
| $G_{w-1}$ | − | − | − | − | −0.296 | −2.41 | − | − |
| $PV_{xj}$ | − | − | − | − | −0.180 | −8.51 | − | − |
| $P_{w-1}$ | 0.374 | 4.86 | − | − | − | − | 0.045 | 2.39 |
| $M_j$ | − | − | − | − | − | − | 0.004 | 1.58 |
| $TB_j$ | − | − | − | − | − | − | −0.005 | −1.69 |
| $Q_{xj}$ | −0.152 | −7.03 | − | − | − | − | − | − |
| $P_{xj-1}$ | 1.123 | 12.60 | − | − | − | − | − | − |
| DBAN-Bananas | − | − | −0.175 | −2.34 | 0.567 | 8.87 | − | − |
| DCOF-Coffee | − | − | −0.098 | −1.66 | −0.032 | −1.69 | − | − |
| DCOC-Cocoa | − | − | 0.040 | 0.64 | 0.755 | 8.40 | − | − |
| DBAU-Bauxite | − | − | −0.116 | −1.56 | −0.071 | −2.06 | − | − |
| DTIN-Tin | − | − | −0.139 | −1.43 | 0.219 | 6.79 | − | − |
| DCOP-Copper | − | − | −0.049 | −0.59 | 0.429 | 7.89 | − | − |
| DWOO-Wood | − | − | 0.004 | −0.06 | −0.027 | −1.53 | − | − |
| DMAN-Manganese | − | − | −0.164 | −0.06 | −0.450 | 9.71 | − | − |
| Constant−(Phosphates) | −0.172 | −7.49 | 0.217 | −2.53 | 0.636 | 8.46 | −0.197 | −2.33 |
| $R^2$ | 0.86 | | 0.38 | | 0.69 | | 0.32 | |
| D.W. | 1.801 | | 2.04 | | 3.56 | | 1.437 | |

somehow surprising fact is that $\dot{P}_{w-1}$'s coefficient (0.371) is substantially and significantly lower than one. In other words, there is an implicit partial system of indexation operating in the world of primary commodities, but it is very far from providing commodity exporting countries with real compensation for world inflation. This finding reinforces Prebisch's terms of trade argument. Assuming that $\dot{P}_{w-1}$ represents expectations of future world inflation, we see that if no additional measures are undertaken, world commodity prices train behind the general world price trend by a widening margin. The possibility of partially correcting such a distortion depends on past commodity price hikes. Although $\dot{P}_{x-1}$'s coefficient is greater than one (1.123), the difference is not statistically significant. Thus, a long-run upward trend of commodity prices only partially offsets a deterioration of the terms of trade.

The exported quantity and world income coefficients ($\dot{Q}_{xj}$ and $\dot{G}_w$, respectively) together with the intersect of equation $^{xj}$(9.1) allow us to estimate average price and income elasticities of demand for the selected commodities, for the mean values of the equation.[7] The computed world price elasticity is −0.225 and the world income elasticity estimate is 1.440; both fall into the range of Behrman's estimates.[8]

The price elasticity estimate confirms an explanation of the fact that the nine commodities were subject to export restrictions. Low price elasticity of demand is a necessary condition for the success of such restrictions, and indeed this condition is satisfied. If one accepts the belief that deterioration in the terms of trade is associated with low income elasticities, the income elasticity estimate contradicts the above finding concerning the deterioration of the terms of trade. We do not believe the finding to be contradictory, however, since the experience of the 1970s showed that world inflation and economic growth do not always go hand in hand.

The export earnings equation (9.2) together with the information obtained in equation (9.1) allows for a more specific analysis of export restrictions. We see in equation (9.2) that commodities have a differential contribution to the growth of export earnings. Commodities such as phosphates, manganese, wood, copper, and cocoa provided their exporting countries with a faster rate of growth of exported primary goods values than do bananas, coffee, bauxite, and tin. These apparently autonomous different trends are probably related to differences in income and price elasticities and thus to the capacity of exporting countries to collude for the purpose of cartelizing their world sales.

The price change ($\dot{P}_{xj}$) coefficient in equation (9.2) reveals a positive relationship between changes in prices and export earnings. This finding again implies low price elasticities for the selected commodities. However, this coefficient does not allow for an assessment of the effect of export restrictions. As we noted in equation (9.1), price changes are affected by a series of variables. Since we are interested in the specific potential effect of quantitative controls on export earnings, we substitute

$\dot{P}_{xj}$ in equation (9.2) with equation (9.1) to obtain equation (9.2a).

$$\dot{V}_{xj} = 0.162 - 0.049\ \dot{Q}_{xj} + 2.230\ \dot{G}_w + 0.121\ \dot{P}_{w-1} + \quad (9.2a)$$

$$+ 0.364\ \dot{P}_{x-1} + \text{Dummies} .$$

Equation (9.2a) accounts for the effect of variables other than the exported quantity changes or export earning changes.
We now define as $\dot{Q}_{xj}$ a coefficient that represents the net effect of quantity changes on export revenues. Clearly this effect, in spite of being statistically significant, is small and exports must be drastically restricted in order to substantially increase the exporting countries' revenues. For example, a 10 percent restriction of quantity exported would lead to an average increase of 0.5 percent of export revenues. It must be kept in mind that this regards nine commodities that are, apart from oil, probably the most suitable for the implementation of such restrictions.
How do export restrictions stimulate economic growth? In equation (9.3) we see that an increase in the growth of export revenues does indeed raise the rate of economic growth. Moreover, this effect is stronger the larger the share of manufactures in GNP and the lower the share of primary goods in total exports. This leads to the conclusion that in terms of economic growth, countries benefit more from an increase in their export earnings, the greater the degree of their industrialization. This finding is in accord with the theoretical hypothesis presented earlier in this chapter, implying that export restrictions have better chances of success the greater the exporting countries' ability for further processing. This ability depends, of course, on the existence of a suitable economic and industrial infrastructure, represented in equation (9.3) by the variable PIN, the share of manufactures in GNP.
Equation (9.3) shows that commodity exports contribute in varying degrees to economic growth. The commodities with a relatively large contribution to economic growth are cocoa, bananas, copper, manganese, tin, and phosphates. This ranking gives a hint about the profitability of manipulating exports of different commodities for the purpose of stimulating economic growth. The efficacy of this tool can be judged with a numerical illustration. If a 10 percent quantitative restriction of exports leads to a 0.5 percent average increase of export earnings growth, this would result in a 1.0 percent change of the rate of overall growth. This is a statistically significant but small change.
Equation (9.4) shows that the rate of inflation in developing countries is positively related to the rate of growth and other traditional variables, such as domestic money supply, world inflation, and the balance of trade. The evaluation of this

undesirable potential side effect of export restrictions leads to the conclusion that it indeed exists. Export restrictions could affect three of the explanatory variables in this equation. They slightly stimulate economic growth, increase money supply, and improve the balance of trade. For the latter two variables the effect of export restrictions has not been estimated. Thus, money supply and the trade balance are considered as exogenous variables. Nevertheless, one of the sources of growth of money supply and of changes in the balance of trade is the change of export earnings. And, as we have seen above, the effect of export restrictions on the growth of export earnings and on economic growth is rather small. Thus, its impact on the rate of inflation can also be considered very small.

To sum up, we found that none of the commodities that were subject to export restrictions are indeed endowed with the appropriate features necessary for the successful implementation of this kind of policy. There is no doubt that such restrictive measures could increase export earnings and indirectly stimulate economic growth. Nevertheless, it appears that the efficiency of this instrument as a lever for economic growth is extremely limited and probably cannot provide an adequate response to problems of world poverty and backwardness.

## APPENDIX
## The Data

World characteristics such as world income, income per capita, and inflation were taken from UN, Statistical Yearbook. New York: 1970-1977. Export variables, prices, and quantities for the selected commodities and countries were taken from UN, Commodity Trade Statistics. New York: 1970-1977. National attributes of the selected countries were taken from IMF, International Financial Statistics Yearbooks. Washington, D.C.: 1970-1976. The exported quantities and commodity export prices for each of the selected countries were computed as quantum and price indices respectively (100=1970) as follows:

$$Q_{xijt} = \frac{\sum_{i=1}^{n} Q_{xijt} P_{ij}^{1970}}{\sum_{i=1}^{n} Q_{xij}^{1970} P_{ij}^{1970}}$$

$$P_{xijt} = \frac{\sum_{i=1}^{n} Q_{xij}^{1970} P_{ijt}}{\sum_{i=1}^{n} Q_{xij}^{1970} P_{ij}^{1970}} \qquad t = 1969-1974 .$$

where,
$Q_{xjt}$ = quantum index of exported primary commodities from country $j$ in the year $t$,
$P_{xjt}$ = price index of exported primary commodities from country $j$ in the year $t$.

NOTES

1. McBean and Nguyen 1980.
2. See Nankany 1979, 38. Nankany bases his arguments on the counter-Keynesian hypothesis for mineral exporting countries, formulated by Jenkins and Gillis (1978).
3. See detailed discussion in chapter 2.
4. Behrman 1977, 58.
5. For statistical sources of data and computing methods of variables see Appendix 1.
6. Rubber is excluded from these estimates due to the lack of suitable data.

7. $\eta_p = \dfrac{\dot{Q}_x}{\alpha_1 + \beta_{12} Q_x}$ and $\eta_I = \dfrac{\alpha_1}{\beta_{12} Q_x} + \dfrac{\beta_{10}}{\beta_{13}}$,

where $\eta_p$ denotes an average price elasticity for the selected commodities and $\eta_I$ denotes the average income elasticity.

8. See Behrman 1977.

REFERENCES

Behrman, J. 1977. International Commodity Agreements: An Evaluation of the UNCTAD Integrated Commodity Programme. Washington, D.C.

Jenkins, G. and Gillis, M. 1978. The Macroeconomic Impact of the Mineral Exporting Sector on a Developing Economy. In Taxation and Mining: Non-Fuel Minerals in Bolivia and Other Countries edited by M. Gillis, Cambridge, Mass.

Mcbean, A.I. and Nguyen, D.T. 1980. Commodity Concentration and Export Earnings Instability: A Mathematical Analysis. Economic Journal 90: 354-62.

Nankani, G.T. 1979. Development Problems of Mineral-Exporting Countries. World Bank Staff Paper 354. Washington, D.C.: The World Bank.

World Bank. 1980. Commodity Trade and Price Trends. Washington, D.C.: The World Bank.

# 10
# Export Controls: An Institutional and Historical Perspective

*Michael Rom*


Before we examine the case of export controls it seems worthwhile first to clarify the meaning, definition, scope, points of view, and types of export restrictions that have been applied.

MEANING

The problem of free access to supply and export controls has been dealt with in the past in the literature as one topic, and comprised mainly issues related to the supply of raw materials and primary commodities. Actually, the subject of supply at present may be much broader, including not only the above mentioned products but also manufactures and even know-how. On the other hand, the object of export controls includes not only prevention of free access to supply but at times is intended to prevent free access to markets.

DEFINITION

The term "export controls" will be used throughout this chapter to cover all trade policy measures adopted by the exporting countries to affect the flow of exports directly: quantitative limitations (including prohibitions), export taxes, duties and the like, as well as administrative measures that have the same effect. "Voluntary" controls are also included.

POINTS OF VIEW

The problem of free access to sources of supply and of export controls can be approached from different points of view -- that of an exporter or importer of raw material and know-how; that of a developed or developing country dependent on the raw material. The approach can be based on the existing world economic order, or on the wish to establish a new one. If the existing world order (at least in its more important principles) is accepted, then it will suffice to seek supplementation, corrections, or relatively minor reforms that will improve the functioning of the existing system. If, on the other hand, one negates the existing world order and strives for some kind of overall global planning based on control and distribution of resources by a central planning authority; or, as suggested by the Club of Rome, one assumes that resources should be treated as a common heritage of mankind, then naturally the approach of relatively small corrections will not be acceptable.[1] Clearly, between these extreme approaches intermediate positions are possible where reforms are introduced to such an extent as to bring about a new economic order of some kind.

The purpose of this chapter is to examine the subject of export controls within the framework of the standards and values embodied in GATT today. While it is difficult to give their precise definition because of the many different points of view held by the present membership, it appears that the ideology of the founding fathers is still preserved and GATT stands for the following fundamental values: free trade, to the maximum extent possible, based on competition between private enterprise, and a market economy in which the price mechanism is the major allocator of resources; elimination of all non-tariff barriers and maximum possible reduction of cost restrictions; maintenance of non-discriminatory treatment in all its various forms (e.g., MFN clause, equitable treatment, national treatment, etc.).

The major change from the original GATT is the acceptance of the principle of differential and preferential treatment of LDCs, as embodied in the Tokyo Declaration and its forerunner, Part IV of the GATT (added in 1966).

Targets of Export Restrictions

The following section presents a list of various targets of export restrictions. The list is by no means all-inclusive. Furthermore, the classification does not differentiate between cost restrictions and quantitative restrictions, such as embargoes and quotas or licensing. In some cases, the export control is only in the form of cost restrictions (such as duty or levy); in other cases, it is only in the form of quantitative controls; while in yet other cases, both forms of control are imposed together.

(1) Export prohibition or restriction in order to ensure supply of materials or products to the domestic market
(a) to supply a scarce commodity to the local consumer;
(b) to prevent a physical shortage from developing during periods of excess demand abroad beyond available local supply;
(c) to build up reserves of stocks for possible future shortage crises or war (e.g., stockpiling of strategic materials, such as oil);
(d) to protect the domestic industry by providing it with easily available and cheaper domestic raw materials (Canadian restriction of pulp exports; the export tax on coffee in Brazil);[2]
(e) to protect lower domestic prices relative to prevailing world market prices of maintenance of domestic price control (for instance, EEC export levies on sugar to isolate domestic prices from world market prices or informal export controls

in the US during 1973-74 in US fertilizers for the purpose of reinforcing price controls;
(f) to prevent the development of inflationary pressure and the import of inflation from abroad (thus, Canada introduced export controls in its soya after the introduction of US export controls);
(g) to prevent unemployment.

(2) <u>Export control for the purpose of increasing export earnings or obtaining fiscal receipts achieved by means of:</u>
(a) An optimum tariff when a country possesses a monopoly position in a commodity. For example, a tax on natural nitrates, in which Chile had a virtual world monopoly, was imposed in 1979 for several years without harming domestic producers. However, in the longrun the high prices (and security considerations) led to the development of a synthetic nitrogen industry;
(b) Joint export controls in order to exert a monopoly price and income, etc. may be contemplated by a few producing countries that together control the supply of the commodity (e.g., OPEC).
(c) Commodity agreements (made often not only to stabilize, but also to increase income) frequently also include export control measures, sometimes alone and sometimes in addition to buffer stocks.[3]
(d) Prevention of excessive and ruinous competition on foreign markets by many small firms in the exporting country. Export control may raise and stabilize the price and income for the entire industry, e.g., agricultural marketing boards, which sell and advertise abroad the products of a multitude of small farmers (possibly under one brand name) and obtain for them a better price in the market.
(e) Imposition of tax or duty on export products as sources of revenue was employed in Europe until the middle of the 19th century; it was forbidden in the US by the Constitution (Art. 1 Sec. 9). Today export taxes for revenue purposes are mainly used in some developing countries since they are easier to administer than other forms of taxation. As a rule such a tax or duty will not be high, since it is widely believed that the duty is at least partially borne by the domestic producer when the world market is competitive.[4]

(3) <u>Export control for the purpose of influencing or counteracting foreign governments' policies:</u>
(a) An export tax may be imposed to counteract escalation of protection in importing countries. It is quite customary for importing countries to protect their domestic industry by imposing increasingly higher duties on the more advanced stages of production while permitting duty-free imports of raw materials. Such a policy discourages the development of domestic processing industries in the exporting countries. An export tax on raw materials to counteract the influence of the escalation of protection in importing countries may

therefore be introduced. The difference between such a tax and an export tax imposed to protect a domestic industry lies in the magnitude of the tax. Whereas here the purpose is only to erode an artificially created advantage in the importing country, there the purpose is to create an artificial advantage at least for the infancy period.

(b) Export controls may be imposed to countervail state trading of centrally planned economy. Export controls imposed to ensure that centrally planned countries that have bilateral agreements with market economies do not utilize the agreements for buying only "essential" commodities but actually purchase the entire range of goods and quantities for which they have committed themselves under the agreement. Switzerland imposed this type of control in the late 1940s. Export controls are also used as protection against state trading central purchasing agencies exercising monopsony power over weak individual exporters. This method is equally applied against other monopolies or transnationals that have a dominant position vis-a-vis individual companies.

(c) Voluntary and "voluntary" export restrictions to prevent the introduction of import controls in foreign countries. During the 1930s Japan maintained export restrictions that were truly voluntary and autonomous in character and were introduced for various reasons, among them the fear that without them more severe countermeasures would be taken by the US. Over the years "voluntary" export controls have developed that are more or less imposed on the exporting countries by the threat of the importing countries to impose import controls. Many of these export controls are based on agreements for "orderly marketing arrangements" that permit a given rate of growth in exports provided it is controlled at an agreed level. Thus, the exporting country will be interested in maintaining "voluntary" export controls rather than being subject to import restrictions that may be more severe.[5]

(d) Export controls may be imposed by a contracting party for the purpose of obtaining the relaxation of another contracting party's import restriction, or to obtain a relaxation of another party's export restriction on a commodity in local or general short supply. These practices were considered contrary to GATT rules by a working party of GATT in 1950. Another example of the bargaining tool is the amendments to the US Export Administration Act of 1969 to permit the use of export controls by the US to counter restrictions by other nations on US access to foreign supplies (added in 1976) and the anti-boycott provisions (added in 1977). As a result of these amendments, many Arab countries made positive changes in their boycott requirements.[6]

(e) Export controls may be applied to influence the behaviour of foreign governments or in response to unfriendly acts. The most prominent case is the US Export Administration Act, which includes foreign policy as one of its three expressed purposes (the others being scarce materials and national

security.⁷ An outstanding example is the ban on wheat exports to the USSR introduced by the Carter Administration after the USSR invaded Afghanistan.⁸ Another example is the OPEC oil embargo against the Netherlands and the US in 1973-74 in an attempt to influence their position in the Israeli-Arab conflict.
(f) Export controls may be imposed for humanitarian purposes or in conjunction with UN sanctions. In the case of southern Rhodesia, export controls were introduced by the US in line with UN charter provisions 25, 39, 41. In the case of Uganda no such collective action was taken by the UN community; the US trade boycott was justified on humanitarian considerations in an attempt to prevent genocide.⁹

(4) <u>Export controls to execute the regular tasks and duties of government:</u>
(a) Export controls for the maintenance of quality, standards and sanitary regulations or public morals;¹⁰
(b) export controls for the prevention of fraud and misrepresentation;
(c) export controls to implement and maintain foreign currency control;
(d) export controls to direct destination of exports in cases of balance of payments problems, exchange control, clearing agreements, etc. Immediately after World War II, for example, export controls were instituted in several countries to ensure that certain "dollar earning" commodities were directed to "hard" currency areas;
(e) export control to monitor supply. For example, the US government currently monitors the supply of many basic commodities through a licensing system that permits it to evaluate and keep abreast of development and avoid unforeseen situations;
(f) export taxes to defray the costs of promoting sales abroad through research, advertising, and governmental control over quality;
(g) export controls on multinationals and their affiliates for the purpose of preventing transfer of capital or earnings, in the form of low prices in inter-company pricing or for the purpose of preventing unjustified market allocations between affiliates.¹¹

(5) <u>Export controls for the purpose of maintaining an advance over foreign countries:</u>
(a) Export controls may be imposed to prevent unfriendly nations from obtaining critical military or economic supplies or technologies. Such an effort is effective only if comparable goods and technologies are not readily available from other sources. Thus, there are constant efforts in the West to coordinate and agree multilaterally on the list of products and technologies whose sales to the Eastern Bloc should be controlled. The US usually examines the foreign availability of products before applying controls.¹²

(b) Many countries maintain controls on the export of know-how not only for strictly strategic reasons but in order to maintain a competitive advantage especially when the R&D invested is substantial. Such control is mainly exercised by private companies, but very often also by governments.

(c) Export controls may be imposed on products for which the exporting country has specific advantages and which it wants to remain the only producer. Staley quotes examples of export embargoes on seeds, animals, and other goods. For example, in 1925 the Philippines prohibited the export of abaca seeds in order to assure continuance of Philippines monopoly on Manila hemp (abaca). Other embargoes imposed have included South Africa's ban on ostriches, ostrich eggs and angora goats; the ban by Egypt and Tunisia on date shoots; and the ban by Cuba on pineapple slippings.[13]

(d) Export controls may be imposed for the purpose of creating a preferential advantage or protection for one country (usually the mother country of a colony) or a number of closely related countries against their competitors. An example was the export tax on tin ore from the Malay States (exports to the Straits settlements and later to the UK and Australia were examples of discrimination against the US).

(6) <u>Export controls for the purpose of conserving exhaustable resources or preventing over-exploitation of natural resources</u>
Such controls are introduced in the field of scarce minerals and oil. Sometimes production rather than export controls (taxes, or quantitative limitations) are introduced. Export control on manufactures from natural resources are sometimes introduced to prevent over-exploitation. For instance, Canada protects its forests by controlling its paper exports.

(7) <u>Export controls as safeguard mechanism built into agreements.</u>[14]

(8) <u>Rationing.</u> The limited amount of raw material available in relation to needs may force major suppliers to ration the export supply available and introduce controls in order to assure sufficient supply to all customers. This occurred during and after World War I and World War II due to destruction of productive capacity.

\* \* \*

The above classification is merely a convenient tool. Many different ways of classification are possible. Furthermore, it may frequently be difficult to classify a particular case according to one purpose only since the same action will have more than one effect. Thus, for instance, a limitation on the export of a raw material in order to guarantee supply to the local market may at the same time raise the price of that smaller part exported, and thus increase the income and gain of the exporting country. Similarly, while the original purpose of the control measure may be to protect the domestic economy from inflation it may at the same time have beneficial effects on the domestic industry and employment. The building up of a domestic stock may, at least partially, strengthen national security; etc. The classification is useful since it gives a clear overview with a broad approach regarding the introduction of controls, but no clear-cut judgement can be made as to its justification, legality, or desirability. The reasons and motives for export controls despite their identified character in the above classification are quite heterogeneous; their justification, at least from the point of view of existing international trade rules of behavior, are of varying degrees of acceptability.

Finally, it should be made clear that the different types of export controls have varied in importance at various times in history and from country to country. Much depends on the specific conditions and circumstances in which the country finds itself. As mentioned in Chapter 1, in ancient Egypt and Greece and during the mercantilist period, the major emphasis was on the maintenance of essential foods and material at home and on preventing essential materials from reaching the enemy or competitor. In developing countries export controls were introduced primarily for revenue purposes. During the two world wars and the period in between, export controls were introduced (1) to allocate scarce raw material among allies and in the domestic market; (2) to prevent essential materials from reaching the enemy; (3) to control clearing agreements; (4) to maximize the quota gain of the exporter; (5) for producer agreements. During the 1920s attempts were made to eliminate quantitative export restrictions and allow only cost restrictions. During the post-World War II period export control was related substantially to foreign exchange and hard and soft currency problems while in the 1970s the primary preoccupation of export controls was the prevention of inflation.

## HISTORICAL BACKGROUND

There is no doubt that policymakers were much more aware of the subject of export control during the first half of this century than during the last thirty years. To a large extent this was due to the condition then prevailing in the developed world. During World War I it was necessary to ensure essential supplies of raw materials and many countries had difficulties in obtaining them, or in paying for them when they could be obtained. Later, when production and supplies increased, there were periods of surpluses and instability in prices of raw materials that required curtailment of supplies through international commodity agreements that were based inter alia on export controls. During the Great Depression extreme protectionism was introduced in order to preserve the domestic market for local producers and preferential trade arrangements were made that adversely affected the ability of several countries to sell abroad and obtain the necessary foreign currency for purchasing essential raw materials. Finally, before and during World War II it was deemed necessary to ensure control over raw material sources and export controls were introduced on a discriminatory basis to preserve the Allies' production potential and to prevent the enemy from gaining access to vital commodities. Clearly, under such circumstances the supply of and access to raw materials were of primary importance. The issue was dealt with in international forums and policymakers were very much aware of it.[15] Opinions on possible solutions of the problem differed according to times and conditions. During the period of shortages some observers suggested rationing of raw material on an international scale; other observers saw the rapid return to a freely competitive economy as the only way to overcome shortage difficulties.[16] The colonial system as well as the restricted access to raw materials was severely attacked by the so-called "have nots", such as Germany, Japan and Italy, who resented what they considered abusive monopoly practices -- export tariffs, export controls, and preferential arrangements -- by the "haves". Italy, in fact, demanded to set up a commission to study and present concrete proposals for the prevention of the monopoly of raw materials, either by states or by great international trusts. The commission was to propose the regulation of the distribution of these materials and assure all states equitable commercial treatment. The UK objected to this principle, according to which the raw material situated within the limits of one country should be treated as the common property of the world.[17] On the other hand, countries such as France, which throughout the years had supported the Most Favored Nation Clause, demanded the elimination of this principle after World War I, when it sought to distinguish between former allies and former enemies, discriminating against the latter.[18] Many of the "have nots" saw the solution in a reallocation of territories and colonies that would assure them of control over sources of raw materials.

On the other hand, there was a group of idealists that regarded the absence of non-discriminating free trade generally, and of raw materials in particular, as the source of all evil. Furthermore, in the 1920s there were those who considered export restrictions, protective export duties, and export control schemes to be more aggressive, more interfering with supply and demand, and ethically less defensible than import tariffs and restrictions.[19]

Some of the idealists argued that one of the central causes of war and commercial and territorial rivalries was the struggle for raw materials. They considered discriminatory customs tariffs and export duties together with systems of colonial preferences to be the principal weapons in such conflicts. The great stress laid on the necessity for their elimination, particularly in the US,[20] found expression in point 3 of President Wilson's 14 points. The group saw in the attempt to bring about a freer trade not only an important principle of the theory of international trade, but also a means of reducing international conflicts. It insisted, therefore, first on non-discriminatory treatment to all countries in access to markets and raw materials; and second on an effort to reduce barriers to trade in order to attain the final goal of free trade although this was not regarded as an immediately attainable objective.[21]

## EFFORTS IN THE LEAGUE OF NATIONS

The attempts and efforts to eliminate export restrictions within the framework of international agreements and treaties in the League of Nations were similar to those of post-World War I negotiations.
In this context, it is interesting to note the report of Professor C. Gini, which formed the basis of the League's discussion on the subject of raw materials. This report indicated three alternative solutions for the problem of raw materials, then in short supply:
(1) the nationalistic solution;
(2) the socialist, or state, solution;
(3) the free trade solution.
In the first solution, the government attempts self sufficiency -- a more suitable solution in a state of war, than in peace, and for many countries completely impossible. The second solution, to some extent already suggested for a transitory period after World War I involves the creation of a central international organization that acquires raw materials and distributes them in accordance with the needs of individual countries. During the League's discussions this idea was dismissed as unsuitable and Gini himself indicated, on the basis of the war experience, that difficulties in practical application made such a plan unworkable.[22]

The third solution thus seemed to be the most suitable and desirable. This was not intended to mean common ownership of raw materials, but only abstention from exercising some sovereign rights that a country has in the field of raw materials that may be to the detriment of other nations. Gini believed that nations would agree on some limitation of their sovereign rights rather than accept outside intervention. However, such a solution would require the existence of an efficient international organization that would ensure its functioning also under conditions of economic crises and the absence of war or preparation for war, which would obviously lead to its elimination.

There was certain optimism after World War I and the League of Nations tried to take steps in the direction of liberalization of trade, especially with respect to raw materials. In October 1927 a diplomatic conference adopted an International Convention for the Abolition of **Prohibitions and** Restrictions, in which the parties undertook, subject to certain exceptions, "to abolish within a period of six months all import and export prohibitions or restrictions, and not thereafter to impose any such prohibitions or restrictions" (Article 2). However, the parties reserved the right to adopt prohibitions or restrictions "for the purpose of protecting in extraordinary and abnormal circumstances the vital interests of the country" but they should not lead to any arbitrary discrimination (Art. 5).[23] Other international agreements were signed by 18 countries following conferences held in 1928. These denounced the prohibition and limitation of exports on hides and skin and on bones.[24]

During the 1930s Gini's preconditions did not exist; all these attempts were thus doomed to fail. It should be emphasized that after World War I (and later after World War II) the supporters of the free trade ideology believed in a better world, where long-lasting, secure peace would reign thanks to the new international mechanism. The hard facts of life very soon upset these optimistic hopes.

Already during the inter-war period, most attempts at establishing international rules -- though still approached from an extremely Utopian point of view compared with the times in which they were voiced -- had to compromise with reality.

The rules accepted at the 1927 conference and those accepted in 1937 as recommendations of the economic committee of the League (demanding, for instance, abolition of quantitative export restrictions on raw materials, save in international commodity agreements, or the imposition of non-discriminatory export duties on raw material for revenue purposes only) were full of exceptions or prefixes that reduced the value of the provisions. There was also a demand for national treatment of foreign investments in natural resources. Yet the committee recommended that a country "is entitled to reserve certain favors to its nationals and to exercise a measure of control over the development of resources by foreigners."[25] Export prohibitions of raw materials were justified in a country producing a small quantity of raw material compared to its needs. Furthermore, the justice of imposing export duties to counter escalation or prohibition of the finished products' import was recognized.[26] The recommendations of the committee also included reference to commodity agreements which were to be judged on the merits of the case. However, special emphasis was put on the obligation to effectively include the interests of the consumers in the agreement.

None of these provisions ever materialized because of the outbreak of World War II. They are, however, of interest, since they are the forerunners of the Havana Charter and GATT.

TRACING THE SOURCE OF THE IDEA OF FREE ACCESS TO SUPPLY IN GATT

The founding fathers of the ITO and GATT belonged to the group of those who believed in the vital need to return to non-discriminatory, multilateral free trade. In particular, we must mention the then Secretary of State of the US, Cordell Hull, who already in 1916 had adopted his life long philosophy that, "unhampered trade dovetailed with peace, high tariffs trade barriers and unfair economic competition, with war."[27] Hull was not only an advocate of free trade but fought for the establishment of appropriate international institutions to implement this policy. He proposed elimination of international trade barriers in 1917 (embodied in Point Three of President Wilson's Fourteen Points), but was not then in as an influential position as when he was Secretary of State.

During his 12 years in office, he fought relentlessly for the liberalization of trade, and the Reciprocal Trade Agreement Act of 1934 was pushed through as a result of his efforts, in a world that was generally moving in the opposite direction, toward higher protectionism. It was under his leadership that the US State Department, even during World War II, started to plan the post-war world of international trade and its institutions.

The fundamental assumption of US foreign policy was "that the creation of a peaceful world order requires economic cooperation among nations and the removal of economic cause of friction and that this can best be achieved in an expanding and relatively stable world economy that provides for all nations non-discriminating access to supplies and markets, to transportation facilities and investment opportunities."[28]

Thus, the State Department, under the leadership of Cordell Hull, was devoted to the idea of the elimination, after World War II, of the highly protective discriminatory treatment and unequal access to market and sources of raw materials. To that purpose they tried, in 1941-42, to insert into the Anglo-American negotiations, an economic commitment to eliminate these highly protective and discriminatory practices. This US objective was opposed by the UK. One of the most dramatic episodes in the negotiations of the Atlantic Charter in 1941 was the struggle between Winston Churchill and US Under-Secretary of State, Sumner Welles, over the question of whether the Fourth Point of the Charter should include a condemnation of discriminatory trading arrangements such as the Imperial Preferences, practiced within the British Commonwealth. Welles proposed a draft that read as follows:

Fourthly, they will strive to promote mutually advantageous economic relations between them through the elimination of any discrimination in either the U.S.A. or the U.K. against the importation of any product originating in the other country; and they will endeavour to further the enjoyment of all peoples of access on equal terms to the raw materials which are needed for their economic prosperity.[29]

Churchill refused to accept this version, claiming that it would require prior consultation with the dominions in view of its prescribing the Ottawa Agreements, adding that there was little hope of it being accepted. President Roosevelt, wishing to prevent serious friction and arrive at a quick joint declaration, did not give Welles his full backing.[30] Churchill avoided specific condemnation. The final version of the paragraph, agreed by compromise, took the British viewpoint on Imperial Preference into account:

Fourthly, they will endeavour, **with due respect to their existing obligations**, to further enjoyment by all states great or small, victor or vanquished of access on equal terms to the trade and raw materials of the world which are needed for their economic prosperity.[31]

Cordell Hull, dissatisfied with the outcome of the Atlantic Charter negotiations, tried to obtain further commitments from the British, first immediately after the end of the meeting and then again during the negotiations on Article VII of the Mutual Aid Agreement between the US and the UK under the Lend-Lease Act of 1941.[32]

After hard discussions with the UK which continued in Washington and London over a period of eight months, the UK finally agreed, in February 1942 to Article VII, which includes inter alia the following binding commitment:
"...To this end they shall include provisions for agreed action, by the US and UK to elimination of all forms of discriminatory treatment in international commerce and to the reduction of tariffs and other trade barriers; and in general to the attainment of all the economic objectives set forth in the joint declaration made on August 14, 1941 by the President of the US and the Prime Minister of the UK."
At an early convenient date, conversation shall begin between the two governments with a view to determining in the light of governing economic conditions, the best means of attaining the above stated objectives by their own agreed action and seeking the agreed action of other likeminded governments."[33]

Seeking to tackle the post-war problems of trade, the US, UK, and other important trading countries discussed the establishment of an appropriate international institution. Negotiations concerning the form and the function of the International Trade Organization (ITO) were first held on a bilateral basis between the US and the UK. The US published its proposals for a Charter of the ITO, which were discussed and amended in successive conferences of the Preparatory Committee (appointed by the Economic and Social Council of the United Nations to the draft of the Charter), held in London, New York, Geneva, and Havana between 1946 and 1948. The final version, drawn up in Havana in March 1948, became known as the Havana Charter.

Meanwhile, the governments that formed the Preparatory Committee agreed in 1947 to sponsor negotiations aimed at lowering customs tariffs and reducing restrictions among the 23 participating countries, without waiting for the ITO itself to come into being. The General Agreement on Tariff and Trade (GATT), drawn up in Geneva in October 1947 was considered a temporary agreement -- the result of the first of a number of tariff conferences to be held under the auspices of the ITO. The General Agreement incorporated part of the provisions of the ITO-draft charter, and when it became clear that the Havana Charter would not be ratified, GATT became the permanent international institution that assumed a large part of the functions that had been assigned to the now-abandoned ITO.

Under Hull the US State Department had continued to be actively involved in planning the future world trade institutions and rules of behavior, including inter-alia the ideas agreed upon in the Atlantic Charter and the Lend-Lease Agreement. In the original US proposals for the ITO charter, references to the access to supply appear twice: A.3 refers to the need "to reach the objectives of the Atlantic Charter and Article VII of the Lend-Lease Agreement." Chapter I, sub.-art. 3 states the objective of "facilitating access by all members on equal terms to the trade and raw materials of the world which are needed for the economic prosperity."³⁴ This last statement is taken over almost literally from the last part of Article 4 of the Atlantic Charter.

In the Final Act of the Havana Charter, chapter 1 (Purposes and Objectives) we find, in Article 1, sub.-art. 3 the objective of furthering "the enjoyment on equal terms of access to the markets, products and productive facilities which are needed for their economic prosperity and development" is set forth. Sub.-art. 4 promotes "on a reciprocal and mutually advantageous basis the reduction of tariffs and other barriers to trade and elimination of discriminatory treatment in international commerce."³⁵

Sub-article 3 does not appear in the preamble of GATT, but as already mentioned, GATT was negotiated during the preparation of the ITO charter. The preparatory committee of the Havana Conference stated, with respect to the draft of GATT, that "desiring to further the attainment of objectives of the conference by making effective among themselves such provisions of the above-mentioned draft charter as are applicable at this stage and thus taking such action prior to the conference as will constitute concrete achievement capable of generalization to all countries on equitable terms.³⁶

In other words, the basis of GATT was the ITO Draft Charter, but only those provisions that were applicable at that stage of the ITO Draft Charter were repeated in GATT. Thus, GATT actually dealt only with chapter IV of the charter and was thus much more limited in scope.

The provisions concerning export control and free access to supply that appear in GATT and in the Havana Charter are scattered and vague. To some extent this can be explained by the fact that unlike the Atlantic Charter, GATT and the Havana Charter represent bodies of rules worked out in negotiation among countries having different interests and points of view. It is nonetheless a historical fact that freer, non-discriminatory access to sources of supply was considered by the founding fathers of GATT and the Havana Charter to be at least as vital as access to markets.³⁷

Nevertheless, the question may be raised whether GATT's export provisions parallel its import provisions or whether there is an imbalance in favor of the latter.³⁸ GATT's major emphasis in the earlier years of its existence has been on freer non-discriminatory access to the world markets mainly because of the need to eliminate (then prevailing) import restrictions and to provide export opportunities in order to overcome balance of payments deficits besetting most of the member countries of GATT.

Furthermore, the reasons that caused the neglect of more elaborate provisions with respect to export restrictions during the last 25 to 30 years are to be found in the atmosphere that prevailed after World War II. A 1946 report argued that the severity of the International raw materials problem is primarily determined by the character of the world trading system.³⁹ There would be few problems of this kind in an expanding world economy sustaining a large and stable flow of commodities, services, and investment funds. Within such an environment importing countries would have no difficulty in financing purchases of foreign raw material; price fluctuation would generally remain within reasonable bounds; and prolonged conditions of excess productive capacities could be expected to occur but infrequently. The problem of raw materials export controls would essentially disappear under the assumed ideal conditions of peace and free trade, if political security, security from economic crises and depression, and restraint of beggar-my-neighbor policies could be maintained. Under these pre-conditions there would be no major problem of raw materials; those problems that did surface would be minor and could be resolved by agreements and rules determined in bilateral negotiations.

However, these preconditions, which idealists believed would prevail after World War II, were fulfilled only to some extent. For instance, the belief that the establishment of the UN would solve the problem of collective security, thus establishing a framework that would enable the treatment of raw materials not as an essential product in time of war, has vanished, and we are still witness to the importance of raw materials in the struggle between the blocs.

True, the narrow nationalist frame of reference has been in many cases broadened to a wider frame of blocs but it is difficult to argue that a struggle for the assurance of sources of supply needed in time of war does not exist or that there are countries that do not have difficulties in purchasing raw materials because of high prices and lack of foreign currency.

On the other hand, some of the assumptions and conclusions of the Staley/Knorr Report of 1946 seem to have been confirmed. The dominant position of the US in the world economy and its role in forming the post-World War trading system and the international commercial policy has doubtlessly moved the world closer to the preconditions, at least with respect to the members of the GATT. These have contributed towards the disappearance of the problem of access to resources and to the elimination of export controls, at least as a serious problem. In concrete terms, apart from a very short period during the Korean War in 1950, export controls and free access to resources did not constitute a problem for GATT until 1973. There were some problems, but for the most part were either outside the realm of GATT (such as export control in connection with international commodity agreements) or did not refer to members of GATT (such as relations with Eastern Bloc countries and OPEC).

## THE REASONS FOR RAISING THE ISSUE IN THE MULTILATERAL TRADE NEGOTIATIONS OF GATT

The primary cause for the recent rise of interest in the problem of export controls and free access to supply of primary commodities was not (as is usually believed) the 1973 oil crisis,[40] but the US imposition of temporary controls on the export of soya and its products, other agricultural products, and metal scrap. The oil crisis merely exacerbated the problem and awoke public consciousness to its existence.

Especially worrisome was the introduction of export controls on soya, that began as an outright prohibition, and later turned into restrictions that essentially licensed about half the export orders accepted up to a given date. The US informed OECD about the measures taken, explaining that these were necessary in view of the unexpected rise in demand without concurrent increase in supply, which created the danger of a shortage to meet the normal requirements of the US. In accordance with OECD procedures, Japan (supported by other OECD members) requested that these measures should be subject to consultations as soon as possible.

Japan, a large consumer of soya, which reduced its own production to one quarter of what it had been in 1960 at the request of the US, produced at that time only 3 percent of its consumption; almost all its imports came from the US. But Japan was not the only country that felt the adverse effects (mainly price rise) of the export controls; in the EEC as well there were shocks of price rises, which caused the Community to shift to the production of substitutes. A chain reaction of export restrictions occurred in other countries as well. The whole subject of export controls and their effects came up for general re-examination. The OECD Secretariat prepared an inventory of export restrictions and analyzed them with regard to types of controls, type of products, duration, motives, correlation, effects, etc., and examined the situation with respect to the existing legislation in international and regional organizations. This task took a number of years. From the beginning, countries such as Canada and Australia were not convinced of the need for a new examination of the subject. The US, which had been instrumental in starting a more thorough examination of the whole subject in the OECD, became less interested at the later stage of the OECD investigation, mainly because of the decision of Congress on the Trade Act of 1974 to take up the matter in GATT.[41] Henry Kissinger also announced at UNCTAD IV, in Nairobi, that "a study should be begun in GATT on the feasibility of an International Code on Export Controls in order to improve reliability of supply.[42]

Thus, although the US concluded from the OECD findings that the practical solution of some problems of international trade suffered from lack of international disciplines or weak procedures, it was willing to transfer the main treatment of the subject to GATT. The EEC, on the other hand, argued the desirability of continuing with work started in the OECD, although at a "measured" pace. Canada and Australia found no justification in the findings for new initiatives since no disruption to trade as a result of export controls had been proven. Other countries, such as Switzerland and Sweden, were of the opinion that there was room to continue with the discussion but within the framework of the Multilateral Trade Negotiations (MTN) in GATT. Since, in fact, no new export restriction had been introduced, it was decided in the OECD to continue and follow up the subject and to return to the problem at a later stage, if necessary.

Meanwhile, within GATT the subject was discussed at the MTN during the discussions in the Non-Tariff Measures (NTB) group.

But several countries (mainly Australia and Canada) argued that it was not within the authority of the group and the subject was referred back to the Trade Negotiations Committee and later transferred to the "framework" group.[43] At the initiative of one delegation (probably the US with support from other delegations) a proposal was submitted that essentially included the following points:
(1) Even permitted export controls may cause difficulties;
(2) some export control provisions in GATT lack clarity and are controversial;
(3) export control notification and publication should be renewed; notification prior to application of a given measure should be introduced;
(4) more efficient and expeditious procedures of consultations, taking account developing countries' interests, should be established. Disputes should be settled by recourse to Articles XXIII:1 and XXIII:2 of GATT, and if unsuccessful, then by new agreement on settlement of dispute;
(5) a review of export controls should be included within periodical surveys of trade development;
(6) an early review should be made of the conclusions on the use of quantitative restrictions adopted in the 1950 Report of the CPs, taking account of Part IV of GATT and other later developments.[44]

The proposal had two annexes. The first contained all existing GATT provisions with respect to export controls. The second contained a list of problems and topics for possible negotiations on export controls that included inter-alia:
(1) Purposes for which export controls may be permitted;
(2) more precise definition of exceptions for use of quantitative export controls and clarification of concepts such as "equitable share";
(3) definition of "temporary", "basic", and "liberalizing" period of restriction;
(4) differentiation in treatment between export prohibitions and export restrictions;
(5) rules on negotiation, concession and bindings, emergencies, and renegotiation of export duties; and
(6) special treatment of less developed countries.

This annex was headed by the remark that all problems could be subject to negotiation only if the major countries, likely to benefit from the new rules, would also be willing to take upon themselves obligations that could be considered to constitute adequate reciprocity to those countries from which the new obligations regarding export controls were demanded.
This remark seems to point to the real source of the difference of opinion among the GATT member countries. Some raw materials producing countries felt that no balance existed between the demands presented to them as exporters and the demands presented to the consuming countries. They therefore resisted every attempt to change the existing rules, and demanded

specifically to include in the agreement the recognition of their right to unlimited control of their resources.[45] In this connection one must recall that GATT constitutes a fragile balance among concessions based on the principle of reciprocity.

Some producing countries do not enjoy free access to the markets for most of their (agricultural) products, because of existing market protection. Other producing countries are mainly suppliers of raw materials and have little to offer in those finished products for which free access to the markets exists. They are therefore unwilling to accept the argument that in return for the obligation undertaken by consuming countries to restrict their sovereignty and permit free access to the market, producing countries should undertake a similar obligation to permit free access to sources of supply.[46]

The objections to the new rules on export restrictions were not always based on the same factors. Thus, the more developed among the primary producing and exporting countries, such as Canada and Australia, objected to changes because of lack of balance. On the other hand, the developing countries based their resistance on the principles of development and diversification embodied in Part IV of GATT and on the principles of the Charter of Economic Rights and Duties.

Therefore, a counter-proposal of the developing countries stated as follows: export control can be used legitimately in order to further economic and social objectives, and developing countries are permitted to use export control measures in order to promote the development and diversification of their trade and industry and to raise the standard of living of their people. This proposal is based on the objectives of Part IV and specified in Article XXXVI and in particular the measures referring to adequate supply for existing manufacturing enterprises and for the establishment of new processing facilities in the context of their development and employment policies.

Several delegations objected to this counter-proposal and negotiations dragged on. The subject matter also did not have top priority with the US delegation, which was tied down with many other topics. When they finally got around to dealing with the subject more intensively, there was not sufficient time for the committee to enter into the subject in depth. It was therefore possible to reach an understanding to continue with the study of the subject and deal with it after completion of the MTN. During the early months of 1979 it was agreed among the contracting parties of GATT to request as one of the priority tasks after the completion of the Tokyo Round a reassessment of GATT provisions relating to export restrictions and their changes, in the context of the International Trading System as a whole, and taking into account the development, financial, and trade needs of the developing countries.

The work program accepted on 29 November 1979 indicates that the subject matter of export control would be dealt with by the consultative group of eighteen, which should be asked to advise the GATT council on the framework and ways of dealing with the subject in the future.

NOTES

1. Long-term proposals are based on the following observations:
(1) Mineral resources are distributed unevenly over the earth.
(2) Their exploitation benefits a small number of countries that have been favorably endowed by nature.
(3) The industrial development of the presently less developed countries will increase their consumption of mineral resources and more and more countries will need these resources.
In view of the above it is important that conditions be created that make it possible to treat mineral resources as a common heritage of mankind and gradually to shift from the exercise of national territorial sovereignty over mineral resources to the exercise of functional sovereignty. The concept of common heritage should imply:
(1) A real world market for all mineral resources.
(2) A world tax system to replace national taxes on mineral resources, the revenue collected to be distributed among developing countries through agencies such as IDM according to a certain criteria.
2. See Bergsten 1975.
3. See Behrman 1977.
4. In the other extreme, when the revenue tax is imposed on top of a world monopoly price, the actual income of the country from abroad and receipts of the government may be smaller than could be obtained by letting the monopoly maximize its profit and tax a fixed sum. The difference between this case and the case discussed in (a) is that there the country possesses a natural advantage but there are a number of producers in the country whereas here one talks of a monopolist.
5. See US Tariff Commission, Non-tariff Trade Barriers Report to the Committee on Finance of the US Senate and its Sub-Committee on International Trade, part 2, 254. A very interesting article on the history and nature of voluntary export controls containing many examples is Smith 1979.
6. See Bertsch 1981.
7. See Branting, 1980.
8. Another instance is the Export Administration's decision to place Cambodia and South Vietnam in the exact category, made "to deny these regimes, which came to power, hostile to the US, by force of arms, to deny them access to US markets and to submit trade with those countries to a licensing procedure." See Testimony of Robert H. Miller, Deputy Assistant to the Secretary of State for East Asian and Pacific Affairs, before the Sub-Committee on International Trade and Commerce of the Committee on International Relations, US House of Representatives, 94th Congress, 4 July 1975. In the debate it is admitted that these countries were not threatening the US directly, and that control was a prudent and orderly way to establish a basis for judging how these new regimes evolved.
9. See Freedman 1979.

10. See, for instance, the Japanese controls listed in US Tariff Commission Non-tariff Trade Barriers, part 2.
11. See Behrman 1970, 136-37.
12. See Branting 1980.
13. See Staley 1937, 78.
14. See Protocol for the Accession of Poland, which includes in Part I paragraph 4:
"(b) The contracting party concerned may request Poland to enter into consultation with it. Any such request shall be notified to the CP. If as a result of this consultation Poland agrees that the situation referred to in (a) (imports of the product from Poland causing serious injury) above exists it shall limit exports or take such other action which may include action with respect to the price at which the exports are sold, as will prevent or remedy the injury." BISD 15th suppl.
15. Some of the same conditions are present today. However, today, many of the problems lie beyond the realm of GATT while others are disputes between members and non-members.
16. For instance, the report that recommended, in October 1918, the establishment of the Central Board of Controls of allies, neutrals, and enemies, under whose supervision commodity countries would ration supplies.
17. League of Nations 1946.
18. Viner 1951, 94-95.
19. For more detailed references with respect to this position and its criticism see Staley 1937, 173-75.
20. Indeed, President Wilson announced "that the passing away of discriminatory tariffs was to be like reduction in national armaments. In the President's mind this proposal was linked to the idea that any economic weapons including refusal of access to strategic raw materials should be entrusted to the League of Nations for purpose of restraining agression. It was, however, realized in many quarters that absence of discrimination and "open doors" in colonies were in themselves no guarantee of access to raw materials. It was necessary for all countries to be able to exchange their products in order to pay for the raw materials they required, which meant that the channels of international trade should be reopened. These various lines of thought were expressed in the third of the fourteen points of President Wilson in the peace conference, which read as follows: "The removal so far as possible of all economic barriers and the establishment of an equality of trade conditions among all the nations consenting to peace and associating themselves for its maintenance." (Staley and Knorr 1946, 22).
21. President Wilson, replying to a charge that he advocated "free trade", explained that he did not emphasize free trade but wanted only non-discriminatory treatment, leaving weapons of economic discipline and punishment to the joint action of all nations (Staley and Knorr 1946, 22).
22. Staley and Knorr 1846, 33-35.
23. The other main provisions were as follows: regulations regarding the manner, form, or place of importation or exportation, or other facilities or conditions "shall not be made

as a means of disguised prohibition or arbitrary restrictions" (Article 3). Certain prohibition and restrictions were excepted if not constituting arbitrary discrimination or disguised restrictions in international trade. These related to those imposed on moral or humanitarian grounds; health, sanitary, and psychosanitary regulations; national treasures, gold and silver, state monopoly, etc. (Article 4). Various temporary exceptions and submissions of claims for further exceptions within a given period were allowed (Article 6). These include situations: (1) of factor law that prevent a country from immediately undertaking, as regards specified products, the obligation of the agreement; (2) the more interesting case of prohibitions or restrictions whose elimination on the one hand would involve the country in grave difficulties and on the other hand would not prejudicially affect the trade of other countries. Article 17 suggested the meeting of a second conference, to deal with these supplementary claims. That conference met and it was decided that the convention (including the additional reservations approached) would come into force if ratified by 18 states before 30 September 1929. Only 17 states ratified. The convention was brought into force by special arrangement by seven states including the UK, Japan and the US but by 1934 it had been denounced by them all. See: Official Paper No. C. 14 M.11 1929 11 (CIAP 19(13)) 1927. Geneva 1st Jan. 1929. Serie de Publication de la societe des Nations Question Economiques et Financieres.

24. League of Nations 1942, 35; 93-94.
25. Staley and Knorr 1946, 61.
26. It should be noted that at the World Economic Conference of 1937 where the last attempt to liberalize trade before World War II was made, all the above principles of the economic committee were included. With respect to the specific point it was mentioned there that export duty on raw materials should never be levied for the special purpose of imposing an additional burden on foreign countries in order to put them in an inferior position as to the production of the finished product.
27. In his memoirs, Hull admits, "Though realizing that many other factors were involved, I reasoned that if we could get a freer flow of trade, freer in the sense of fewer discriminations and obstructions so that one country would not be deadly jealous of another and the living standard of all countries might rise thereby eliminating the economic dissatisfaction that breeds war -- we might have a reasonable chance of lasting peace." To what extreme has the same approach been extended, can best perhaps be illustrated by his own argument claiming that those countries with whom the US entered into trade agreements there was no war; on the contrary, they joined together in war "because the political line-up follows the economic line." Hull 1948, 81; Gardner 1969, 9-12.
28. Brown 1950, 1.
29. Welles 1947, 8.
30. "Time being of essence, I think I can stand on my own former formulae, to wit: access to raw materials. This omits

entirely the other subject which is the only one in conflict -- discrimination in trade." Welles 1947, 13.

31. Welles 1947, 140-41.

32. In the final analysis his preoccupation with the Ottawa Agreements on Imperial Preference was exaggerated, since the reservation dealt only with the existing obligations, which were limited in time. Gardener 1969, 51.

33. Gardener 1969, chapter IV.

34. In addition, export control provisions are specifically elaborated in the General Commercial Policy Chapter, Buchanan and Lutz 1947, Appendix 3.

35. The similarity of the original draft prepared by Sumner Welles for the Atlantic Charter (probably with the assistance of other officials in the State Department, such as Harry Hawkins, who also participated in the negotiations of the ITO) is apparent. Gardener 1969, 56. The article in the Havana Charter and the second part of the Welles sentence are practically identical except for the changes in the words "market products" and "productive facilities", instead of "raw materials," the last two probably made at the insistence of the developing countries, which also probably insisted on the addition of the world's development after prosperity. See Brown 1950, 97-100.

36. During the first preparatory committee in London, the discussion of the purpose of the organization was "postponed until the structure of the organization can be seen as a whole."

37. See, for instance, Roosevelt's instruction to Sumner Welles during the negotiations of the Atlantic Charter. "He (the president) was firm in the conviction that equal opportunity to enjoy the world's natural resources must be available to all people" Welles 1947, 16.

38. For a summary of the existing export control provision in GATT, see chapter 11.

39. Staley and Knorr 1946, 108-9.

40. At the Tokyo Round of Multilateral Trade Negotiations in April 1979 it was emphasized that the growing interest in the problem of export restrictions was in part the result of the oil crisis and temporary restrictions in other products. It is true that the oil crisis has made the problem more severe and caused the public to become more conscious of the problem, but the primary cause for the discussion of the subject were the US export restrictions mentioned above.

41. From a press release of the committee on finance of the US Senate it is evident that it was Senator Walter Mondale's amendments that added two additional items to Section 121 of the Trade Bill, dealing with the reform of GATT. These items would direct the President to enter into negotiations to improve rules governing access to supplies of food, raw materials, and manufactured products and to establish multilateral rules against the denial of equitable access to supplies. The items appeared in the Trade Act 74 (Public Law 93-168) in section 121(a)(7) and (8) p. 9. The text reads as follows:

Section 121 <u>Steps</u> <u>to</u> <u>be</u> <u>taken</u> <u>toward</u> <u>GATT</u> <u>Revision;</u> <u>Authorization</u> <u>of</u> <u>Appropriation</u> <u>for</u> <u>GATT:</u>

The President shall as soon as practicable take such actions as may be necessary, to bring trade agreements heretofore entered into the application thereof into conformity with principles promoting the development at an open non-discriminatory, and fair world economic system. The action and principles referred to in the preceding sentence include, but are not limited to the following:
...(7) The improvement and strengthening of the provisions of GATT and other international agreements governing access to supplies of food, raw materials and manufactured or semi-manufactured products including rules, and procedures governing the imposition of export controls, the denial of fair and equitable access to such supplies and effective consultative procedures on problems of supply shortage.
(8) The Extension of the Provisions of GATT or other international agreements to authorize multilateral procedures by contracting parties with respect to member or non-member countries which deny fair and equitable access to supplies of food, raw materials and manufactured or semi-manufactured products and thereby substantially injure the international community.

42. UNCTAD IV 1976.
43. GATT, Tokyo Round 1978, 8-9.
44. Several delegations had reservations on this point since they considered that the findings of the working group of 1958 had no current validity in view of Article XXXVI and part IV of GATT as a whole and the Charter of Economic Rights and Duties accepted by the General Assembly of the UN recognizing the sovereign rights of a country on its natural resources.
45. Neue Zuricher Zeitung 1979.
46. GATT, Tokyo Round of MTN 1979.


BIBLIOGRAPHY

Allan William R. 1933. The International Trade Philosophy of Cordell Hull, 1907-1933. American Economic Review XLIII.
Behrman, J.R. 1977. International Commodity Agreements: An Evaluation of the UNCTAD Integrated Commodity Programme. Washington, DC: ODC, NIEO Series.
Bergsten, F.C. 1975. Completing the GATT, Towards New International Rules to Govern Export Controls, British North American Committee. In F.C. Bergsten (Ed.) Toward a New International Economic Order. Lexington, Mass.
Bertsch, Gary K. 1981. US Export Controls in the 1970's and Beyond. Journal of World Trade and Law 15.
Branting, Luther Karl. 1980.Reconciliation of Conflicting Goals in the Export Administration Act of 1979: A Delicate Balance. Law and Policy in International Business 12: 415-60.
Brown, William Adams, Jr. 1950. The United States and the Restoration of World Trade. Washington, D.C.: The Brookings Institution.

Buchanan, Norman S. and Lutz, Friedrich A. 1947. Rebuilding the World Economy. New York: The Twentieth Century Fund.
Freedman, Steven J. 1979. UD Trade Sanctions Against Uganda: Legality Under International Law. Law and Policy in International Business 11.
Gardener, R.N. 1969. Sterling Dollar Diplomacy. Expanded edition. New York: McGraw-Hill.
GATT. 1950. General Agreement on Tariffs and Trade. Geneva.
\_\_\_\_ 1950. The Use of Quantitative Restrictions for Protective and other Commercial Purposes. Geneva.
\_\_\_\_ 1979. Basic Instruments and Selected Documents. 26th Supplement. Geneva.
\_\_\_\_ Basic Instruments and Selected Documents. 15th Supplement. Geneva.
\_\_\_\_ 1947. Document E/PC/T/34. Geneva.
\_\_\_\_ 1979. Document of Canada. Geneva.
\_\_\_\_ Document MTN/FR/W/20/Rev. 1. Geneva.
\_\_\_\_ 1979. The Tokyo Round of Multilateral Trade Negotiations. Geneva.
Gilbert, R. and Noguchu, Tetsuo. 1976. Energy Ores and Minerals. In RIO - Reshaping the International Order, A Report to the Club of Rome coordinated by Jan Tinbergen. New York: Dutton.
Hull, Cordell. 1948. The Memoirs of Cordell Hull. Vol. I. New York: MacMillan.
Jackson, J.H. 1969. World Trade and the Law of GATT. New York: Bobbs Merril.
League of Nations. 1946. Raw Material Problem and Policies in the Council of the League 1920. Geneva.
Roessler, 1975. Gatt and Access to Supplier. Journal of World Trade Law. 9:
Smith, Malcolm D.H. 1979. Voluntary Export Quotas and US Trade Policy - A New Non-Tariff Barrier. Law and Policy in International Business. 5.
Staley. E. 1937. Raw Materials in Peace and War. New York: Tenth International Studies Conference Council of Foreign Relations.
Staley, E. and Knorr, K.E. 1946. Raw Material Problems and Policies. Geneva: League of Nations.
Taussig, E.W. 1943. Memorandum on the International Allotment of Important Commodities, American Economic Review. XXXIII; 877-81.
UNCTAD 1976. UNCTAD (IV) Plenary Meeting. Vol. II.
UN 1974. General Assembly A. 9946. New York.
US Congress. 1975. Trade Act 74 (Public Law 93-618).
Vertragsabweichungen - Legalisierte und Problematische Varianten - Exportbeschraenkungen, ein Heikles Thema. 1979. Neue Zuricher Zeitung. December 29, 1979.
Viner, Jacob. 1951. The Most Favored Nation Clause. In International Economics. Illinois: Free Press.
Welles, Sumner. 1947. Where Are We Heading? London: Hamish and Hamilton.

# 11
The Analysis of the GATT Provisions

*Michael Rom*

The previous chapter attempted to give a historical perspective to the issue of export controls and access to supplies in GATT. This chapter will first give a short account of the existing export control provisions and then analyze the issue in detail, by comparing these provisions with the import control provisions of GATT. Thus, the relevant articles of the Agreement will be systematically examined and, where necessary, proposals for further clarifications, elaborations, or new provisions will be suggested.

We can summarize briefly[1] the existing GATT provisions on export controls as follows:
(a) Export duties and taxes may be raised when they are not bound. In principle, export prohibitions and restrictions of any other kind are prohibited (Article XII) except in the cases identified below.
(b) Discrimination is prohibited and export duties must be imposed in accordance with MFNC (Article I).
(c) Negotiations toward reducing tariffs is permitted (Article XXVII bis). Developed countries do not expect reciprocity from developing countries and concessions are to be made by the former, consistent with their individual development, financial, and trade needs. The results of these negotiations are included in the schedules of Article I. State trading enterprises can also negotiate reduction of duties and other changes (on exports Article XVII 3 ad.). As to the safeguarding of the value of concessions negotiated, there are both general principles in the field of valuation for customs purposes to serve as guidelines (Article VII 1) and instructions concerning the changing of fees and formalities with respect to exportation (Article VIII). These fees should be restricted to what it costs to give the service, and procedures and for matters should be minimized and simplified.

Although in principle export restrictions are prohibited, there are circumstances under which they are permitted:
(a) in case of critical shortage of foodstuffs and other products essential to the exporting country (Article XI, 2(a));
(b) in case of application of standards (Article XI, 2(b));
(c) in case of export control for foreign exchange control purposes (Article XV, 9b);

(d) in case of misrepresentation of trade name (Article IX 6).[2]

Article XIII,1 requires non-discriminatory treatment of export restriction. Article XIII,5 requires that, where applicable, the principles of this article which refer to the non-discriminatory administration of quantitative restrictions shall also extend to export restrictions. Nevertheless, there are cases where Article XIV is applicable, for instance Article XIV, 4 which permits direction of export of a country applying import restriction if the directed export is done in such a manner as to increase its earnings of currencies, which it can use without deviation from Article XIII.

The non-discriminatory treatment in exports of state trading enterprises is stipulated in Article XVII. A note to Articles XI, XII, XIII, XIV and XVIII states that the term "export restrictions" includes restrictions made effective through state trading operations. In general exceptions to Article XX most paragraphs include provisions permitting in fact export control whether in the form of quantitative restriction, cost restriction or other measures. These refer to measures necessary for the protection of public morale (Article XXa); human, animal, or plant life or health; gold and silver; compliance with laws and regulations such as monopolies (in accordance with Articles II4 and XVII); patents, trade marks, copyright, etc.; national treasures; natural resources conservation made effective, together with restriction on domestic production or consumption; inter-governmental commodity agreements conforming to criteria accepted by GATT or not disapproved by them; materials essential to domestic industry; (when domestic price is below world price and the move is part of a government stabilization plan, provided it shall not increase exports or protection of the industry, and the exports are restricted in a non-discriminatory manner); products in short supply, provided all CPs are entitled to an equitable share of the international supply of such products and that measures, in consistence with other provisions of the agreement, will be discontinued as soon as the conditions causing them cease.

Article XXI, which deals with security exceptions, contains important provisions permitting export control relating to fissionable materials and their raw materials; arms munitions and military supplies in time of war or other international emergency; and in pursuance of obligations under the UN Charter for the maintenance of international peace and security. With respect to developing countries, export restriction seems to be permitted for the sake of raising and stabilizing income for primary products (see Article XXXVIII, 2(a), Article XLII, 4) although this has not been stated specifically.

In addition, there is the requirement for publication of laws, regulation, judicial decisions, and administrative rulings relating to exports (see Article Xl). These must be published promptly in such a manner as to enable governments and trades to become acquainted with them. The laws and regulations mentioned above should be administered in a uniform and impartial manner and permit prompt review by independent tribunals of customs matters

(Articles X3 and X4). It thus becomes evident that there is no lack of provision relating to export controls. Why then has the issue been raised? It seems that criticism has emanated for a number of reasons and from different quarters.

First, there were those that argued that export provisions are too liberal[3] and the number of exceptions is so large that practically any export control measure undertaken can be justified by a GATT provision. Therefore, time has come to obligate exporting member countries to abide by commitments as are doing the importing countries. On the other hand, it is argued that the export provisions in the agreement are much fewer than those for importers, thus preventing exporting countries from obtaining equal treatment in many respects.[4] Finally even those provisions that do exist, are very often not explicit and precise enough. Although the original intention was to ensure equally free access to markets and to sources of supply,[5] in time, due to the reality of serious problems with access to the markets, the emphasis was put on the treatment and elaboration of those rules for that aspect, and the treatment of export controls and freer access to supply was relatively neglected.[6]

Article II is more problematic. The first paragraph, 1(a), reads: "Each contracting party shall accord to the commerce (i.e., including exports (M.R.)) of the contracting parties treatment no less favorable than that provided for the appropriate part of the appropriate schedule annexed to this Agreement." Thus,. prima facie concessions mentioned in the schedules relate also to export duties. On the other hand the continuation of the Article, i.e. 1b and 1c refers specifically only to imports, as do Sub-Articles 2 and 4.

Based on Sub-Articles 1b and 1c, Jackson (1969) claims that Article II refers only to import duties. Roessler (1975), looking at Article II, 1(a) and Article XXVIII, bis, and on actual examples of export duty bindings (in the schedules) claims that export duties are included in the Article. The major practical difference in the positions of the two occurs in the case of a withdrawal of concession. If it is included in the schedule, it can be withdrawn only after the interests of affected third countries are safeguarded (through certain procedures that sometimes give them compensation rights). On the other hand, if it is not included, then the concession can be withdrawn by bilateral agreement of the two parties concerned without regard for third parties.

Roessler's position appears correct. Some of the relevant provisions included in Article XXVIII bis (at a later stage in GATT) were discussed together with Article I of Most Favored Nation (MFN)[7] and actually appeared together in the International Trade Organization (ITO) draft charter prepared for the second session of the ITO preparatory committee.[8] Although the US draft on the subject of negotiations was kept to a separate section, there was no attempt to exclude negotiations of export tariff reductions. The real preoccupation with import tariffs; the neglect of export tariffs; the inclusion of the schedules in the GATT; and the fact that (as originally intended in the US ITO draft) the negotiation article in GATT comes only after substantive provisions have created this apparent distinction between export and import tariffs that did not exist in principle when the articles were read or discussed during the negotiations. It therefore would be appropriate to introduce amendments and refer explicitly also to exports in Article II. The same ought to be done with respect to the preferences in Article I, although at present this is probably of marginal value if not meaningless altogether.

Article III relates to national treatment and does not refer to export duties and restrictions. Thus, theoretically it is possible for a country to grant a concession in the form of a reduction or elimination of an export duty and then circumvent such a concession or cancel its value through an administrative regulation or the imposition of an internal tax. Generally, the absence of the obligation to extend national treatment to exports seems logical since such an obligation would in many cases be detrimental to the exporting country.

Let us take the example of domestic technical standards that exceed those demanded abroad. If as a result, the price of the exported product rises, thus pricing the product out of the market, the exporter will want to produce according to the less strict requirements of the country of destination and thus reduce the cost of the product. This he could not do if the national treatment clause applies. This, one of many examples, is sufficient to justify generally the absence of national treatment in the case of exports.

Nevertheless, in order to meet the objection raised earlier, a limitation to the above should be introduced, namely that national treatment should apply in cases of concessions granted on exports to the extent necessary to prevent circumvention of that concession.

Article VII contains a specific reference to exports in its first paragraph: "...contracting parties recognize the validity of the general principles of valuation set forth in the following paragraphs of this Article and they undertake to give effect to such principles in respect of all products subject to duties or other charges or restrictions on importation and exportation based upon or regulated in any manner by value."

However, again Sub-Articles 2, 3 and 4 relate specifically only to imports elaborating what the value of imported products should be, and how it should be determined. No similar detailed provisions exist for export duties. The latter should also be specified, otherwise here as well concessions granted on export duties may be circumvented. It is true that implicitly the elaborations of Sub-Articles 2, 3 and 4 are (in view of Sub-Article 1) of general validity. However, in their application there is room for different interpretations and a more specific elaboration of the value of exported product for customs purposes and how it should be determined would seem desirable.[9]

Article VIII deals with fees and formalities associated with both imports and exports. Paragraphs 1 and 4 condemn the use of exchange taxes or fees as a device for implementing multiple currency practices. If, however, a contracting party uses multiple currency exchange fees for balance of payments reasons, with the approval of the IMF, the provisions of section 9(a) of Article XV fully safeguard its position. In other words, under special circumstances export taxes may be permissible as an alternative to multiple currency practices.[10]

Article X deals with the publication and administration of trade regulation of both imports and exports. However, there is a distinction in Sub-article 2, which requires official publication of measures affecting imports, but not exports, prior to enforcement. The subject will be discussed below in conjunction with the topic of notification.

Article XII relates to restrictions to improve the balance of payments and refers almost exclusively to import restrictions instituted in order to prevent a severe deficit in the balance of payments. There are no corresponding rules for export restrictions to deal with a balance of payments surplus. A possible exception is contained in Sub-article 5, which refers to cases in which a persistent disequilibrium exists which restricts international trade, and where CPs are encouraged to initiate discussions to consider other measures (apart from the widespread application of import restriction). The injunction also includes those contracting parties which tend to have an exceptionally favorable balance of payment. Yet even in this sub-article no specific recommendations regarding measures that should be applied are included. It would seem desirable to elaborate in which specific cases revaluation or alternative measures could be applied.

Similarly a careful reading of the "framework" group discussions (see MIN/FR/W 20 Rev. 2(b)) proves, that in the future not only import restrictions but also surcharges on imports would be permitted if this were the method "that least disturbs trade" (GATT, Tokyo Round, 1979, p. 150). No similar reference exists with respect to export surcharges. That such situations should be taken into account can best be illustrated by the case of West Germany, which in 1969 levied a 4 percent export tax in order to adjust its balance of payments (Roessler, 1975, p. 38). Yet many narrower cases should also be considered and not only those involving restrictions imposed to reduce surplus. Sometimes an export surcharge or control is the best method of improving the foreign exchange deficit by raising prices and revenue from export.[11] Otherwise cutthroat competition would diminish the entire industry's chance of selling abroad (Rom 1980, pp. 110-111).

Article XIII deals with the non-discriminatory administration of quantitative restrictions. The first paragraph refers explicitly to exports as well as to imports, ensuring non-discriminatory treatment in both cases. However, Sub-articles 2, 3 and 4 refer explicitly only to imports when discussing the methods of administration of quantitative restrictions. Although at the end of Sub-article 5 it is stipulated that "insofar as applicable, the principles of this article shall also extend to export restrictions", the reference is rather vague, and open to different interpretations.

In the OECD findings it is argued that "in cases where there is a quota system or quantitative controls the methods used to determine the allocation of exports vary."[12] Sometimes these measures are analogous to those that have been employed for import restrictions. Thus, some countries have allocated licenses on the basis of contracts recorded at a certain date, or firm orders for which exporters could provide evidence. In other cases the allocation has been made among importing countries on the basis of exports during a reference period or has been based on consultation with the main customers and in the light of their requirements. The same country has, in some cases, used different methods depending on the product in question and the circumstances prevailing at the time. Sometimes there was no pre-determined official allocation plan, but before granting export licenses the exporting country's government ensured that a certain part of the production had been delivered to domestic consumers. In fact, there is no internationally accepted criterion as to the method to be used in allocating exports. It would, moreover, be very difficult to lay down such criteria in the abstract since to be fair, the particular circumstances of each individual case would have to be taken into account, and it is impossible to say in advance what those circumstances would be. Certain principles embodied in the GATT may, however, be applicable to such cases.

We believe that, in general, the GATT instruction for non-discriminatory administration of import restrictions are broad enough to be applicable, in most cases, to non-discriminating treatment of export restrictions particularly in view of the phrase "due account being taken of any special factors which may have affected or may be affecting the trade of the product." Obviously the interpretation of this phrase in the case of exports needs amendment since there the cross-reference to GATT Article XI, 2c is to relative productive efficiency among producers, which does not apply here. If an amendment is introduced the order of emphasis should be changed and a reference to exports together with imports should be included in the texts of the Sub-articles XIII and V, leaving a loophole permitting special treatment where others are not applicable, and then explaining why.

In addition, it might be useful to adopt certain general guidelines to be observed for those cases in Sub-article V where the earlier provisions are not applicable. These would include guidelines aimed at avoiding arbitrary or unjustified discrimination; ensuring an equitable share of supply to all countries; avoiding unnecessary damage to the interests of other countries (which implies, inter alia, the abolition of restrictions as soon as they are no longer necessary); avoiding the introduction of disguised restriction in international trade; and encouraging accepting consultation among mainly interested countries.

The provisions of Article XIV have undergone substantial changes since the original GATT article, which corresponded roughly to the Havana Charter (although there were some differences that permitted even contracting parties a choice of applying restrictions on the basis of the ITO or the GATT.[13] The existing article includes only a small part of the provisions included in the past. The US opposed the extension of exceptions in the discriminatory restrictions, knowing that all these restrictions will be directed primarily against itself - and that such restrictions are particularly severe in view of their being quantitative and not cost restriction, that many of the original suggestions, have not been accepted.

However, certain compromises were needed, such as an increase in the list of items of the general exceptions and a more flexible provision for the balance of payments exception (which in substantial part was of a temporary nature).

This explains why the discriminatory treatment in Artivle XIV refers to the balance of payments and why preoccupation at the time was similar to Article XII itself, with import restrictions. While there may be other justified actual discriminatory treatment not referring to the balance of payments (for instance in Article XXI or some of the general exceptions) this article is reserved to discriminatory treatment based on Article XII.

In view of the fact that it was suggested to correct that article in order to take account of export restriction, it would seem worthwhile to consider whether it is not desirable to permit similar changes in this article also. This may be relevant in circumstance where a discriminatory export restriction or levy may be the solution to an excessively high surplus in the balance of payments, resulting from extremely efficient exports, to a particular region of the world[14] and where revaluation may not be desirable or possible.

Most of the provisions of Article XV are not particularly relevant to our discussion here, since the article deals primarily with the relations between GATT and the IMF. It is however interesting to mention the Addendum to Sub-article IV, which refers, inter alia, to "a contracting party which as a part of its exchange control operated in accordance with the Articles of Agreement of the IMF requires payments to be received for its exports in its own currency or currency of one or more members of the IMF, will not thereby be deemed to contravene Article XI or Article XIII". This in spite of the article itself, which stipulates that contracting parties shall not by exchange action frustrate the intent of the provisions of this agreement.

Article VI refers to anti-dumping and countervailing duties. While the subject of subsidies is more explicitly defined and discussed in Article XVI of GATT, the subject of dumping is discussed only in Article VI. Therefore we will discuss first the subject of dumping.

Where subsidies are granted by the government, dumping is carried out by an individual economic enterprise. As Kindleberger (1958) states, "Most economists regard dumping as a vicious policy much more than ... the intervention of the government. The reason being that the producer in a position to discriminate ... is a monopolist in whole or in part working for his own interest," whereas government intervention usually is charged with the general good.[15]

Dumping can be carried out only if separate markets exist and the producer has some control over the price at which he sells. If he has no influence over the price and is one of many sellers adjusting output to a given price, it pays him to continue selling up to the point where price equals marginal cost in his own country rather than sell abroad at even lower prices and a loss. It can therefore safely be assumed that dumping is carried out mainly by monopolies and cartels (although some quasi-monopolies, which through advertising and other means influence the demand for their product at home, may also engage in dumping).

Article VI of GATT stipulates with respect to dumping that if a) the products of one country are introduced into the commerce of another country at less than the normal value of the products[16] and b) it causes or threatens material injury to an established industry in the territory of the importing country or materially retards the establishment of a domestic industry, then that country may impose an anti-dumping duty to offset the dumping.

The question arises if it is not similarly justified to take steps to prevent what Kindleberger calls "reverse dumping", i.e. the setting of the export price at a level higher than that set for the domestic market.[17]

Not every rise in price abroad above the price in the domestic market can be seen as objectionable: there are many good economic reasons that justify the raising of prices in the foreign market above the price of the internal market and this practice is not condemned by GATT.

But just as dumping as such is not condemned unless it causes or threatens to cause material injury, so it seems that the same rule should apply to the abuse of a monopolistic dominant position, or to a cartel that raises export prices excessively and causes or threatens to cause material injury to the domestic industry in the importing country and/or materially retards the establishment of an industry. In such a case there are three elements which ought to be considered: a) the distortion of competition by the establishment of a cartel or the existence of a monopoly that holds a dominant position; b) the material injury to the importing member country; and c) the fact (mentioned earlier) that the action is carried out by an enterprise or enterprises that are pursuing only "their own interest" and not the national good. Perhaps in addition to the article ought to be introduced that would permit taking action when, as a result of abuse of a dominant position or a cartel, unjustifiably differential pricing in export as compared to the domestic market is taking place.

Admittedly this subject is related to enterprises employing restrictive business practices and should really be treated within the broader context of restrictive practices. But the same argument is also true with respect to dumping, which is carried out largely by cartels and monopolies. Therefore, from a strictly balancing point of view there is sense in including also the opposite side of the case. Secondly, for the time being at least, Chapter V of the Havana Charter (or its substitute) has not been concretely absorbed into the GATT and recent treatment in UNCTAD within the new code is of a voluntary nature and not contractually binding as is the case with the GATT. It would therefore seem desirable if, at least in the specific case mentioned above,[19] some protection within the framework of GATT could be provided. The problem already bothered the US during the ECA, where they attacked the European practice of charging higher prices for steel in the export trade than those charged at home (Kindleberger 1958, 268).[20] It is certainly typical today (particulary in customs unions or free trade areas) with respect to export cartels,[21] which compete internally and raise prices jointly abroad, thus preventing equal access to raw materials or semi-manufactures. Obviously, the solution in such a case is not the same as that which exists for dumping. Here the solution would probably be along the lines of what could be termed in terms of the subsidies code the second track; complaint to the committee, consultations dispute settlement including the possibility of taking counter measures, etc.-- all this is compatible with the new Anti-Dumping Code (BISD 26th Supplement).

A second case in which it would seem justified to use the above article and refer to the committee is the case of nullification or impairment of benefits that should arise from concessions given within the framework of the agreement. If by raising the export price through a cartel or a monopoly an export duty concession granted by the exporting country is circumvented or the value of mutual concessions of reductions of tariffs is impeded or negated (for instance, within an interim agreement towards the creation of a customs union or free trade area where the export cartel reaps the difference between reduced customs duty paid on imports from the export cartel country and third member countries), then a provision should exist within the article to permit specific action with the committee of dumping and reverse dumping.[22]

Bergsten refers also to a third problem, which he calls "reverse dumping" but which seems more correctly referred to as "predatory dumping in reverse." According to Bergsten, this phenomenon retards the development of substitutes in the field of energy. The solution to the problem, if one exists at all, is in joint anti-dumping action.

As to subsidies, their main provisions are included in Article XVI although the countervailing duty is discussed in Article VI. It should be noted that the definition of export subsidies was in the past similar to that of dumping -- "the sale of such product for export at a lower price than the comparable price charged for the like product to buyers in the domestic market." Thus, the opposite of such a case is the sale of such a product for export at a higher price than the comparable price charged in the domestic market. As we have noted early, this practice in and of itself may not be objectionable.

However, the difference between a subsidy and dumping is that subsidization is possible through government grants and assistance. The opposite of a subsidy is an export tax, or duty, which are permissible under the GATT unless a concession was bound that limits or eliminates the duty. But with respect to export duties, even bound ones, a country may raise the internal export tax on the particular bound export product since as we saw for the time being NT does not apply in such a case (this is the reason for the suggested change).

On the other hand, it should be noted that at present the definition of an export subsidy, within the code of subsidies, has been changed and is no more related to the price abroad compared to the price at home (see Annex 1 of the Code of Subsidies). What distinguishes an export subsidy is the fact of government assistance distorting competition and materially injuring or threatening to injure domestic industry in the importing country. If this criterion is accepted, one could observe the exact opposite situation if, as a result of an excessive payment to the government, exports materially injure the importing countries.

Such a case justifies treatment at least comparable to that of general subsidies of the GATT which, though permissible per se may have harmful effects and therefore ought to be the subject of consultation as stipulated in Part I of Article XVI.

Other possibilities would be to negotiate for a reduction or binding, in return for other concessions, or in extreme cases to request adjustment, in the light of Article XXIII, 1b and 2. But it is legitimate to impose an export duty, tax, or any other payment on exports as compared with the domestic prices.$^{23}$ Finally, the case of import subsidization as opposed to export subsidization deserves mention. Such cases have been known to exist in order to encourage larger imports of raw materials at lower prices. Exporting countries might at times find such action harmful to their domestic economy; naturally they should be permitted to impose a countervailing export duty to counteract this import subsidy. Provisions similar to those on countervailing duties on imports should be included in the agreement.

Article XVII deals with state trading and refers to both export and import provisions. There are, however, two exceptions. The first relates to government procurement, where no identical provisions exist for government sales. Thus, it is not clear whether government sales to governments have to be affected by the standard of the first paragraph which (accepting Jackson's arguments) is MFN (based on the fact that only government purchases have been exempt from that treatment) or whether the same fair and equitable treatment that applies to government purchases should also be applied to government sales, and that the omission is simply an oversight, as in some other places.$^{24}$

The second exception that relates to imports alone is in Article XVII, 4(b), which states that "a contracting party establishing or maintaining ... an import monopoly of a product which is not the subject of a concession under Article II shall, on the request of another contracting party having a substantial trade in the product$_{25}$concerned, inform the contracting party of the import mark up."$^{25}$ No similar requirements exist, at least explicitly, for export monopoly. Such a distinction is unjustified since the information may be very important in cases of dumping or reverse dumping or for the purpose of negotiations mentioned in **sub-paragraph** 3 of Article XVII or of Article II 4 (which also refers only to imports).[26]

It should be mentioned that negotiations regarding export monopoly were much more explicitly stipulated in Article 31.1 of the Havana Charter. That document stipulates that if a member establishes or maintains a monopoly of the exportation, the member shall upon request of any member having a substantial interest ... negotiate ... with the object of achieving:

"In the case of an export monopoly, arrangements designed to limit or reduce any protection that might be afforded through the operation of the monopoly to domestic users of the monopolized product, or designed to assure exports of the monopolized products in adequate quantities at reasonable prices."

These provisions were not carried over to GATT and only in 1957 some of the article provisions were added to GATT (see Article XVII, 3 and 4 and Addendum).[27] However, the specific reference quoted above was omitted. It seems that the inclusion of such explicit reference is of interest, in view of its relationship to export monopoly negotiations, concerning adequate quantities of supply and not only reasonable prices (as may perhaps be understood from the Add. XVII.3).

Another point with respect to Article XVII relates to the Add. to paragraph 1 (third sub-paragraph). This sub-paragraph stipulates that the charging by a state enterprise of different prices for its sales of a product in different markets is not precluded by the provision of this **article**, provided that such different prices are charged for commercial reasons to meet conditions of supply and demand in export markets. A monopolist interested in maximizing profits will always equalize his[28] **marginal revenue** from sales and thus charge **different prices** in different markets with differently sloping demand curves. However, such an approach is contrary to the basic principles of GATT, which stipulate unconditional MFN treatment and non-discrimination.

Although it was agreed during the **negotiations** of the ITO in New York, that state enterprises could charge different prices for commercial reasons, and the Havana Charter provisions have been taken over into GATT, it seems that the time has come to reconsider them. The maximization of profit of a monopolist is really an abuse of a dominant position, distorting competition. A more limited abuse, through flat pricing, prevents unequal access to raw materials and products, at least as far as the foreign competitors among themselves are concerned. Not all situations are similar and exception might be justified, for instance, in certain non-essential products where the income to the exporting country is much more vital than the commodity in question in the various importing countries. But it seems that while exceptions should be permitted the rule should be flat pricing for all foreign customers.

The discussion up until now related to rules for state trading enterprises in free market economies.[29] However, in centrally planned economies state trading exists in a completely different form. In some of these countries the foreign trade monopoly is an integral part of the overall economic plan in physical terms, and prices are determined centrally. The cost of goods may not bear any relation to the cost of production but may be fixed according to the requirements of the collective plan. Prices of imported goods may be controlled by the government, which may fix sales prices in terms of internal requirements rather than profit. A government monopoly may push prices up by withholding supply and invade markets by selling at a loss. It may also exact lower prices from dependent suppliers by threatening to withhold purchases.

Even if only commercial considerations are permitted and the political considerations (which often play a role) are excluded, the danger exists that state trading enterprises in centrally planned economies can practice monopolistic discrimination as the natural result of their economic system; it may not be possible for a complaining country to prove that any actual violation of GATT rules has been committed.[30]

At the time of the negotiations of the Havana Charter, the USSR chose not to participate in the ITO. As a result, the problem of state monopoly of foreign trade in centrally planned economies (which was discussed separately in the early stages of Havana and distinguished from the issue of state trading enterprises) was dropped at the time; the separate provision on "complete state monopolies" in foreign trade was excluded.[31]

The problem became relevant when some centrally planned economies wanted to join GATT, because while they would reap great benefits if granted most favored nation treatment, their obligation to reciprocate would be practically meaningless in view of their monopolistic trade regime. Furthermore a free, competitive market system is at a disadvantage facing a monopolistic trade regime. Thus agreements had to be concluded along lines that were outside the accepted GATT provisions (see for instance protocols with Poland). These agreements are not in accordance with any specific articles of GATT; furthermore, the problem has not been squarely faced and some of the treatment provided is really an attempt to duck the issue.[32]

Until overall rules are developed specifically for trade relations among countries having different economic systems, the free market economy GATT members should be safeguarded against special problems that might arise in their trade relations with state trading economies.[38] Such safeguards should also include export controls, for instance, to prevent monopolistic pressure on weak exporters.

Article XVIII deals with government assistance to economic development. Sub-article 2 recognizes the fact that protective measures may be necessary for the implementation of economic development plans and policies, but refers to imports only. Export control measures (e.g., on raw materials that can contribute to industrialization by encouraging the domestic processing of the raw materials) are not explicitly mentioned. Furthermore, the contracting parties on the basis of a GATT report in 1950 determined inter alia that "restrictions used by a contracting party on export and of raw materials in order to protect or promote a domestic fabricating industry falls outside the exception provided for in the general agreement."[34] In other words, the use of quantitative export restrictions for this purpose was not permitted. Yet, in the new Part IV of Article XXXVI, it is stated explicitly in sub-article 5 that "the rapid expansion of the structure of the less developed contracting parties will be facilitated by diversification of the structure of the economy and the avoidance of an excessive dependence on the exports of primary products..." An addition to sub-article 5 elaborated that "a diversification program would generally include the intensification of activities for the processing of primary products...".

It is true that the primary emphasis at the end of sub-article 5 is on increased access to markets for the processing and manufacturing industries. But in the light of the above objectives and in view of the parallel provisions for imports would it not also be justified to permit the introduction of export control measures.[35]

Sub-article XVIII, 2 also refers to the maintenance by developing countries of sufficient flexibility in their tariff structure to be able to grant tariff protection required for the establishment of a particular industry.

The text, which generally relates to imports, does not take into account that sometimes the best protection for the development of industry is the imposition of a duty on the export of raw materials. In some cases this may only be a counter measure to "escalating duties" applied by the importing countries or manufacturers to protect their own industries; in other cases it constitutes a protective device to encourage infant industries.

Article XXXVII, 1a in Part IV of GATT refers to this phenomenon. There is a general commitment by the developed countries "to accord high priority to the reduction or elimination of barriers to products currently or potentially of particular interest to less developed contracting parties ... which differentiate unreasonably between such products in their primary and in their processed forms." However, it would seem appropriate specifically to permit developing countries to maintain additional flexibility in their export tariffs also for counter-escalation and infant industry protection. This was a justified exception recognized already during the negotiations in the League.

Article XVIII, Section B refers to balance-of-payments restrictions in the case of developing countries. The same criticism voiced with respect to Article XII above applies to this section.

Article XVIII, Section C permits special measures, not consistent with other provisions of the agreement, yet sub-article 14 refers only to measures affecting imports, despite the introduction in 1979 of the safeguard action for development purposes that has loosened the requirements of the procedures for application of that section's provision. Deviation from sub-article 14 is permitted only if delay in application according to the procedures raises difficulties; in other words, the deviation refers to the time element. It seems necessary to correct the decision taken 28 November 1979 to permit deviations from sub-article 14, including also application of export control measures if necessary. This seems to be the case in Section D of this Article, which does not refer to developing countries under 4(a) but only 4(b). There the measures in sub-article 13 are not restricted by sub-article 14.

Article XIX deals with emergency action on imports of particular products. Many aspects of this complex subject of safeguards relate to our topic only indirectly. Therefore we shall not dwell on the various positions and opinions debated.

From our point of view, Article XIX raises several problems. First, there is no reference to disruptions resulting from export commitments and permission to apply an exception in such a case. As a result -- it is claimed by Roessler -- very few export duty concessions have been granted, since "in the absence of escape clauses, countries will be reluctant to commit themselves."[37] To what extent the issue is really an important one in practice is difficult to say, since the number of export duties is small compared to the number of import duties imposed by member countries. There is no doubt, however, that formally there is an imbalance between the treatment of imports and of exports that ought to be corrected.

Secondly, Article XIX formulates a strict cumulative criterion for its application as a safeguard. Injury or threat of injury to domestic producers must stem from (1) a tariff concession; (2) unforeseen developments; or (3) increases in imports (in relation to domestic sales). The article also talks of conditions that threaten serious injury and since in practice today the major danger of injury is not necessarily the direct result of tariff concessions given, the article in fact is applied without the stringent test of the cumulative criterion. There are therefore those who suggest changing the criterion in order to facilitate the application of this safeguard.[38]

In view of the fact that the existing article however modified will still be used, sub-article 2, which stipulates that those contracting parties having a substantial interest as exporters of the product concerned should have an opportunity to consult, is very meaningful. But since there is no reference to the possibility of an export control as a safeguard measure, there is also no reference to the opportunity to consult and to examine how such an "export control" may affect the importing countries. There is no doubt that situations may arise where continuation of an export commitment could seriously disrupt the situation in a specific industry in the exporting country. Therefore, parallel to changes relating to imports, similar criteria should be developed for the application of safeguards to exports; consultation in cases of exports should also be stipulated.

Thirdly, Article XI paragraph 1 prohibits quantitative export controls apart from some definite exceptions. If no specific provision will permit such quantitative controls in the case of an emergency they cannot be applied.[39]

Fourthly, the article does not define precisely the meaning of such terms as "serious injury, or threat thereof", or "in critical circumstances" it is evident that they refer to imports. It is desirable that the effort to interpret these terms in the framework of current discussions should also include more precise interpretations of terms relevant to exports.

Fifthly, Article XIX does not refer explicitly to the topic of selective or MFN treatment in applying the import safeguard, but until today the accepted practice in GATT has been to apply the safeguard provisions on an MFN basis, in accordance with Articles I and XIII of GATT, as well as based on the interpretative note add. 40 of the Havana Charter.[40] As long as no change has been made in this practice, the same should apply to safeguard provisions in the field of exports.[41] In other words, export safeguard measures should be applied on a MFN and non-discriminative basis.[42]

Sixthly, the text of Article XIX does not clarify whether the agreement to be reached according to sub-article 3(a) requires compensation. The custom which developed in GATT is that a country applying the emergency measure is required to pay compensation.[43] There are many convincing proposals suggesting that in certain justified cases there should be no need to pay compensation. The treatment afforded imports should be applied to exports as well.

All the above relates to Article XIX in the agreement. But the major problems of export controls are the Voluntary Export Restrictions (VER) and Orderly Marketing Agreements (OMA), which very often result directly from Article XIX, although the issue is not dealt with there. The difference between "export controls" as discussed above and VER is that VER are usually imposed on the exporting country by the importing country, threatening to apply Article XIX unilaterally and to introduce more severe import restrictions.[44] Unlike true voluntary export restrictions. which grow out of the interests of the exporting country, VERs are a substitute for import restrictions.[45] Different observers give different motives for VER: in the US, VERs have been explained by the reluctance to compromise the US commitment to GATT through import controls "which might weaken her negotiation position ... The VER solution transfers the responsibility for the breach of an international obligation from the importing to the exporting nation."[46] It has also been argued that Article XIX must be applied on a multilateral, i.e., MFN basis, whereas the disrupting country or countries are only one, or few in number.[47] VER have also been adopted to avoid payment of compensation, or risk retaliation, especially from the medium cost producers who might be hit by the application of the safeguard provision directed mainly against newly industrialized countries.[48]

Since the requirements of Article XIX are too strict and reality does not conform to the established criterion for its application, it is feared that the safeguard application would not be approved by GATT.[49] On the other hand, countries applying VERs are often afraid that if Article XIX or other import restrictions are applied unilaterally by the importing countries, these would be more severe. Furthermore, once compensation has been paid, the restriction could be dragged on indefinitely, since the provision "for such time as may be necessary" for the protective action has no time limit.[50] For these reasons, many countries succumbed to pressure and agreed to introduce VERs.

It would be useful to determine which of the above motives is dominant. If VER is used mainly in order to avoid the application of Article XIX on an MFN basis, then the answer could perhaps be: more selectivity in applying the safeguard. However, if VER is used in order to avoid the need to pay compensation, then the answer could perhaps be: the elimination (or reduction) of the compensation in justified cases of emergency, and to examine whether there is room for rules regarding the conditions under which compensation is justified. If the argument is that the criteria are too severe, then the answer lies in the modification of the criteria.[51]

In any event it is evident that the first motive causes the exporting country to breach its international obligation, since according to Article XI (with certain exceptions not applicable here) export restrictions are prohibited.[52] To justify this it is argued that the "breach" is only "technical", since in fact the "injured" party is the nation that sought the export quotas of goods to its market. The two parties to the agreement are not likely to file a complaint with GATT; according to the present procedures of GATT, a violation can be examined only at the motion of an aggrieved party.

Yet, there is no doubt that in the present state of affairs this system of voluntary export restriction is much inferior to outright import restriction. On the other side, importers and consumers have no opportunity to voice their opinion about the system and its effect. On the export side, the effects on the exporting country itself are not always examined or taken into account, since the imposition comes from abroad. Third party countries may be harmed from the resulting trade diversion of excess supplies to their markets and no prior consultation with them is required, i.e. import restrictions and VERs are not equivalent.[53]

It follows that, on the one hand, changes are required in Article XIX to make its application more attractive to member countries, and reduce the pressure to use VER and OMA. On the other hand, provisions relating to VER, which would promise more protection to the interest of the exporting countries and third countries, ought to be explicitly included in the agreement.

Several points are worth mentioning with regard to VER. First, one of the drawbacks is the lack of multilateral surveillance or examination procedures of these restrictive methods, which enables the stronger nations to impose whatever they want on the weaker, exporting countries. Had there been obligatory provisions they would, for instance, require countries applying VER to report to GATT and obtain its approval before or after entering into such VER agreements.[54] Such a requirement would reduce the pressure on the exporting countries to use this method of control as an alternative to comport controls and strengthen their hands by enabling them to claim that they have to gain the approval of the GATT. Furthermore, to the extent that the method of VER is nevertheless applied it will then have to be in accordance with certain provisions that ought to be elaborated.

In this connection it is important to note that there could arise situations in which VERs are the correct policy within the general framework of a safeguard action, e.g., a situation in which the source of serious injury is only one or very few countries that seriously disrupt the market in one or more countries. Then, the best solution would be precisely the VER rather than an import safeguard, on condition that its application undergoes prior scrutiny and approval of a surveillance body in GATT. This body would examine the agreement and its applications for the economy of the exporting country as well as on third countries, i.e., to what extent there would be trade diverting effects. It would also examine the justification of the request of the importing country for the introduction of a VER and determine to what extent the particular import was causing or threatening to cause serious disruption. It would examine what measures of adjustment in the importing country would be undertaken and the length of period considered reasonable to maintain the safeguard; examine whether the rate of increase of exports stipulated in the agreement is reasonable and satisfactory; etc.[55]

It has been argued that it is difficult to establish criteria for the existence of VER and that it is therefore desirable to establish sets of principles[56] to be observed in the process of arriving at such a judgement. On the other hand Dam (1970) has argued in another context that committees do not take positions in the absence of substantive provisions. The solution, therefore, would seem to be to determine criteria without regarding them as mandatory but rather to be used as guidelines by the surveillance body.

It is clear that if a VER would be required to undergo such a procedure of approval, its use would be made more difficult; but if approved and used it would be applied in a more appropriate fashion. Both results seem desirable.

One comment with respect to selectivity. By the nature of things a VER is selective since it applies to the particular disruptive source.[57] It is therefore suitable for those cases where attempts are made to apply "selective" import safeguards. Since import safeguards are and ought to be applied on a MFN basis, the more orderly and institutionalized VER may constitute a way out.[58]

On the other hand, the discussions on import safeguards will, it is hoped, lead to more lenient requirements with respect to compensation in real emergency cases, modification of criteria of application, etc. As a result, more use will be made of this tool, eliminating solutions outside the Agreement and permitting further liberalization of international trade.

In most of Article XX's sub-paragraph reference is made implicitly, if not explicitly, to exports. It seems justified to examine to what extent these exceptions are adequate and whether they are not too broad so as to permit abuse. Already during the negotiations of the ITO draft the UK suggested a qualification to precede the list of specific exceptions that would ensure that such measures are not applied arbitrarily or in an unjustifiable discriminatory manner between countries where the same conditions prevail.[59] This qualification was accepted and prefaces the article. Nevertheless objections were raised that it is not sufficiently precise. One objection is the difficulty of applying the measures selectively, for instance, for the protection of lives.[60] On the other hand, the US delegate in the "framework group" demanded more precise and new formulations of the qualification in order to eliminate or reduce the possibility of discrimination.

It would seem that at present, Jackson's suggestion requiring that parties to GATT report all instances where regulations or requirements restricting exports that are based solely on Article XX is one possible course of action that would reduce abuse and permit evaluation by the international community in the light of Article XX and the purpose of GATT.[61] As experience accumulated the contracting parties would then be in a position to formulate new proposals. However, against it should be weighed the drawback of the overflow of notification.[62]

As to the article's specific provisions, there appears to be a limitation in paragraph (g) that does not always make sense, namely the condition relating to domestic consumption or production restriction in conjunction with conservation of exhaustible natural resources. Very often the exporters of raw materials are not or are only marginal consumers of the product, but this should not prevent them from introducing restrictions in favor of conservation, as may perhaps be gathered from the provision.

The reference in paragraph XX (h) to add. Article XX(h) that extends the exception to any commodity agreement that conforms to the principles approved by the economic and social council in its resolution 30(IV) of March 1947 actually in a round about way refers to the Havana Charter provisions on international commodity agreements, which consisted of some sixteen articles.[63] These provisions based on the original US proposals tried to develop criteria under which commodity agreements should be accepted. In particular, based on the pre-war experience and discussions, it emphasized the protection of consumer's interest in such agreements.[64]

However, since the Havana Charter has not been ratified and thus failed to enter into force, the above reference which was at the beginning in the exception itself of GATT was in 1955 shifted to the Add. The text of the provision permits also two other alternatives (1) conforms to criteria submitted to the CP and not disproved by them (2) submitted itself and not so disproved.

While the hope that GATT would develop its own criteria failed to materialize, since contracting parties could not agree, there is no record of commodity agreements, submitted and disproved by the second alternative.[65] The position of GATT with respect to international commodity agreements was a passive one,

permitting commodity agreements but not promoting them.[66] The US's attitude changed in 1962, after it entered the international coffee agreement, the first agreement where the commodity concerned was not produced in the US.
Yet, paragraph one of Article XXVIII states explicitly that "the contracting parties shall collaborate jointly, within the framework of this agreement and elsewhere..." and while a more active role was taken by GATT (for instance, during the Kennedy Round) in the discussion of some commodity agreements, GATT's approach remains "self denying", leaving this subject matter to other organizations, such as UNCTAD and others. This is probably in view of the different character of such arrangements that do not adhere to the basic principle of GATT and more so in view of the global character which such agreements require in order to be successful.
Provision (i), which permits a contracting party to adopt a measure involving restrictions on exports of domestic materials necessary to ensure essential quantities of such material to a domestic processing industry during periods in which the domestic price of such materials is held below world price as part of a governmental stabilization plan, was introduced by New Zealand in the Geneva Conference.[67] It referred to a specific situation, in which a country maintains price stabilization schemes covering the economy as a matter of permanent policy. If, as was the case in New Zealand, the foreign price of the raw material is above the level of the price maintained internally for the industry (e.g., leather), it becomes necessary to ensure, by means of export controls, that the local requirements are satisfied; otherwise there would be no leather for the local market, or alternatively, the price would have to rise.[68]
It is interesting to note that the possibility of imposing an export tax instead of restrictions was considered, but experience has shown this to be unsatisfactory and impracticable in view of the wide price fluctuations of primary commodities, which would require too frequent variations of the tax. The provision was accepted with the proviso (as the request of the Netherlands) that such a restriction should not operate to increase the export of, or the protection attached to, the domestic industry. It is clear that this provision is strictly limited to cases where general schemes of internal price stabilization are in operation. Yet, as has been pointed out earlier (Articles VI and XVI) even without such a scheme, export restrictions may be needed to prevent the outflow of raw materials needed by the domestic industry when, for example, another country subsidizes the import of the raw material.
With respect to provision (j), this was in its original form a temporary measure that related to the immediate post-war period.[69] It was extended several times and revised in 1955; included for another five-year period; and extended again and again. If, however, the origin of the provision is disregarded, the exact difference between Articles XI, 2(a) and XX, j(1) is not entirely clear. Both talk of temporary shortages of products, although in the first the reference is to "critical" shortage of

food and other products essential to the exporting country while Article XX, (j) refers to products in "general or local short supply".[70] But these differences do not seem to justify differentiation, unless one understands that in the case of essential products and critical shortage complete prohibitions are permitted, whereas in the second case, according to a proviso in Article XX (j) all contracting parties are entitled to an equitable share of the international supply of such products.

Article XXI, which related to export controls permitted as exceptions, was referred to earlier; only brief comments will be included here. A substantial part of current discriminatory export controls are carried out under this exception.

An examination of the provisions indicates that taken literally the exceptions for security reasons are rather strict. Unfortunately, in practice the clause is much more broadly interpreted and applied. Thus, for instance, as formulated the text does not seem to permit the maintenance of a stock of essential foods and other essential raw materials as a permanent policy of government for security reasons or the export restriction of these commodities[71] because these are neither fissionable materials, nor products necessarily supplied to military establishment. Nevertheless, many countries follow such a policy for security reasons, at least with respect to some products.

The most elaborate contemporary law on export controls for security reasons exists in the US. It includes, for instance, the prevention of export of any material that could contribute to the military (and earlier, economic) power of the enemy. The Export Control Act underwent many changes over the years yet even today after some of the previous broader prohibitions that tried to limit the economic potential have become more restricted, the new approach of a "critical technologies" list is being used to prevent transfer of manufacturing know-how and design in areas that may, if acquired by the potential enemy, contribute significantly to its military potential. However, such an approach may cause the prevention of exports of sectors engaged in advanced research and development for the civil population. If the technology and know-how is (as is often the case) an extremely advanced one, it follows that the definition of GATT is again more restrictive than the law.

The Act also authorizes the President to prohibit or curtail exports in line with US foreign policy. No such reference existed in GATT unless the US foreign policy export restrictions are applied in the context of Article XXI(c) which refers to the obligation under the UN Charter to maintain international peace and security. This is not always the case, as many examples can indicate. The only time that Article XXI(c) has been applied was in the case of the embargo on Rhodesia (Zimbabwe).

However, as we have noted, the US applied export controls against, for example, Uganda and South East Asia; MFN status was not applied to Czechoslovakia. All of these actions conflict with Article XXI and are sufficient to indicate that despite the rather restricted exceptions in the GATT, in practice a much wider use is made of them. Furthermore, from the text of the provision it becomes clear that no surveillance or guiding provisions as to conditions of application are included. In this respect it seems worthwhile to refer to Jackson, who argues:

> One purpose of GATT ... is to bring a medium of law and order into international economic relations, i.e., to reduce the danger and the damage of arbitrary exercise of economic power. The GATT security exception (as well as certain other clauses, such as Article XXXV and the waiver clause of Article XXV), can reopen the door to arbitrary abuse, (by a country possessing the advantage of such economic power). For this reason it might be wise to try to put Article XXI invocations on a more multilateral basis. For example, it might be made clear that although wide leeway will be granted on individual contracting party's decision to take measures under Article XXI exceptions, whenever these come to the attention of GATT they will be subject to review by a GATT working party which may report on its views.[73]

Such a proposal does not seem useful for the following reasons:
(1) Experience (the case of the US and Czechoslovakia, for example) indicates that GATT itself, in authorizing the suspension of mutual obligations of both contracting parties, has abstained from making any judgment. As one GATT official commented, such disputes could not be settled by GATT because of their "political economic nature". The General Agreement was a technical instrument with which to deal with "technical trade problems" and this question "was of a different order altogether".
(2) The representatives of GATT are not purely technical experts but representatives of countries with political considerations and interests that might affect their judgment.
(3) There are really no substantive criteria guiding GATT. Although the danger of abuse appears to exist and one precondition for the successful functioning of GATT is the acceptance by the more powerful members of GATT of the Rule of Law--instead of their economic and political power of leverage --it would be naive at this stage to introduce more restrictive provisions in this vital field of security exception.

Bergsten has stated, "It must always be remembered that trade or other international economic rule cannot be used mechanically to deal with issues of high politics. Efforts to do so usually destroy the rules rather than solve the political problem".[74]

The most that can be done at present in order to improve the situation somewhat is to add a provision that recognizes that the legitimate action of applying a security exception might have unintended and harmful effects. Therefore, the affected contracting party shall discuss the possibility of limiting those effects with the other party. Such an amendment, while not submitting the country applying the measure to requirements of international surveillance and judgment, would try to take account of grievances in this field.[75] During such consultations issues might be raised regarding the effectiveness of the particular control in leading to the desired objectives, or whether less harmful alternatives could achieve the same goal. To some extent there is room here for guidelines similar to those developed by the US Congress with respect to the foreign policy control in the Export Administration Act of 1979. However, such guidelines are to be seen strictly as a tool assisting in the discussions and not as criteria to which the applying country must abide.

Articles XXII and XXIII deal with consultation, nullification, and impairment.[76] Articles XXII requires contracting parties to agree to consultation on any matter affecting the operation of the agreement -- which naturally refers also to export controls to the extent that they affect the operation of the agreement.[77]

The question, however, may be raised whether the reference includes all those matters for which at present there are no provisions in the agreement (for instance, levies for balance of payments reasons). It can be argued that the question is of little relevance since although bilateral consultations are carried out on the basis of Article XXII. Nevertheless, according to Article XXIII, if a country feels that any benefit accruing to it directly or indirectly under this agreement is being impeded as a result of (1(b)) the application by another contracting party of any measure whether or not in conflict with the provisions of this agreement or (1(c)) the existence of any other situation, it can make a written representation or proposal to the other party and should be given sympathetic consideration by that party. If no satisfactory adjustment is effected within a reasonable time, the matter can be referred to the contracting parties for investigation, recommendations, or ruling, and in serious enough matters they may authorize suspensions of application of concessions or other obligations of the agreement. In other words, Article XXIII provides the possibility for consultations and complaint procedures including redress for export control measures not mentioned in the agreement.[78]

Nevertheless, it was argued by Dam that
> the breadth of jurisdiction conferred by the 'any measure' language of paragraph 1(b) -- and for that matter by the 'any other situation' language of paragraph 1(c) -- creates for the panels that pass on Article XXIII complaints, problems of a jurisprudential order... To rely on paragraph 1(b) jurisdiction is to attempt to resolve disputes without reference to specific substantive rules... The panels faced with these dilemmas have intuitively drawn back from the bases of jurisdiction contained in paragraph 1(b) and 1(c) in favor of an approach that would make the legality of the trade measure under the substantive provisions of the General Agreement the crucial factor in determinations of nullification and impairment.[79]

In view of the above it is obvious that the use of these two general articles will become more effective in the case of export controls if the substantive provisions on the subject are more elaborated in the agreement.

During the Tokyo Round Negotiations, the entire subject of notifications, consultations and dispute settlement came up for discussion since member countries, and in particular developing countries, were dissatisfied with the existing provisions. Despite differences of opinion, on 28 November 1979 a compromise was reached that to some extent takes account of the demands of the developing countries but puts its emphasis on improving the procedures of dispute settlement and on increasing the efficiency of the panel system. A detailed annex clarifying the existing procedures in GATT on the subject was added and certain improvements were introduced in the procedure of notifications and consultations as well as in the setting up and work of the panels. Developing countries were permitted to continue to use the good services of the Director General and were subject to special procedures of dispute settlement with developed countries. While the adopted "understanding" of 28 November 1979 improved somewhat the procedure with respect to consultation, it did not on the whole change the existing situation except, perhaps with respect to notifications. Here the following provisions were included: (1) the commitment to existing obligations under GATT regarding publication and notifications was reaffirmed; (2) the contracting parties agreed, to the maximum extent possible, to notify the contracting parties of their adoption of trade measures affecting the operation of the General Agreement, it being understood that such notification would of itself without prejudice to views on the consistency of the measures with, or their relevance to, rights and obligations under the General Agreement; (3) contracting parties that have reason to believe that such trade measures have been adopted by another contracting party may seek information on such measures bilaterally from the contracting party concerned.[80]

We see in this new provision some advance over the existing notification requirements; since they refer to trade measures it is evident that export measures are included. Yet at the same time the existence of several qualifiers ("to the maximum extent possible", "affecting the operation of the agreement", "notification not prejudicing consistency of the measure") must be noted. The first two leave notification open to the judgement of the member country, but there is the safeguard of the obligation to provide information at the request of another contracting party. Nevertheless it seems the requirement is too broad.

By comparison, the OECD requirements on notification with respect to export controls appear less severe. There, the duty to notify changes relates only to an illustrative list, which in the field of export control was restricted to "abolition or introduction of quantitative restrictions on exports" and to legislation or administrative regulations that should be notified in summary form.

Furthermore, in many cases although measures might theoretically have an effect on the operation of the agreement, in practice the effect is negligible. It would therefore seem more appropriate to limit notification requirements to an agreed illustrative list of measures on which notification would be required and certain criteria such as serious injury or threat thereof to industries abroad; the importance of the commodity in the economy of the contracting parties abroad; and sufficient time to notify.

This will naturally not prevent a country desiring to obtain information on an export measure from the contracting party applying it from requesting it in line with the above mentioned understanding on notification. It will nevertheless prevent an overflow of unimportant notifications on measures that are more of internal concern.

As to consultations it is worthwhile mentioning that OECD documentation mentions the idea of prior **consultation**, (i.e., before the measures are **applied**) because when several countries are confronted with the same structural or sectoral problems, ad hoc consultations could facilitate the pursuit of positive and mutually acceptable solutions. Furthermore, that documentation emphasizes that "it is desirable to develop prior consultations, where member countries envisage making important changes in their trade practice and the interests of other members are involved." The aim of these prior consultations is not to prevent governments from giving effect in the last analysis to contemplated changes in trade practices, but to allow them to make their final decision in the light of the views expressed by other member countries."[81]

It is impracticable to expect that in every case of important change envisaged by a contracting party to GATT, prior consultation should be carried out. Yet it would seem a good idea to make such prior consultations possible by introducing a provision to that effect in the "understanding" or in the text of GATT itself, since at present the provision is for post factum consultation of the measure taken.

The provisions of Article XXIV relate mainly to customs unions and free trade areas, as exceptions from MFN and non-discriminatory treatment of other restrictive regulations to commerce.

The issue whether the Article XXIV exception clause also applies to quantitative restriction, or whether these should be dealt with on a non-discriminatory manner, was raised at one time, but has since been refuted. This naturally refers also to export restrictions.

There is no doubt that a customs union or a free trade area should be permitted to eliminate substantially all restrictive regulations on commerce (as well as duties) on its internal trade without having to do the same with respect to third parties (the above provision permits also internal exceptions based on Articles XI, XII, XIII, XIV, XI and XX, many of which may be relevant in the case of export restrictions).

The two major examples of a customs union and a free trade area are the EEC and EFTA, respectively. The EEC eliminated internal export controls by providing first a standstill and then abolition of duties and restriction within a very short period.[82]

Nevertheless, toward third countries (or in exceptional cases also) generally export control measures are applied and internal regulations to that effect have been issued in addition to the

list of products to which export controls are applied. This list is changed and supplemented from time to time.
The EFTA provisions on export restriction may still be largely used whenever really needed to combat shortages of essential foodstuffs and shortages of raw materials necessary for domestic industries. Apart from these two exceptions, the EFTA Articles 8 and 11 follow closely the principles laid down in the EEC Treaty.
Since in a free trade area different member countries have different external trade relations with third countries, there is danger of circumvention when one member country imposes control on exports to third countries while another does not. To prevent such circumvention and evasion both articles in EFTA contain sub-articles (8(2) and 11(2)) prohibiting re-exportation to third countries via a member country.
The fact that differential treatment is permitted between a customs union or free trade area and third countries does not necessarily imply that this should continue to be the case, as Bergsten has noted.[85] However, it is difficult to see why in this particular case a change should be introduced. Article XXIV has been criticized for much more serious drawbacks, yet the chances of revising the article are not good.[86]
Finally, a relevant issue in the case of export controls is (as it was in 1927) the question of the observance of GATT provisions by regional or local authorities.[87] This issue is discussed in sub-article XXIV, sub. 12. In a number of countries, provinces, or states have their own export control provisions and their laws are independently legislated. Therefore, steps should be taken by the federal or central government to ensure that every reasonable measure be taken to ensure observance by local authorities in accordance with GATT provisions. If ways could be found to strengthen this provision so as to avoid other possible interpretations this would be desirable.[88]
Article XXVIII bis relates also to export tariffs and charges. Article XXVIII, on the other hand, refers to modifications in imports only. This by way of implication, since the definition of countries with whom a contracting party has to negotiate a modification includes, apart from the country with which the concession was "initially" negotiated, also the country with the "principal supplying interest." If the modifications referred to export tariffs and charges, the negotiations would have to be conducted with the country having the "principal buying interest," in addition to the country with which the concession was initially negotiated. This oversight was probably due to the insignificance of actual export duty concessions in the schedules. But this minor correction is nevertheless required to balance the treatment of export concessions with that of import concessions.
Such a correction would also respond to some of the criticisms of Roessler.[89] He claims that the legal framework for the protection of countries granting and binding export duty concessions is missing, and thus deterring countries from making them. By entering the correction here and elsewhere in the

agreement as suggested, many more possibilities for export duty concessions would be created, including some of Roessler's ideas, including a unified export levy on all stages of the production process in oil by the oil exporting country in return for import concessions by the oil importing countries in other products of labor intensive industries of long-run interest to that oil exporting country.

Another question altogether refers to whether export control concessions should only refer to tariffs. In GATT, there were precedents during the Kennedy Round -- more within the MTN--of negotiations of existing non-tariff rights (see, for instance, the US grandfather clause in the case of subsidies in return for concessions by other contracting parties on the definition export subsidies, within the second track).

Such possibility, with respect to export control measures legally permissible under the provisions of the agreement yet perhaps undesirable to other contracting parties should also be provided for by the inclusion of a provision which also permits negotiation of nontariff measures including export restriction. (For instance, with respect to state trading supply commitments).

Article XIX should have been deleted after the ITO Charter failed to be ratified. Unfortunately, at the 1955 review session of GATT where Article XXIX's deletion proposed together with other amendments, one vote was missing for the unanimous decision required by Article XXX. The article therefore remained in the text, although it is virtually never applied.[90] This does not mean that the issues mentioned in Article XXIX (dealt with by the ITO charter and not included in GATT) are not relevant to international economic policy. It means rather that GATT considered these to be on the whole outside its realm of activities.[91] Since some of the isses dealt with in the ITO charter and excluded by GATT are of extreme importance to export control and access to supplies, it is important to emphasize that within GATT the subject can be dealt with only partially and that international provisions are required that extend beyond GATT and therefore beyond the limits of the present article.[92] These include (1) some new rules on international investments that, on the one hand, encourage foreign investment in the development of raw materials, yet prevent the control or monopolization of the sources of supply. This should also lead to the re-examination of complementary agreements whereby in return for the development of a source of supply, payment is received in kind, a procedure that might also prevent equal access to sources of supply; (2) agreements to transfer technology and know-how (presently under discussion in UNCTAD) since access to supply should relate not only to raw materials and primary commodities but also include access to technology and know-how of particular importance to developing countries. It would seem that a "zebra code," which would make some provisions mandatory (on which all parties could agree) while others remained voluntary guidelines, ought to be sought. Furthermore, in this context it is perhaps noteworthy to point out that in the case of transfer of technology and know-how, some export restrictions are justified since otherwise the owner of know-how would not be willing to part with it; (3) the new code on Restrictive Business Practices (RBP) in UNCTAD, which refers also to many practices relevant to our subject, serves only as voluntary guidelines. Further attempts to achieve a mandatory code would be desirable since abusive RBPs are increasingly being substituted for government measures, though it would not necessarily have to include all the provisions of the voluntary guidelines; (4) closely related to the above is the subject of multi-or transnational enterprises, whose share in international trade is constantly increasing and which may control exports for a variety of reasons that are contrary to the assumptions, interests, and principles of free trade evolved within GATT.[93] Therefore rules must be developed for a world in which such enterprises are becoming an increasingly dominant feature; (5) the subject of international commodity agreements, including the export restriction that they evolve are one of the prime subjects presently pursued by UNCTAD. The Common Fund and Integrated Commodity Program are still in the process of being evolved. It seems that in the international commodity agreement field GATT will remain rather passive in the near future;[94] (6) Chapter IX of the ITO Charter also contained an Article (No. 98) on relations with non-members. While its contents are not generally relevant in the present context, it is important to emphasize Sub-article 98:5, which requests the executive board to make periodic studies of general problems arising out of the commercial relation between member and non-member countries and with a view to promoting the purpose of the charter, requests it to make recommendations to the conference with respect to such relations. Any recommendation involving alterations in the provisions is to be dealt with in accordance with the article on amendments (Article 100).

Such a general article as well as this specific Sub-article 5 is missing in GATT, more precisely in the case of export restrictions applied by non-members not obligated by GATT's provision and adversely affecting GATT's members.

Throughout this chapter various amendments to GATT provisions have been presented but little attention has been given to the questions of whether or how such amendments could be introduced. Various opinions exist. Roessler seems to prefer the development of a pre-negotiations set of rules for export concessions, which would by themselves not be legally binding but which could be referred to by individual contracting parties in a brief note in their schedules and thus be binding for the commodities to which they referred to.[95] Such a method would mean, however, that many topics not specifically referring to a product would not be included in the rules negotiated. Another method, suggested by Bergsten, is to set up a "Code of Export Conduct" similar to the "Anti-Dumping Code". However, the problem with such a code -- as with so many of the now existing codes -- seems to be how to treat member countries of GATT that are not members of the code, in view of the non-discriminatory obligations of Articles I and XIII. A third possibility (also mentioned by the two previous writers but considered to have little chance for implementation) is to amend GATT itself. Roessler's argument is that some of GATT's contracting parties are interested in the changes and, furthermore, that such fundamental change should be introduced only after more experience has been gained.

It should, however, be mentioned that the amendments suggested here are mostly of a parallel character, intended to balance existing provisions with regard to imports, and may also take into account the balanced interests of all parties.[96]

Furthermore, the amendments are mainly in Parts II and III of the agreement, therefore only a two-thirds majority would be required. As to the very minor correction in Part I the possibility of amendment by certification seems to be possible. It should be added that not all amendments are of equal importance, and prior negotiations may work out a balanced package that could be accepted by all and that would constitute an improvement over the existing situation.

In the present chapter the subject of export controls has been discussed within the existing framework of GATT. By the nature of this limitation many issues have been avoided or mentioned only in passing.

For instance, there exists the question of what happens to trade rules based on nation states and national enterprises, as in GATT, in a world in which trade will be increasingly governed by multinational enterprises, where production itself will be internationalized, and where the interests of these enterprises will not necessarily be in line with those of the countries in which they are located.[97] Obviously, a whole new set of rules will have to be evolved.

Another issue is, for instance, export controls as well as other trade relations with non-member countries. It may very well be that a whole set of rules can be developed within a broader framework -- with a more limited set of agreed provisions based on the lowest common denominator that could be accepted by such a varigated multitude of countries having different values, social structures, and degrees of development. The issue is best illustrated by comparing the stricter rules on RBPs prevailing in a more closely-knit organization such as the EEC or EFTA with the RBP code of UNCTAD or the suggested Chapter V of the ITO. The closer cohesion of accepted objectives and values in the first group enabled it to agree on more binding commitments than is possible within the larger group, yet the one does not exclude participation of the same group also in the broader circle. However, the above are only by way of illustration. Many other issues were mentioned and they certainly do not cover all that could be dealt with.

Furthermore, within the GATT agreement we have dealt primarily with the substantive provisions regarding export controls and their inadequacy, and have suggested changes. Little attention has been paid to the fact that even where provisions exist, they were, at times, little heeded. It should therefore be clear that the possible contribution of an improvement in substantive provisions is limited to the assumption that the more powerful economic and political member countries recognize the desirability and value of "rule-oriented" rather than "power-oriented" behavior in GATT.[98] Even then it should be obvious that in the current world situation an important part of the subject of export controls will be excluded from GATT rules. Nevertheless, where certain improvements are possible, they will reduce unnecessary conflicts and adverse effects.

NOTES

1. A more detailed summary is annexed to GATT Doc. MIN/FR/W 20 Rev. 1.
2. Although not stated explicitly, (d) follows from the provision.
3. See H. Jackson, World Trade and the Law of GATT (New York: Bobbs Merrill, 1969), 502. Also Bergsten 1975, 25.
4. See Roessler 1975, 27.
5. See p. 9.
6. That subject was raised concretely up to the Multilateral Trade Negotiations (MTN) only four times with respect to export concessions and discriminatory treatment between India and Pakistan in 1984 and in 1952 (see Jackson, op. cit., pp. 491-501), and Czechoslovakia against US in 1949 (see Roessler, op. cit., p. 30). It was raised again in 1950 when the contracting parties decided to discuss quantitative restrictions for protective and other commercial purposes (Geneva 1950, p. 4-6). The question was discussed in GATT.
7. See UN Conference in Trade and Employment (UNCTE), Report of the First Session of the Preparatory Committee. London: 1946.
8. See Report of UNCTE Preparatory Committee: Second Session. 1947. Where Chapter IV Article 16 on the most favored nation treatment, and Article 17 on the reduction of tariffs and elimination of preferences appeared in Article 24 of the London, and Article 18 of the US Draft. In all drafts references to negotiate tariff reduction relate to exports as well.
9. Interestingly enough the new code on valuation also does not include any reference to the subject. The most probable explanation seems to be the relatively few export duties in existence and perhaps the fact that on primary commodities, which are the most natural candidates for export duties (being exported from developing countries) the duty or tax usually is a specific one in view of the severe fluctuations in price of the commodity.
10. A case in point, for instance, is the export tax in Paraguay. See IMF 1951, 128.
11. The (1950) GATT report on quantitative restrictions considered such practices as illegitimate.
12. It is true that such an activity may be considered as contrary to what was argued on Articles VI and XVI, but here a) the intention is not abuse; b) the country suffers from a severe deficit in the balance of payments; and c) no normal free competition is possible without destroying the industry. This is the case for many of the export marketing boards controlled by government restriction.
13. For a detailed account of the negotiations, see Brown 1950, 84-89; 149-152; 197-203.
14. Discriminatory voluntary export restrictions (VER) are generally applied for reasons other than balance of payments difficulties. However, the latter also exists, e.g., Europe's pressure on Japan to apply VER in view of Europe's $ 10 billion deficit.
15. See Kindleberger 1958, 271.

16. The article defines what is meant by "less than the normal value."

17. Kindleberger defines reverse dumping as the case where the manufacturer sells at higher prices abroad. Bergsten, on the other hand, has predatory dumping "in reverse" in mind when he talks about reverse dumping, namely, first selling at high prices as long as no competition appears, then dumping abroad to destroy competition. Predatory dumping involves selling at very low prices abroad in order to destroy the competition, after which prices are raised. Here, the opposite is the case.

18. Some of these are discussed by Kindleberger (1958, 263-69). But even under conditions of competition an enterprise that may benefit from a temporary excessive profit in a new market should do so according to the theory and there is no reason why it should demand a lower price (this is all the more so if his marginal cost of exports is above the price in his domestic market).

19. Some vague reference to that chapter is maintained through Article XXIX, 1, which states, "The contracting parties undertake to observe the fullest extent of their executive authority the general principles of Chapter I to VI inclusive and of Chapter IX of the Havana Charter pending their acceptance of it in accordance with their constitutional procedure". In practice, the GATT has avoided dealing with the subject.

20. This is also becoming very relevant in view of the raising role of the transnational firm in international trade (see further discussion).

21. In the GATT there is no obligation that the price at home and abroad should be identical. The price abroad may be higher--and there will be no equal access to local and foreign producer--for instance, also as a result of an export duty. Furthermore at least in the opinion of this writer, not every cartel is objectionable per se--if one talks of products in which otherwise would be a destructive cut-throat competition, or where there are other justifiable reasons. See BISD, 171-88.

22. It is interesting to note that complaints of restrictive BP have not been dealt with by the GATT on the grounds that no substantive provisions for the application exist in GATT. See BISD, 9th Supplement, 170-71.

23. It is important here to emphasize the difference between our approach and Bergsten's. According to Bergsten, "export controls", so defined as to include export duties, should be prohibited from use unless the exporting country can prove material injury if not used. Regarding cost restrictions, we disagree with this opinion. Exactly like in import duties, a country is free to impose them unless bound in GATT. However, if material injury can be proven to other contracting parties then and only then it should be subject to consultations and some measures of adjustment.

24. The difference, for instance, is to sell based on past trade rather than to the highest bidder in free competition among potential users.

25. As Article XVII, 4(b) states, "The term import mark-up in this paragraph shall represent the margin by which the price charged by the import monopoly for the imported product (exclusive of internal taxes, transportation, etc.) exceeds the landed costs."

26. Marginal suggestions on the export side were made earlier by the US delegate (see Brown 1950, 113) but were not accepted by the preparatory committee (see Kock 1969, 50).

27. See Jackson 1969, 335-36, who argues that the lobbying of war-ravished nations pushing for temporary periods of transitions, together with the expectation that Article 31 will be applied in the ITO, persuaded the drafters of GATT to omit the Article.

28. See the discussion in Kindleberger 1958, 262-64.

29. See Kock 1969, 184-85.

30. Seyid 1958, 233, 240.

31. Thus the US in its original proposals for the charter, suggested that members having a complete state monopoly of foreign trade should undertake to purchase annually, products valued at not less than an aggregate amount agreed upon. This global purchase arrangement would be subject to periodic adjustments in consultation with the organization - the proposal was dropped in Geneva when the Soviet Union failed to be present. Regarding some of the objections and counter arguments, see Seyid 1958, 241.

32. For instance, the continuation of "temporary" quantitative controls by some free market economies (Dam 1970, 327).

33. See the attempt made by Seyid 1958, 327.

34. GATT 1950.

35. In fact many delegations during the framework discussion were of the opinion that the 1950 conclusions of the CP were no longer applicable.

36. It is interesting to note that the draft on import and export prohibitions of 1927 is parallel to Article XIX here. There, in Article 5, the possibility of serious disruption or unforeseen situations in exports is specifically taken into account.

37. Roessler 1975, 37-38.

38. See, for example, Merciai 1981, 50-51.

39. The acceptance of Modification of Export control measures in the agreement would generally require some modifications of Article XI.

40. Dam 1970, 104-5.

41. Although this practice has been questioned, we believe that the safeguard should continue to be applied on an MFN or non-discriminatory basis. This prevents a country from making too easy use of safeguard actions. In view of the large number of countries involved which may take retaliatory measures in unjustified circumstances, sometimes individual countries are too weak to do so effectively. However, certain exceptions should be possible, for instance, differential and preferential treatment of newly established and small supplying countries or in highly

extreme and strictly defined and multilaterally supervised circumstances.

42. Nondiscriminatory treatment of quantitative export controls may raise problems if the controls are the results of "disruptive purchases of one country" --in such a case Bergsten suggests to set an earlier enough base period as "representative period" for the allocation (Bergsten, p. 46). The problem is complicated, however, by the fact that in allocation of supplies the historic record is not always the just and fair treatment. See discussion of Article XIII.

43. Tumlir 1973, 9.
44. Smith 1973, 193.
45. See, for instance, VER imposed by Japan for the sake of changing the image of its product quality.
46. Smith 1973, 26-29.
47. GATT, Tokyo Round 1979, 90.
48. Merciai 1981, 47.
49. Smith 1973, 49; Tumlir 1973, 6.
50. Tumlir 1973, 7.
51. Merciai 1981, and Tumlir 1973, 16.
52. However, it is interesting to quote US Secretary of Commerce Maurice Stans: "The only thing that is overriding in favor of voluntary agreements is that they are permitted under our international agreements such as GATT without any penalties applied. At any time that we use legislative force or other unilateral type of action to impair trade, there is a right under the agreement for the other countries to take equivalent action against our goods " (Smith 1929, 39). It is true that there are not specifically stipulated penalties or retaliation, but it is contrary to the Agreement's provisions and VERs are not permitted (Smith 1929, 29).
53. See Bergsten 1975.
54. Smith 1979 is not satisfied with reporting by applying country and suggests including in the agreement provisions that would enable any member country of GATT, or even the GATT secretariat, to inform about the VER agreement that includes an alleged breach of either country's GATT obligations. He admits, however, that this may be regarded as an undue infringement of sovereignty at the present time. But if there is a country that thinks that any benefit accruing to it by this agreement is being impaired or that the attainment of any objective of the agreement is impeded it may resort to Article XXIII. Therefore, the suggestion by Smith seems superfluous, especially if the agreement will be amended to obligate applying countries to report on VER.
55. Such length of period determination is vital in order to force adjustment, and ensure the temporariness of the safeguard measure.
56. Tumlir 1973, 16.
57. The difference between the export measures discussed on pages 349-50, which should be applied in a MFN basis, and the VER here, which are to be applied selectively, is that here the measure is not applied autonomously by the exporting country but is demanded by the importing country from the exporting country.

58. The suggestion of Tumlir (1973, 9) to distinguish between MFN and multilaterality and apply the latter meaning of multilaterality, i.e., common responsibility, joint decision, and international surveillance, does not solve the problem of effective protection of the weak countries against whom a safeguard is applied selectively. The fact that a country can complain to an international forum and seek adjustment does not mean that members of the forum will protect the interest of the complaining country, in the same way as they would do so if the general interests of all member countries were at stake.

59. UN Document EPCT/C 11/50.
60. Freedman 1979.
61. Jackson 1969, 744.
62. Later in the chapter we present a suggestion on Notifications.
63. See Havana Charter, chapter 6.
64. For the pre-war experience, see Staley 1937, chapter 7.
65. Jackson 1969, 727.
66. Dam 1970, 245.
67. Jackson 1969, 504-5.
68. Roessler 1975, 32 argues that in cases of short supply, rather than introducing export controls it might be more desirable to let prices rise, since in the long-run supply would adjust to the world need; something controls prevent. However, it is difficult to discuss such an argument in the abstract without reference to the specific conditions under which the market price stabilization schemes take place. This is also true with respect to his second argument, that introduction of controls makes the source unreliable and buyers may develop import barriers to increase their self-reliance. Although this may be true and exporting countries ought to take it into account, situations might be conceived where the exporting country has no choice.
69. Jackson 1969, 746-47.
70. The concept of "critical shortage" deserves further examination and clarification; see, for instance, Prof. Helmut Hesse's paper on the subject, in particular his argument with respect to the so-called "risk pool function". Hesse argues that through trade greater price stability (defined as low price variance) is effected for a given product because of the different and compensatory developments in other countries. Source: "Export restrictions as a means of avoiding critical shortages". Hesse 1980, 9-11.
71. This was a policy recommended by Condliffe (1950, 804) as an alternative to domestic uneconomic production of essentially needed goods.
72. The reader interested in subsequent changes in this act is referred to Branting 1980.
73. Jackson 1978, 750.
74. Similarly, Bergsten suggests that the use of the export controls for "national security purposes should be subjected to the notification, consultation, and survaillance procedures to avoid egregious abuse". Bergsten 1975, 32.
75. Branting 1980, 442.

76. According to Jackson (1969, 165) in all there are 19 provisions in the agreement for consultation (mainly in specific cases) and 7 for compensation or withdrawals of concessions. Of these 13 are relevant to exports and hold provisions for consultations: II:5, VII:1, VIII:2, IX:6, XIII:4, XVIII:7, XXII, XXIII, XXIV:7, XXVII and four provisions for compensation and withdrawal of concessions II:5, XVII:7, XXIII, XVII.

77. Jackson, describing the complicated history of the articles on nullification and impairment and dispute settlement in the Havana negotiations, points out among other things that in London (in 1946) the original proposals of the US on nullification and impairment were extended and this clause was considered to be more than just a complaint procedure and settlement of dispute. "Not only did the original draft explicitly allow complaints against a measure taken by another government whether or not it conflicts with the terms of this Agreement, but the London delegates added a phrase allowing redress when there arises any situation... which has the effect of nullifying or impairing any object of this charter." The explanation was: that there may be labor below the standard labor conditions, etc. so that then it definitely was possible to go beyond the specific provisions. In New York the committee did not change the text and included it also in the GATT text, but in the meantime the US Congress criticized the provisions of the "Interim Organization" of the GATT draft, and whole introducing changes, changed the wording from "objective of the agreement" to "affecting the operation of this agreement".

78. It would seem that in the light of Article XXIII bilateral consultations based on Article XXII should also be possible since it might be argued that they are a preliminary step to avoid reaching the procedure of Article XXIII, which may affect the operation of the agreement.

79. Dam 1970, 359-60.

80. Both publication and notification requirements are less stringent in the case of export restrictions (Articles X and XIII).

81. TC (77, 7A pp. 5-6 and 13-14).

82. See EEC Treaty, Articles 16 and 34.

83. See OECD Documentation on metal scrap, where the UK and Denmark seem to apply export control measures also internally (TC/WP (76)8 (1st Rev.) 29.11.76; also, Regulation EWG No. 2603/69 of the Council published in the official Journal Nr. L324/25.

84. See Treaty of EFTA Articles 21 and 26 with regard to foodstuffs and Annex G paragraph (7) with regard to raw materials in the case of Portugal.

85. Bergsten 1972, 46.

86. See Rom 1978.

87. See Article 2 of the League of Nations International Convention for the abolition of import and export prohibitions and restrictions (Official No. C14MII 1929 II C.I.AP 19 (3) 1927), para. 3: "Further the high contracting parties undertake to adopt the necessary measures to ensure that the provisions of the present convention (will be) strictly observed by all authorities

central or local and that no regulation is issued in contravention thereof."

88. In the code of Technical Barriers to Trade (see BISD 26th supp., for instance, page 11 Art. 2.9) there are two formulations, one positive (to take reasonable measures to ensure) and one negative (not to take measures that have direct or indirect effect of encouraging such bodies to act in a manner inconsistent with those provisions).

89. Roessler 1975, 33-39.

90. Jackson 1969, 512-14.

91. Some attempts were made to deal with the subject of RBPs up to 1960. Some provisions on international commodity agreements were also independently included in Article XX (12). The question arises whether this approach should not be reconsidered. However, in view of the fact that most of the issues are at present dealt within UNCTAD, there is little likelihood that GATT may reconsider its approach.

92. Article XXIX:1 related to chapters I to VI inclusive and chapter IX of the Havana Charter. This includes, inter alia, such issues as full employment, international investment for economic development, and industrial economic development, including transfer of skills, arts and technologies. Restrictive BP Chapter V, inter Gov. Commodities Agreements Chap. VI, relations with non-members Ch. IX (98).

93. See, for instance, RIO op. cit. Annex 7, 274. In 1975, US transnational enterprises and their foreign subsidiaries alone were estimated to account for 28 percent of world exports.

94. There is, of course, always room for re-examining this position (this may be true also of other subjects discussed under this heading, such as the RBP issue) but it is unlikely.

95. Roessler 1975, 140.

96. Thus, suggested amendments favoring mainly exporting countries are in Articles 1a, XII, XIV, XVI, import subsidy protection; XVII.5, XVIII, 1, 2, XIX.1, XX.g, XXII and XXIII, reduced notification obligation as compared with understanding;" XXVIII by interest should be included, will encourage making of concessions. Amendments suggested favoring mainly importing countries are II, III, VII, XIII, XVI, except import subsidy XVII, 1, 2, 3, 4, XIX.2, XX notifications XXI, XXII, XXIII prior consultation possibility, XXIV 1,2, XXVIII concessions other than tariffs, XXIX protection against non-members.

97. There exist predictions that the future points to internationalization of production since labor is less mobile than capital or know-how and enterprises will transfer production to countries with cheaper labor.

98. Jackson 1978.

REFERENCES

Behrman, Jack N. <u>National Interests and Multinational Enterprises</u>, New Jersey: Prentice Hall Inc. 1970.

Bergsten, C.F. 1975. Completing the GATT, Towards New International Rules to Govern Export Controls, British North American Committee, October 1974. In Toward a New International Economic Order, edited by C.F. Bergsten, Lexington, Mass.
Bertsch, Gary K. 1981. US Export Controls in the 1970s and Beyond. Journal of World Trade and Law 15: ___.
Branting, Luther Karl. 1980. Reconciliation of Conflicting Goals in the Export Administration Act of 1979: A Delicate Balance. Law and Policy in International Business 12: 415-60.
Brown, William Adams Jr. 1950. The United States and the Restoration of World Trade. Washington, DC: The Brookings Institute.
Condliffe, D.R. 1950. Commerce of Nations. New York: Norton.
Dam, Kenneth Wa. 1970. The GATT Law and International Economic Organization. Chicago: University of Chicago Press.
Freedman, Steven J. 1979. US Trade Sanction against Uganda: Legality under International Law. Law and Policy in International Business 11:3.
GATT. 1950. General Agreement on Tariffs and Trade. Geneva.
_____. ----- Basic Instruments and Selected Documents.
_____. 1979. 26th Supplement.
_____. ----- 15th Supplement.
_____. 1979. The Tokyo Round of Multilateral Trade Negotiations. Geneva.
_____. 1950. The Use of Quantitative Restrictions for Protective and Other Commercial Purposes. Geneva.
_____. ---- Doc. MTN/FR/W/20/Rev. 1.
_____. 1947. Doc. E/PC/T/34.
Hesse, H. 1980. Export Restrictions as a Means of Avoiding Critical Shortages. Ibero-America Institute, Goettingen University, Discussion Paper.
Kindleberger, C.P. 1958. International Economics. Revised Edition, Homewood Ill.: R.D. Irwin Inc.
Kock, Karin. 1969. International Trade Policy and the GATT 1947-67. Stockholm: Aimqvist & Wicksell.
IMF. 1951. 2nd Annual Report, Exchange Restrictions. Washington, D.C.: IMF.
Jackson, John H. 1969. World Trade and the Law of GATT. New York: Bobbs and Merrill.
_____. 1978. The Crumbling Institutions of the Liberal Trade System. Journal of World Trade and Law 12.
_____. 1980. GATT-MTN System. Law and Policy in International Business 12.
League of Nations. 1927. International Convention for the Abolition of Import and Export Prohibitions and Restrictions. Official No. C14MII II C.I.AP 19(3).
Merciai, Patrizio. 1981. Safeguard Measures in GATT. Journal of World Trade Law 15.
OECD. 1974. British-North American Committee on Export Control of Metal Scrap in Many Countries. Paris, OECD.
_____. 1970. TC/WP(76) 8 (1st Rev.).

RIO: Reshaping the International Order: A Report to the Club of Rome. 1976. New York: Dutton.
Roessler, Frieder. 1975. GATT and Access to Supplier. Journal of World Trade Law: 9.
Rom, Michael. 1978. The Role of Tariff Quotas in Commercial Policy. London: MacMillan.
Seyid, Muhammad. 1958. The Legal Framework of World Trade. London: Stevens and Sons Ltd.
Smith, Malcolm D.H. 1929. Voluntary Export Quotas and US Trade Policy - A New Non-Tariff Barrier. Law and Policy in International Business. 5:
Staley, E. 1937. Raw Materials in Peace and War: A Report of the Tenth International Studies Conference Council on Foreign Relations. New York.
Tumlir, Jan. 1973. Proposals for Emergency Protection against Sharp Increases in Imports. London: Trade Policy Research Centre Guest Paper 1.
UN Doc. EPCT/C Article 7 (1946) and Article 101 (1947).
US Congress. 1979. Sub-Commission on International Trade of the Senate Committee on Finance, 96th Congress, 1st Session.

# 12
# Summary of Findings and Main Conclusions

*Helmut Hesse*

Since the beginning of the 1970s a large number of states have imposed product specific export restrictions aimed at achieving various national political and economic goals. Although the phenomenon of export restrictions itself is not new, their rapid increase in recent years does pose a serious threat to the functioning of international trade. Contrary to existing trade agreements on admissable and inadmissable import restrictions, regulations on the export side are almost totally lacking and those that do exist are so vaguely formulated that they can hardly be called on to exercise the relevant sanctions on the case of dispute. As is evident from the inventories of trade restrictions drawn up by various international organizations, developing countries as well as industrial countries impose controls on their exports if there are national welfare or employment gains to be had from doing so. Developing countries adopt measures of this nature mainly with a view to the long range goal of redistributing world income in their favour and promoting their own raw material processing industries; industrial countries on the other hand are more interested in avoiding short term price increases resulting from shifts in supply or demand.

The papers in the present volume concentrate on the longer term goals of export restrictions. They show that in the main it is illusory for developing countries to believe that unilateral interventions in raw material markets as well as monopolistic export price increases and limitations on export quantities will enable them to achieve long term improvements in their economic welfare. Even given very favourable conditions for the success of such restrictive measures, the market power of possible raw material supply cartels will only be sufficient to increase longer term export revenues in the case of very few products. This can be seen from the empirical estimates for the ten "UNCTAD core commodities" presented in Chapter 4 of this book. The success of such restrictive measures is altogether questionable if one is realistic in considering the consequences of continually increasing prices: raw material consumers are sure to seek ways of economizing on their consumption and producers outside the cartel will heavily increase their production to make up for the drop in supply by the cartel. Furthermore, the very existence of cartels is in constant danger of being undermined due to the considerable divergence among the economic and political interests of the raw material exporting member countries.

Even if the conditions of individual raw material markets were extremely favourable to the success of export restrictions, there would still be the problem of the growth promoting allocation of the increased export revenues in the developing countries. Only if these revenues are destined for additional investment can the goal of accelerated growth be realized. As indicated by the empirical estimates in Chapter 9, the incidence of increased revenues from raw material exports do indeed have a growth promoting effect; however, if such increased revenues are compelled by unilateral export restrictions, raw material production has to be cut back so sharply that the resulting growth losses may be just as high as the growth gains from additional investment, without even mentioning the problems of structural adjustment unleashed by moves in this direction.

Thus, the minimal positive effects of export restriction measures in developing countries are outweighed by the negative effects felt in the world economy as a whole. Raw material price increases have an inflationary impact on the economies of the importing countries, and monetary policies can convert this impact into a world-wide acceleration of the inflationary process. Sooner or later, restrictive monetary policies will attenuate the level of economic activity throughout the world and it is here that the least developed raw material countries will suffer the most. There is already evidence that the two waves of oil price increases in the 1970s especially contributed to such effects. Though on the basis of the available empirical data other raw materials cannot be considered as equally important sources of the current economic difficulties being faced throughout the world (see here the empirical findings of Chapters 6 and 7) they can have similar consequences. There is, however, no doubt that widespread export restrictions on raw materials will lead to a world-wide acceleration of the inflationary process and to greater economic adjustment pressures. The necessary adjustments will serve to worsen resource allocation in the world, this in turn implying a fall in world income and thus reduced capacity for redistributing this income at the international level. On these grounds export restrictions with the long term aim of forcedly redistributing world income are to be rejected.

Up to this point no consideration has been given to the dangers involved in cumulative trade interventions. However, it is precisely in the field of international trade that one can expect retaliatory measures on the part of those states not prepared to accept the "beggar-my-neighbor" policy of their trading partners. Export restrictions in the case of some individual raw materials could release a spate of world-wide state interventions in trade, thus causing the collapse of the already very labile balance so gradually and delicately built up over the years. The resulting damage will affect all those participating in the international economic system.

It would nevertheless be wrong to make an outright rejection of export restrictions aimed at redistributing world income without considering some alternative solution for promoting the interests of developing countries in achieving free access to markets in industrial countries. The processing of raw materials in developing countries is even today hindered by the import tariff structure in the industrial countries, especially since effective protection increases with the grade of raw material processing. The relocation of raw material processing industries in developing countries could in quite a number of cases be an efficient means of achieving the industrialization of these countries. A corresponding reallocation of resources must also eventually follow, meaning that the industrial countries will have to forfeit some of their traditional lines of production irrespective of the fact that the associated adjustment problems are particularly difficult to deal with in times of economic stagnation. A recommendable solution would be the provision of state and private assistance in the setting up of profitable processing industries in the developing countries, thus accelerating the growth rate and stimulating import demand for other products, lending support in this way to overcoming the burden of the adjustment process in the industrial countries.

Similarly, in the case of product specific export restrictions aimed at the short term stabilization of domestic supply, an appropriate balance of interests should be sought between suppliers and consumers [1].

In the case, for example, of an external demand boom for certain key products one can not totally prevent exporting countries from imposing export restrictions aimed at reducing possible price increases which threaten to cause a lasting disturbance on their domestic economies. On the other hand, however, the risk pool function of international trade should not be allowed to be disturbed at will by individual states just because it happens to be in their national interest to act in this way.

Although export restrictions have been discussed in all negotiations in trade agreements, they are not satisfactorily regulated within the GATT-Treaty. This point is dealt with in more detail in Chapters 10 and 11 of the book, where the fundamental goals of the GATT- Treaty are discussed with a view to possible addenda and amendments aimed at staving off any further damage to the world economy through export restrictions.

It is hoped with this book to convey the view that **export restrictions are harmful to the world economy and that action should be taken to regulate them through some form of international treaty.**

NOTES

1. Export restrictions of this type do not enter into the theme of the present book, but they have been investigated within the framework of the project as a whole. See Helmut Hesse, Exportbeschrankungen - ein neues handelspolitisches Problem? (Export Restrictions - A New Trade Policy Problem?), in: Knut Borchardt and Franz Holsheu (Eds.), Theorie und Politik der International Wirtschaftsbeziehungen, Stuttgart/New York 1980, pp. 257-282; Helmut Hesse, Export beschrankungen zur Vermeidung eines "kritischen Mangels" (Export Restrictions as a Means of Avoiding "Critical Shortages"), in: G. Bombach, B. Gahlen, A.E. Ott (Eds.), zur Theories und Politik Internationaler Wirtschaftsbeziehungen, Schriftenreihe des Wirtschafts- wissenschaftlichen Seminars Ottobeuren, Vol. 10, Tubingen 1981, pp. 103-130; Hubertus Schenkel, Wirtschaftstheoretische und wirtschaftspolitische Probleme von Ausfuhrbeschrankungen (Theoretical and Policy Problems of Export Restrictions), Arbeitsbericht 19, Ibero-Amerika Institut fur Wirtschaftsforschung der Universitat Gottingen, Gottingen 1980.

# Contributors

**Z.Y. Hershlag**, Ph.D., Professor Emeritus of Economics, Tel Aviv University, and former Director the the David Horowitz Institute for the Research of Developing Countries, Tel Aviv, Israel.

**Helmut Hesse**, Ph.D., Professor of Economics, University of Goettingen and Director of the Ibero-Amerika Institute for Economic Research, Goettingen, Federal Republic of Germany.

**Horst Keppler**, Ph.D., Member of the Economics Department, University of Goettingen, Federal Republic of Germany.

**Roberto Nathanson**, Ph.D., Senior Economic Advisor, The Histadrut, Israel's General Labor Union, Tel Aviv, Israel.

**Miriam Rodrik-Farhi**, M.A., Economist.

**Michael Rom**, Ph.D., Economic and Commercial Attache, Israel Embassy, Vienna, Austria.

**Nora Schrager**, M.A., Economist, Tadiran Electronic Industries, Tel Aviv, Israel.

**Jimmy Weinblatt**, Ph.D., Senior Lecturer of Economics, Ben Gurion University of the Negev, Beer Sheva, Israel.

# Index

Abaca seeds. See Hemp
Absorptive capacity, 182
Adams, J. F., 144
Afghanistan, 201
Agricultural goods, 10, 11, 12, 14, 16, 26-31, 79, 163, 179, 183-184. See also Food commodity group; individual crops
Aluminum, 18-19(table), 20, 32-37(table), 42-47(tables)
  prices, 28-30(tables)
Angora goats, 202
Anti-inflationary measures, 73, 75, 154
Arab oil producing countries, 72, 201
Argentina, 32-47(tables), 179
Atlantic Charter (1941), 207, 208
Australia, 11, 13, 15, 16, 32-37(table), 42-45(table), 140, 202, 211, 212, 213
Austria, 140

Balance of payments, 145, 182, 201
  and GATT, 224, 226, 232, 241
  surplus, 14(table), 16, 27(table), 32-37(table), 74(table), 116, 122, 133, 182
Balance of trade, 192, 193
Bananas, 16, 32-47(tables), 141(table), 185-186(table), 190(table), 191, 192
  prices, 28-30(tables)

Bangladesh, 179
Baron, Stefan, 97, 104-105, 106(table)
Bauxite, 13, 15, 22, 32-47(tables), 48(n2), 141(table), 179, 185-186(table), 190(table), 191
  prices, 28-30(tables)
  processed. See Aluminum
Beef, 26, 32-37(table)
Behrman, Jack N., 191
Belgium, 140
Bergsten, C. F., 228, 240, 246
Bhagwati, J., 161
Bolivia, 11, 32-47(tables), 179, 184-186(tables)
Botswana, 179
Boycotts, 200, 201
Brazil, 11, 12, 13, 15, 25(table), 32-47(tables), 75, 179, 183, 184-186(tables)
Bretton Woods System, 48(n8)
Burma, 179
Burundi, 77(table), 179

Cameroon, 32-47(tables), 179, 183, 184-186(tables)
Canada, 11, 12, 15, 16, 32-37(table), 42-45(table), 71, 140, 198, 199, 202, 211, 212, 213
Cancun Fund, 7
Cancun Summit (1982), 7
Capital, 182
  flows, 144-145, 146
Capital-intensive industries, 22
Caribbean, 179

Cartels, 1, 2, 3, 6, 7, 13,
  26, 32-37(table), 51, 52,
  71, 80, 97-98, 163, 175,
  191, 259
  and GATT, 227-228
  See also Equilibrium model;
    Organization of Petroleum
    Exporting Countries
Central Africa, Republic of, 179
Centrally planned economy,
  200, 231
Chad, 179
Charter of Economic Rights
  and Duties, 213
Chile, 32-47(tables), 179, 183,
  184-186(tables), 199
Churchill, Winston, 207
Club of Rome, 76, 198
Cocoa, 3, 13, 18-19(table),
  22, 32-47(tables), 71, 79,
  90-92, 94, 95-96(tables),
  141(table), 185-186(table),
  190(table), 191, 192
  export taxes, 93, 97
  prices, 28-30(tables),
    102-103(tables), 105,
    106-108(tables), 109,
    110(table)
  processed, 20, 91(table)
"Code of Export Conduct," 246
Coffee, 3, 12, 13, 21, 22,
  32-47(tables), 71, 79,
  90-92, 93, 94, 95-96(tables),
  141(table), 185-186(table),
  190(table), 191
  export taxes, 75, 97, 198
  prices, 28-30(tables),
    102-103(tables), 105,
    106-108(tables), 109,
    110(table)
  processed, 20
Cold War, 72
Colombia, 11, 13, 25(table),
  32-47(tables), 77(table),
  179, 184-186(tables)
Commodity Trade and Price
  Trends (World Bank), 108
Common Fund, 6, 246
Consumer goods, 21, 31
Consumer Price Index (CPI),
  166(table)
Consumption, 55
Copper, 13, 18-19(table),
  32-47(tables), 90-92, 94,
  95-96(tables), 141(table),
  179, 183, 185-186(table),
  190(table), 191, 192
  prices, 28-30(tables), 93,
    102-103(tables), 106-107
    (tables)
  scrap, 73
Copra, 16, 18-19(table),
  32-45(tables)
  prices, 28-30(tables)
Copyright (GATT), 221
Corden, M. W., 88
Core commodities, 17. See also
  Ten core commodities
Costa Rica, 179
Cotton, 18-19(table),
  32-47(tables), 90-92, 94,
  95-96(tables)
  prices, 28-30(tables), 93,
    102-103(tables), 105,
    106-107(tables)
CP, 212, 221, 224
CPI. See Consumer Price Index
Crockett, A. D., 152
Cuba, 107(table), 202
Currency exchange rates, 11-12
Customs (GATT), 220, 223, 228,
  243
Czechoslovakia, 239, 240

Dam, Kenneth Wa, 236, 241
Date shoots, 202
Decolonization, 161
Demand
  aggregate, 15, 16, 148
  disaggregation model, 99-100
  domestic, 15, 23, 75
  in equilibrium model, 54, 55,
    56, 59, 67
  foreign, 15, 16, 21,
    32-37(table), 75, 94,
    101-103, 161, 173-174
  in partial equilibrium model,
    80, 81(fig.), 84, 86, 88
  in simultaneous equations
    system, 187, 188, 189-191
  supply, 161, 173-174,
    176-177(table)
  See also Elasticities of
    demand
Denmark, 140, 253(n83)
Deutsche Mark, 16
Devaluation, 116

Developed importing countries, 2, 128-140, 143, 147, 151-153, 166(table), 169
See also Employment; Export restrictions; Inflation; Price, commodity; individual countries
Direct transfer effect, 120-121. See also Foreign aid
Domestic market, 73, 74(table), 117, 154, 198, 202
Dominican Republic, 13, 32-47(tables), 77(table), 179
Dumping (GATT), 226-227, 228, 230
reverse, 227, 228, 230, 250(n17)

Eastern Bloc, 210
ECA, 228
Economic growth, 4, 5, 6, 7, 73, 74(table), 143, 147, 150, 151, 152, 153, 155-156, 161-178, 181-193, 259
and GATT, 232-233
Economic Report of the President of the U.S., The (1977), 128
Ecuador, 32-47(tables), 77(table), 184-186(tables)
EEC. See European Economic Community
EFTA. See European Free Trade Association
Egypt, 179, 202, 203
Elasticities of demand, 3, 15, 23, 26, 48(n1), 92, 116, 172. See also under Price
El Salvador, 25(table), 179
Employment, 3, 26, 73, 74(table), 128-138, 145, 203
Endogenous variables, 57, 61, 64, 66(table), 68, 190(table)
Equilibrium model, 2, 52-69, 71, 117, 130-131
partial, 72, 80-89
Ethiopia, 179
European Economic Community (EEC), 16, 18-19(table), 32-37(table), 198, 211,
243, 244, 247
European Free Trade Association (EFTA), 243, 244, 247
Exogenous variables, 190(table), 193
Export Administration Act (1969), (U.S.), 200, 241
Export Control Act (U.S.), 239
Export embargoes, 10, 11(table), 12, 20, 26, 27(table), 32-37(table), 79, 183, 201, 202
Export-Import Permits Act (1974) (Canada), 12
Export licensing, 10, 11(table), 13, 26, 27(table), 32-37(table), 75, 78
and GATT, 225
Export profits, 88, 90, 94, 95-96(tables), 97, 98
Export quotas, 1, 11, 12, 16, 20, 26, 27(table), 32-37(table), 79, 89, 183
and GATT, 225
Export restrictions
ancient, 1, 203
conditions for, 117-125, 126
defined, 197
development of, 3, 203-210, 211
and foreign policy, 13, 72, 200-201, 202, 209, 240-241
impact, 2, 3, 5, 6, 7, 26-31, 32-37(table), 65-68, 118-120, 128-138, 139(fig.), 181-193, 203, 259-260
monetary effects, 3-4, 143-156, 182, 203
peak (1972-1973), 23
reasons for, 1, 2, 13-17, 20-23, 26, 27(table), 32-37(table), 72-79, 198-203, 258
types, 10-13, 32-37(table). See also specific types
See also General Agreement on Tariffs and Trade; Macro-economic analyses; Micro-economic analyses
Export revenues, 2, 3, 4, 5, 6, 7, 13, 14(table), 17, 22-23, 26, 27(table), 32-37(table), 67, 71-72, 90, 93-98, 104-110, 137, 162, 163, 167, 168, 169,

Export revenues (cont.)
  182, 187, 189, 191-192,
  199, 203, 258, 259
  currencies, 11, 21, 182,
  201, 203. See also Foreign
  exchange
  and GATT, 221
  and public expenditure, 182
  stabilization, 15-16, 21,
  32-37(table), 89
  surplus, 16
  See also Equilibrium model,
  partial
Export tariffs, 204
  and GATT, 244-345
Export taxes, 2, 10, 11(table),
  12-13, 16, 18-19(table),
  20, 26, 27(table),
  32-37(table), 51-52, 68,
  72, 74(table), 75, 76-78,
  79, 90-98, 182, 183, 198,
  199-200, 201, 202
  and GATT, 220, 222, 223, 224,
  228-229, 233, 238
  See also Equilibrium model
Export value, 165(table), 166,
  167, 168, 170(table),
  171, 172

Ferrous scrap, 12
Fertilizers, 11, 20, 32-37
  (table), 199
Figs, 1
Findlay, R., 144
Finland, 13, 32-37(table),
  42-45(table), 140
Fishmeal, 28-30(tables),
  38-41(table)
Fissionable materials (GATT),
  221, 239
Food commodity group, 4, 11,
  15, 16, 32-47(tables),
  162(table), 163, 164, 165,
  167, 168, 169, 170(table),
  171-172, 173, 174(table),
  175
  and GATT, 220, 239
Foreign aid, 3, 26, 116,
  124, 125-126
Foreign exchange, 1, 94, 97,
  98, 104, 105, 117, 144,
  145, 147, 182, 201, 203
  fixed, 182
  floating, 146, 182
  and GATT, 220, 223-224
Foreign reserves, 144, 145, 146,
  147, 149-150, 151, 152, 154,
  155
Foreign trade tax, 23. See also
  Export taxes
France, 42-45(table), 140, 204
Free trade areas, 228, 243, 244
Furniture, 20
"Future exhaustion cost," 21

Gabon, 32-47(tables), 183,
  184-186(tables)
Gambia, 179
GATT. See General Agreement on
  Tariffs and Trade
GDP. See Gross Domestic Product
General Agreement on Tariffs and
  Trade (GATT) (1947), 2, 5, 6,
  32-37(table), 79, 198, 200,
  206, 208, 209, 210, 211-213,
  260
  provisions, 220-248
General System of Preferences, 68
Geneva Conference, 238
Germany, 204. See also West
  Germany
Ghana, 13, 32-47(tables), 179,
  183, 184-186(tables)
Gini, C., 205, 206
GNP. See Gross National Product
Gold, 221
Gordon, R. J., 144
Government intervention. See
  State trading
Great Britain, 15, 32-37(table),
  42-45(table), 72, 73, 140,
  202, 204, 207-208, 254(n83)
  and ITO, 237
Great Depression, 203
Greece, 140, 203
Gross Domestic Product (GDP),
  166(table), 172
Gross National Product (GNP),
  133, 134, 135, 136,
  138(table), 139(fig.), 172,
  175, 176-177(table), 178,
  189, 192
Guatemala, 32-47(tables),
  77(table), 179
Guinea, 179
Guyana, 13, 32-47(tables), 179,
  184-186(tables)

Haiti, 11, 13, 32-47(tables), 179, 183, 184-186(tables)
Havana Charter (1948), 78, 206, 208-210, 225, 227, 230, 231, 234, 237
Havana Conference, 5
Heller, R. H., 152
Hemp, 202
Hicks-Mosak general equilibrium analysis, 117
Hides and skins, 12, 15, 16, 32-47(tables), 205
  prices, 28-30(tables)
  See also Leather
High technology exports, 71
Honduras, 11, 32-47(tables), 77(table), 179, 184-186 (tables)
Houthakker, H. S., 124
Hufbauer, G. C., 169
Hull, Cordell, 206-207, 208
Hume, David, 1, 144

IBA. See International Bauxite Association
ICAs. See International Commodity Agreements
IMF. See International Monetary Fund
Imperial Preferences, 207
Import demand. See Demand, foreign
Import duties, 76
Import restrictions, 234, 235
Import tariff, 13, 17, 20, 68
  and GATT, 222, 223, 224, 229, 232, 233
Income
  deflator, 55
  elasticities, 22, 174, 178, 191
  national, 4, 116, 120, 121, 123, 126, 181
  national, real, 2, 55-56, 59
  per capita, 124
  real, 3, 52, 54, 124, 125, 163
  redistribution, 1, 3, 7, 26, 76, 88, 98, 116, 123, 124, 125, 156, 163, 260
  transfer, 4, 121-122, 124, 125, 126, 163, 181
Indexation. See under Price

India, 25(table), 32-47(tables), 179
Indonesia, 15, 16, 32-47(tables)
Industrial goods
  exports, 7, 8, 79, 116, 124, 156, 162, 163, 164, 165, 167, 168, 170(table), 171-172, 176-178, 181, 192
  imports, 23
Industrialization, 4, 8, 17, 165, 167, 192, 260
Industrial sector, 4, 8, 13, 75, 169, 198, 203
Infant industry protection, 232
Inflation, 1, 4, 5, 14(table), 16, 22, 27(table), 32-37 (table), 132, 133, 134, 135, 136, 138(table), 139(fig.), 144, 145, 146, 147, 148, 149, 150, 151, 152, 153, 154, 155, 156, 165-166, 182, 188, 189, 190(table), 191, 192, 193, 199, 203, 259
  cost-push, 26, 124, 128, 134, 143
  demand-pull, 124, 137, 182
Input-output ratios, 52, 53, 145
Integrated Commodity Programme, 90, 94, 104, 246
Interest rates, 21
Inter-governmental commodity agreements (GATT), 221
Internal distribution, 75
International agreement
  compliance, 14(table), 21, 27(table). See also League of Nations
International Bauxite Association (IBA), 13, 20
International Code on Export Controls, 211
International Commodity Agreements (ICAs), 6, 163, 238
International Convention for the Abolition of Prohibition and Restrictions (1927), 205
International free trade, 5, 125, 198, 204, 205, 206
International Monetary Fund (IMF), 2, 76, 77(table), 79, 132
  and GATT, 224, 226

International Trade Organization (ITO), 206, 208, 222, 226, 230, 231, 237, 245, 246, 247. See also Havana Charter
International Trading System, 213
Investment, 16, 31, 68, 147, 245, 259
Ireland, 32-37(table), 140
Iron ore, 15, 32-47(tables)
  prices, 28-30(tables)
Israel, 72, 73, 140
Israeli-Arab war (1973), 73, 201
Italy, 42-45(table), 140, 204
ITO. See International Trade Organization
Ivory Coast, 25(table), 32-47(tables), 179, 184-186(tables)

Jackson, John H., 222, 229, 237, 240
Jamaica, 13, 25(table), 32-47(tables), 179, 183, 184-186(tables)
Japan, 12, 15, 18-19(table), 32-37(table), 42-45(table), 140, 204, 211
  export restrictions, 73, 200
Johnson, H. G., 144
Jordan, 179
Jute, 3, 18-19(table), 32-47(tables), 71, 79, 90-92, 93, 94, 95-96(tables)
  export taxes, 97
  prices, 28-30(tables), 102-103(tables), 106-107(tables)

Kennedy Round, 245
Kenya, 25(table), 179
Keynesian economics, 117, 124, 144
Kindleberger, C., 7, 226, 227
Kissinger, Henry, 211
Kuznets, S., 124

Labor, 22, 146, 182. See also Employment; Unemployment
Law, A. D., 163

LDCs. See Less developed countries
Lead, 28-30(tables), 38-41(table)
League of Nations, 5, 205-206
Leather, 12, 18-19(table), 20, 32-37(table), 75
Lend-Lease Act (1941), 207, 208
Lerner symmetry theorem, 23
Less developed countries (LDCs), 1-2, 153-156
  export share, 17, 32-47(tables), 102-103(tables), 141(table), 161-179, 183, 184-186(tables)
  higher-income, 7
  intra, trade, 4, 7, 169, 170(table)
  lower-income, 8
  middle-income, 7, 8
  See also Export restrictions; Export revenues; Raw materials; individual countries
Lewis, S., 7, 8
Lewis Hypothesis, 124
Liberia, 179
Linder, S. B., 168-169
Liquidity, 146, 152, 153
Lome Convention, 68

McNicol, David L., 97, 104, 105, 107-110
Macroeconomic analyses, 2, 3, 116, 117-120, 124-125, 126, 144, 161, 181
Madagascar, 179
Malawi, 179
Malaysia, 13, 15, 21, 25(table), 32-47(tables), 77(table), 179, 183, 184-186(tables), 202
Mali, 179
Manganese, 22, 32-47(tables), 141(table), 183, 185-186 (table), 190(table), 191, 192
  prices, 28-30(tables)
Manufactures. See Industrial goods
Marginal propensities, 122, 123, 124
Market economy, 198, 230, 231
Marshall-Lerner elasticities, 116

Mauritania, 179
Mauritius, 179
MDCs. See Developed importing countries
Meat, 13, 18-19(table), 26. See also Beef; Pork
Metal scrap, 12, 73, 79, 254(n83)
Mexico, 25(table), 32-47(tables)
MFN. See Most Favored Nation
Michaely, M., 7, 8
Microeconomic analyses, 2, 116, 123, 126, 181
Military supplies (GATT), 221, 239
Mineral sector, 10, 11, 12, 13, 14, 16, 27, 31, 179, 183, 184. See also individual minerals
Molasses, 16, 32-37(table)
Money market, 129-130, 147, 155. See also Export restrictions, monetary effects
Money supply, 3, 4, 132, 133, 134, 136, 137, 138(table), 139(fig.), 143, 145, 146, 147, 148-149, 150, 151, 152, 153, 154, 155, 156, 192, 193
Money value, 76, 168
Monopolies, 20, 22, 78, 143, 145, 199, 200, 245
and GATT, 221, 227-228, 230-231
Morgan, D., 16
Morocco, 11, 21, 25(table), 32-47(tables), 179, 184-186(tables)
Most Favored Nation (MFN), 198, 204, 220, 222, 229, 230, 234, 235, 236, 239, 251-252(n41)
"Moving averages," 108
Mozambique, 179
MTN. See Multilateral Trade Negotiations
Multilateral Trade Negotiations (MTN), 211, 213, 245. See also Tokyo Round on Multilateral Trade Negotiations
Multinational corporations, 68, 200, 201, 247

Multiplier effects, 117, 121-122, 178, 181
Mutual Aid Agreement (Lend-Lease Act) (1941), 207
Myrdal, Gunnar, 7, 8

Namibia, 179
Nankani, G., 154, 182
National treasures (GATT), 221
National treatment clause (GATT), 223
Nepal, 179
Netherlands, 72, 140, 201, 238
New International Economic Order (NIEO), 6, 78
New Zealand, 32-37(table), 140, 238
Nicaragua, 32-47(tables), 179
Nickel, 12, 15, 32-37(table)
prices, 28-30(tables)
NIEO. See New International Economic Order
Nigeria, 32-47(tables)
Nitrates, 199
Non-discriminatory treatment (GATT), 224-225, 226, 230, 234, 243, 246, 251-252 (n41&42)
Non-Tariff Barriers (NTB), 211
North-South relations, 1-2, 161
Norway, 13, 32-37(table), 42-45(table), 140
NT, 229
NTB. See Non-Tariff Barriers
Nurkse, R., 7

OECD. See Organization for Economic Cooperation and Development
Oil, 15, 17, 21, 38-47(tables), 75, 79
embargo, 201, 210
imports, 23
prices, 22, 23, 128, 151, 165, 259. See also under Organization of Petroleum Exporting Countries
supply boycotts, 72-73
Okun, 144
Oligopolies, 98
OMA. See Orderly Marketing Agreements
OPEC. See Organization of Petroleum Exporting Countries

Orderly Marketing Agreements
(OMA), 234, 235
Organization for Economic
Cooperation and Development (OECD), 2, 17,
42-45(table), 211, 225,
242-243
Organization of Petroleum
Exporting Countries (OPEC),
6, 13, 199, 210
 export restrictions (1973),
 71, 201
 prices, 1, 26
Ostriches, 202
Ottawa Agreements, 207

Pakistan, 16, 25(table),
32-47(tables), 75, 179
Panama, 21, 25(table),
32-47(tables), 179, 183,
184-186(tables)
Paraguay, 179
Patents (GATT), 221
Perfect competition, 53, 54,
67, 81, 83, 88, 89
Peru, 11, 32-47(tables),
77(table), 179, 183,
184-186(tables)
Petroleum-based synthetics, 73
Phelps, E. S., 144
Philippines, 16, 21, 25(table),
32-47(tables), 179, 202
Phosphates, 21, 22, 32-47
(tables), 141(table), 179,
185-186(table), 190(table),
191, 192
 prices, 28-30(tables)
 processed. See Fertilizers
Pineapple slippings, 202
Plywood, 20, 26
Poland, 231
Poole, W., 144
Pork, 26, 32-37(table)
Prebisch, Raul, 7, 8, 22, 191
Price
 booms, 21-22, 156
 commodity, 3, 11, 21-22, 23,
 26, 27, 31, 74(table), 75,
 76, 104-109, 124, 128-138,
 139(fig.), 143, 144,
 145-156, 162, 164, 165-166,
 172, 175-176, 182, 189,
 191, 258, 259, 260

 control, 73
 demand, elasticity of, 2, 4, 5,
 7, 92, 101-103, 120, 121,
 174, 175, 178, 181, 184, 191
 differential, 32-37(table)
 domestic, 14(table), 16, 26,
 27(table), 32-37(table), 51,
 145, 146, 148, 151, 154,
 182, 198
 factor, 65
 and GATT, 221, 223, 227, 228,
 229, 230, 238
 import, 144
 indexation, 22, 191
 relative, 6, 23, 52, 116
 stabilized, 2, 7, 14(table),
 16, 199
 supply, elasticity of, 4, 13,
 55, 56, 61, 63, 65, 67, 73,
 74(table), 75, 92, 101-103,
 120, 121, 129, 175, 178
 world market, 14(table), 16,
 21-22, 26, 27(table), 32-37
 (table), 51, 64, 71,
 74(table), 93, 124, 163,
 188-189
Primary commodity exports, 1, 3,
4, 7, 8, 17, 22
 substitutes, 3, 6, 7, 31, 163,
 183, 184
 See also Price; Raw materials:
 Ten core commodities
Private sector, 75, 198
Processing industries, 2, 4, 13,
14(table), 15, 17-20, 26,
27(table), 32-37(table),
51-52, 65, 67, 68, 71,
74(table), 75, 78, 116,
126, 181, 184, 187,
199-200, 260
 and GATT, 232
Production controls, 11, 202
Protectionism, 203, 207
Public morale (GATT), 221
Public sector, 75, 182
Pulp exports, 198

R&D. See Research and development
Rationing, 202, 204
Raw materials, 6, 7, 17, 26, 51,
76, 79, 124, 162(table), 163,
164, 165, 166, 167, 170(table),
171-172, 173, 174, 175, 203, 258

Raw materials (cont.)
  access, 2, 197, 204, 206, 207, 208-209, 210, 213
  allocation, 1, 6, 78, 83, 125, 203-204, 259
  conservation, 21, 27(table), 32-37(table), 202
  depletion, 76
  distribution, 78, 83, 197, 205
  domestic consumption, 15, 20, 21, 198
  and export licensing, 13
  and GATT, 221, 229, 231-232, 239
  processing, 78. See also Processing industries
  production, 11, 17, 21, 65, 88, 90-92
  reserves, 74(table), 143, 145, 198
  supply, 2, 11, 14, 15-16, 26, 27(table), 32-37(table), 52, 71, 89, 98, 144, 145, 203, 204, 205, 245, 259, 260
  See also Price, commodity; Ten core commodities
RBP. See Restrictive Business Practices
Recession, world (1975), 164
Reciprocity, 220
Regression analysis, 171-178
Research and development (R&D), 202
Restrictive Business Practices (RBP), 246, 247
Rhodesia. See Zimbabwe
Rice, 12, 32-45(tables)
  export taxes, 75
  prices, 28-30(tables)
Rodriguez, C. A., 144
Roessler, Frieder, 222, 233, 244, 245, 246
Roosevelt, Franklin D., 207
Rubber, 3, 15, 16, 18-19 (table), 32-47(tables), 71, 79, 90-92, 93(table), 94, 95-96(tables), 141(table), 185-186(table)
  export taxes, 97
  prices, 28-30(tables), 102-103(tables), 106-107(tables)

Rwanda, 179

Schenkel, Hubertus, 79
Senegal, 179
Shortages, 73, 74(table)
Sierra Leone, 77(table), 179
Silver, 221
Singapore, 140
Sisal, 3, 18-19(table), 32-41(tables), 71, 90-92, 94, 95-96(tables)
  export taxes, 93, 97
  prices, 28-30(tables), 102-103(tables), 106-107(tables)
South Africa, 72, 140, 202
South Korea, 140
Soviet Union, 15, 42-45(table), 231. See also under United States
Soybeans, 13, 15, 16, 32-37 (table), 42-47(tables)
  export restrictions, 71, 73, 199, 210, 211
  prices, 28-30(tables)
Spain, 21, 32-37(table), 42-45(table), 75, 140
Sri Lanka, 77(table), 179
Stagflation, 3, 6, 26, 128, 134, 143, 153, 165
Staley, E., 202
Staley/Knorr Report (1946), 210
State trading, 10, 11-12, 27(table), 32-37(table), 72, 78-79, 200
  and GATT, 220, 221, 229, 230-231
Statistical Yearbook (UN), 171
Steel exports, 228
Subsidies, 26, 58, 74(table), 75, 78
  and GATT, 228-229, 238, 245
Substitution. See Primary commodity exports, substitutes
Sudan, 179
Sugar, 12, 21, 32-47(tables), 90-92, 94, 95-96(tables), 198
  prices, 28-30(tables), 93, 102-103(tables), 105, 106-108(tables), 109, 110(table)

Supply elasticity, 15, 59, 92, 99-100. See also Price, supply, elasticity of
Supply shock, 143-145, 147, 152
Surinam, 13, 42-47(tables)
Swaziland, 77(table)
Sweden, 32-37(table), 140, 211
Switzerland, 140, 211

Tanzania, 25(table), 32-47(tables), 77(table), 179, 184-186(tables)
Tea, 3, 71, 79, 90-92, 94, 95-96(tables)
  export taxes, 93, 97
  prices, 102-103(tables), 105, 106-108(tables), 109, 110(table)
Technology, 22, 68, 143, 201-202
  critical, 239
  transfer, 245
Ten core commodities, 3, 4, 71, 90-92, 98, 132, 138, 141(table), 183. See also individual commodities
Terms of trade, 4, 13, 22-26, 76, 80, 116, 162, 191
Thailand, 13, 32-47(tables), 75, 179
Timber, 13, 15, 21, 26, 32-41(tables), 141(table), 183, 185-186(table)
  prices, 28-30(tables)
Tin, 3, 13, 15, 21, 32-47(tables), 71, 90-92, 94, 95-96(tables), 141(table), 179, 185-186(table), 190(table), 191, 192
  export taxes, 93, 97
  prices, 28-30(tables), 102-103(tables), 106-107(tables)
Tobacco, 28-30(tables), 32-47(tables)
Togo, 11, 32-47(tables), 179, 184-186(tables)
Tokyo Round on Multilateral Trade Negotiations, 20, 198, 213, 217(n40), 242
Trade Act (1974) (U.S.), 211, 217-218(n41)

Trade marks (GATT), 221
Trade name (GATT), 221
Transnationals. See Multinational corporations
Transport, 68
Tube exports, 72
Tunisia, 11, 25(table); 32-47(tables), 202
Turkey, 16, 32-37(table), 42-45(table)

Uganda, 179, 201, 239
UNCTAD. See United Nations Conference on Trade and Development
Unemployment, 3, 4, 14, 21, 26, 68, 123, 124, 128, 133, 134, 135, 136, 137, 138(table), 139(fig.), 143, 145, 147, 151, 152, 156
United Nations, 210
  Charter, 20, 221
  General Assembly, 78
  See also Charter of Economic Rights and Duties
United Nations Conference on Trade and Development (UNCTAD), 3, 5, 67, 78, 79, 89, 228, 238, 245, 246, 247
  IV (1976), 6, 17, 48(n7), 211
  See also Integrated Commodity Programme
United States, 12, 13, 15, 16, 18-19(table), 26, 32-37(table), 42-45(table), 72, 140, 202, 207-208, 212, 213, 240, 241
  export restrictions, 71, 72, 73, 199, 200-201, 210, 211, 239
  and GATT, 226, 234, 238, 245
  and ITO, 222, 237
  and Soviet Union, 71, 72, 73, 201
Upper Volta, 179
Uranium, 71
Uruguay, 16, 32-41(tables), 179

Van Duyne, C., 144
Venezuela, 13, 32-47(tables)
VER. See Voluntary Export Restrictions
Voluntary Export Restrictions (VER), 200, 234-236

Wages, 22, 143, 144
Walras' Law, 56, 58
Welles, Sumner, 207
West Germany, 16, 42-45(table), 72, 140
 and GATT, 224
Wheat, 11, 12, 32-45(tables)
 export restrictions, 71, 201
Williamson, J., 146
Wilson, Woodrow, 204, 215(n21)
Wilson's Fourteen Points, 204, 206, 215(n20)
Wood, 13, 15, 16, 32-47(table), 190(table), 191
 processed, 20

World Bank, 108, 109
World Economic Conference (1937), 216(n26)

Yemen Arab Republic, 179

Zaire, 77(table), 179
Zambia, 13, 25(table), 32-47(tables, 179, 183, 184-186(tables)
"Zebra code," 245
Zimbabwe, 73, 201, 239
Zinc, 18-19(table), 32-47(tables), 179
 prices, 28-30(tables)